THE WESTERN FRONT

RP

LS

M

Liège

Namur

Coblenz

G
E
R
M
A
N
Y

Rhine

L
U
X
E
M
B
U
R
G

Sedan

Meuse

Luxemburg

E

Saarbrücken

Verdun

Metz

St Mihiel

Nancy

Avricourt

Toul

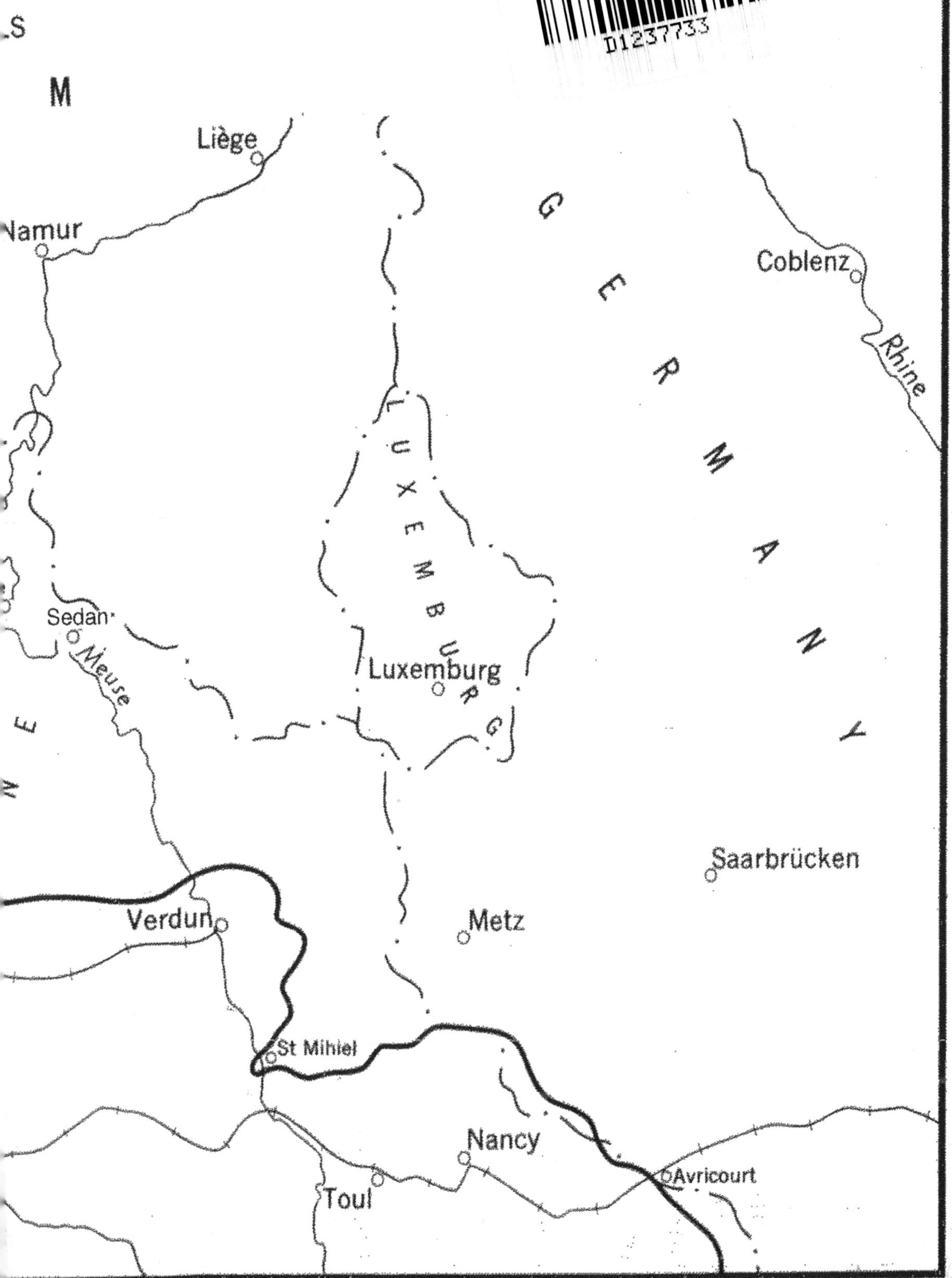

Oswald Boelcke

To my lovely wife, Carole,
and the cadets at the Air Force Academy

Oswald Boelcke

Germany's First Fighter Ace and Father of Air Combat

R.G. HEAD
Brigadier General, USAF

Foreword by General Ron Fogleman
USAF Chief of Staff 1994-1997

Grub Street · London

Published by
Grub Street
4 Rainham Close
London
SW11 6SS

Copyright © Grub Street 2016
Copyright text © R.G. Head 2016

A CIP record for this title is available from the British Library

ISBN-13: 9-781-910690-23-9

Printed and bound by Finidr, Czech Republic

TABLE OF CONTENTS

PROLOGUE

Early in the morning on a cold and bleak January day in 1916, Oswald Boelcke, a German pilot, takes off from eastern France and climbs toward the front. He is in search of two English planes that had been reported to his base. After ten minutes of cruising in the bitter cold, he sees distant specks. Soon they morph into forms of aircraft heading home. As Boelcke gets closer, he recognises the machines as English reconnaissance biplanes.

Instinctively Boelcke checks his guns and closes on the rear aircraft from its blind spot. Now! He squeezes the two triggers, and the English machine is riddled from stem to stern. The pilot banks suddenly and tries to dive away – to no avail. Boelcke is still there, firing at every turn. The Englishman's controls are hit. He begins to descend in barely controllable flight, still behind German lines. Thousands of feet below, the pilot of the disabled aircraft manages to lift the nose, but not enough to avoid a complete crash into the frozen German-held French soil. Both crewmembers survive.

The German pilot, Ltn Boelcke, follows the English plane down and lands nearby. He runs to the crash site and finds the enemy machine surrounded by a crowd from the nearby French village.

Oswald Boelcke inspects his seventh victim. (Michael Seamark, *Mail Online*, 26 November 2012, BNPS by permission)

Boelcke recalled later in a letter to his parents:

'I went straight up to the Englishmen, shook hands with them and told them I was delighted to have brought them down alive. I had a long talk with the pilot, who spoke German very well. When he heard my name, he said with a grin, "We all know about

7

you!" I then saw to it that they were both taken in a car to the hospital where I visited the observer[a] today – the pilot had already been sent off – and brought him some English papers and photos of his wrecked machine.'

Ltn Boelcke asked the English observer, Lieutenant Formilli, if there was anything he could do to help him. "Yes," replied Formilli, who then wrote a letter to his squadron commander to tell his mates that he and his pilot were alive and being looked after. Boelcke took the letter, and the next day, he risked his own life by flying low over the English aerodrome. He dropped the letter to the Royal Flying Corps and returned safely.

The German pilot, Leutnant Oswald Boelcke, was 24 years old, and this was his seventh victory, 5 January 1916. The English pilot was Second Lieutenant William E. Somervill, Royal North Lancers, and the observer was Lieutenant Geoffrey C. Formilli, Royal Garrison Artillery, from 2nd Squadron, Royal Flying Corps (RFC).

Boelcke was flying his Fokker E.IV monoplane, and the English crew was flying their B.E.2C reconnaissance aircraft. Lieutenant Formilli wrote the letter to Captain Babington of the RFC. The letter read:

'P.S. It was Boelcke who brought us down.

'My Dear Babington, just a line to say that Somervill and I are all right. We had a scrap with a Fokker. Willy got a graze on the side of his head and I got one through the shoulder, halfway through. We had most of our controls shot through and had to land and crashed very badly. I am in hospital now & Willy is in Germany. Will you let my people know please.

Yours, G. C. Formilli'

Lieutenant Formilli's letter, 5 January 1916, to his friend, Babington, 2nd Squadron, RFC. (Michael Seamark, *Mail Online*, 26 November 2012, BNPS by permission)[1]

The squadron commander drafted a letter to Formilli's parents and enclosed their son's letter. The commander wrote:

'With your son's note came another from a pilot lost on the same day to say he is undamaged: his engine stopped after being hit. "Boelcke" is a rather famous German pilot. This news has given us all great pleasure, and I rejoice to be able to send it on to you. I hope that you have almost by now got a telegraph for I phoned to the Flying Corps Headquarters and asked them to let you know.

Yours sincerely
C. F. Murphy'

---

[a] The observer is a crew position in a biplane. He was usually an artillery officer whose job it was to locate and map the positions of enemy guns.

ACKNOWLEDGMENTS

The author is indebted to the large number of people who helped with this project. General Ron Fogleman, graduate of the USAFA Class of 1963 and former Chief of Staff of the USAF, wrote the foreword and provided excellent advice. Colonel Gert Overhoff, former commander of Tactical Air Force Wing 31 Boelcke, and president of the Boelcke Tradition Association, wrote the afterword and added his personal insight into the legacy of Oswald Boelcke in the Luftwaffe. Colonel Stefan Kleinheyer, commander of Tactical Air Force Wing 31 Boelcke, hosted our group and reaffirmed the enduring legacy of Oswald Boelcke. Heinz-Michael Raby, member of the Boelcke Tradition Association became a personal friend and was an immensely valuable co-conspirator in the research surrounding the building of the six-foot model of Oswald Boelcke's Albatros D.II aircraft. Our exchange of Boelcke information and research continued into several presentations the author made to audiences in California and the preparation of the book's manuscript.

Admiral Bud Edney was one of the early reviewers and provided invaluable advice on the manuscript. Walter Waiss shared his Boelcke artefacts and provided the Fokker logbook. Norman Franks, noted World War I aviation expert and author, read several sections and provided an introduction to Grub Street. John Davies at Grub Street was a gracious host and wonderful editor of the work. Natalie Parker was the untiring military editor at Grub Street. Tom Leary read each of the drafts and provided numerous suggestions that were both helpful and timely. Virginia Andersen read the final manuscript and provided unique insight. Howard Fisher, World War I expert and curator, provided advice and access to his voluminous library of WWI original material. Brigadier General Mark Wells, retired professor and head, department of History at the USAF Academy, and a World War I expert, took a personal interest in the manuscript and assisted with professional advice and assistance. Charles D. Dusch, Jr., Deputy Command Historian for the Air Force Academy read one of the early drafts and provided a host of valuable comments and suggestions. Kai Erdmann translated important letters and other artefacts to and from the German language.

Sam Tangredi provided excellent advice and contacts. Terry Brennan, curator, and Al Valdez, archivist, at the San Diego Air & Space Museum were the project managers supporting the Albatros model construction, presentation and display. Debbie Seracini provided access to the museum's wonderful library of research material and permission to reproduce some photographs.

Jonathan Fallon, editor, *World War I Aero*, printed two articles on the Albatros model. Laura Taylor, Darlene Quinn and Barbra Drizin provided valuable encouragement and professional advice. Mike Hanlon, Rebekah Wilson and Kim Jindra of the US World War I Centennial Commission endorsed the project.

The entire archival staff at the Royal Air Force Museum Hendon, led by Peter Devitt and Brian Legate, were extremely helpful in identifying and locating historical material from their vast files on Oswald Boelcke and World War I. John Weaver at Discount Hobby Warehouse and Arnett at Frazee Paint, San Diego, provided both materials and advice on the Albatros model construction.

Most of all, my wife, Carole, provided continuous support, motivation, proofreading and substantive suggestions throughout the project.

God bless them all.

Brigadier General (ret.) R.G. Head

FOREWORD

Beginning in 2014, and continuing through the end of 2018, there will be many opportunities to commemorate the 100th anniversary of events associated with World War I. It was an important conflict for many reasons, but from a military perspective it was the introduction of many new weapons that had the greatest impact. These weapons rendered historical thinking and tactics obsolete. One of those weapons was the airplane. For that reason, it gives me great pleasure to introduce this marvellous book about Oswald Boelcke and the early days of military aviation. With the current state of airline transportation, supersonic fighters and remotely-piloted drones, it is difficult to recall that aviation is merely a few more than 100 years old. It is important to review what it was like in those early days, when everything was new and untried. There are many lessons that history can teach us.

Like R.G., I grew up reading books about the airplanes, pilots and aces in the First World War. They were somewhat distant heroes who helped motivate me to attend the Air Force Academy and become a fighter pilot. I flew the F-100 Super Sabre and the F-4 Phantom in combat. During my first tour in South East Asia, I was fortunate to be a MISTY forward air controller flying missions in North and South Vietnam. This mission was a new application of fighter aircraft in a role dictated by the enemy threat. In that mission, we were constantly relearning old tactics and developing new ones.

Oswald Boelcke was a pioneer pilot. He was one of the first pilots in WWI, flying monoplanes and biplanes in an open air cockpit. After several combat tours, interrupted by "rest breaks", he was inspired to put on paper the lessons he had learned while developing a proven set of tactics. Fortunately, as outlined in this book, we have an authoritative record of his exploits and tactical thinking from his letters and German air service documents. Additionally, the book provides an excellent narrative on the state of military aviation among the opposing sides. On one level, the book is an excellent history of the overall war in the air in WWI. It rises to this level because we are treated to five aviation stories: a definitive biography of Oswald Boelcke; a very informative description of his Albatros aircraft; the general state of aircraft manufacturing; the personal and physical challenges to be a pilot during WWI and a comparison of Boelcke's thinking about leadership and tactics at that time, to those of leaders of modern fighter operations. R.G.'s personal insights from his own career add value to the story. Indeed, this is the only book on WWI aviation I know of that was written by a combat fighter pilot from the jet era.

I believe this book is important for three reasons: 1) It is excellent military/aviation history; 2) It describes the early air-to-air regime and tactics in a way that modern readers can understand; and 3) It shows how a set of values (dicta) can be developed and adopted by a large organisation. Let me elaborate.

When I was teaching the History of Airpower at the Air Force Academy, I tried to impress upon the cadets that we could learn both good and bad lessons from those who had gone before us. One such discussion involved the disparate views on the introduction of the parachute in fighter and bomber aircraft. Having personally ejected from a burning aircraft in a combat environment, this was a subject near and dear to my heart. I especially enjoyed reading and discussing the British refusal to use parachutes and the German adoption of them to save lives during WWI. R.G. tells that story brilliantly.

Throughout my career from service as a jet-fighter pilot, flight lead, director of operations and wing commander in both air-to-air and air-to-ground units, I came to appreciate the value of having published tactics and procedures manuals for each aircraft and its various missions. The contribution and effect Boelcke's Dicta of combat tactics had on his squadron, his contemporaries and future aviators was without peer. This is a significant part of his legacy.

On a different level and at a different time, I had a similar experience. When I became Chief of Staff of the US Air Force, I was concerned about an apparent loss of focus on the mission and a decline in integrity within the force. I worked hard to communicate the crucial role the air force would play in the security of the nation in the post-Cold War environment. At the same time, I put emphasis on earning the trust and respect of the American public as a precursor to public understanding and support of the air force. The centrepiece of this effort was the introduction of what we called "Air Force Core Values". The USAF adopted these values as a guideline for personal behaviour, 'Integrity First; Service above Self; Excellence in all we do'. Like Boelcke's Dicta these core values give young men and women, new to the air force, a solid foundation on which to build a professional career in the service of the nation.

R.G. has done all of us a great service by writing this book on an extraordinary man, Oswald Boelcke, who did great things at the dawn of military aviation.

Ronald R. Fogleman
Chief of Staff, USAF 1994-1997
Durango, Colorado
2016

INTRODUCTION: THE BIRTH OF AERIAL WARFARE

The Theme of the Work

The purpose of this volume is to provide the definitive biography of Oswald Boelcke, Germany's first ace. He was the Red Baron's instructor, friend, squadron commander and mentor, and Boelcke's legacy has spanned a century of dramatic advances in aviation.

Oswald Boelcke deserves consideration as the most important fighter pilot of any era, including the present one. His character, inspirational leadership, organisational genius, development of air-to-air tactics and impact on aerial doctrine still resonate in modern air forces around the world. He is the central figure in air warfare across a century of history.

Aviation in WWI is a paradox. In the middle of the most mechanised, impersonal killing fields of Western Europe, there arose a technology that at one fell swoop highlighted the individual – the lone aviator. This technology – the airplane – enabled men to fight the raw elements and each other in small groups and one-on-one combat. It is no wonder that we study and idolise these men; they are the pioneers of aviation. They were real, but they had mythological elements that catapulted them into the imagination of the public. They remind us that we are not just a cog in a modern society's machine of senseless complexity. We are, each of us, a samurai whose individual contribution matters.

This view of the combat airplane as something different, something that brought back the worth of the individual, was both romantic and appealing to the soldiers and civilians of the First World War. Oswald Boelcke's competitor in the ace race, Max Immelmann, felt the same way. His biographer, Franz Immelmann, described Max's attitude, 'My brother Max saw it in his first combat patrols ... as a knightly duel between two evenly-matched opponents'.[1] The image and the idealism of these aerial duels continued into the 1940s and beyond. Boelcke, Bishop and Ball all contributed to the establishment of this concept – this myth.

Richard Hillary, a British Spitfire pilot of the Battle of Britain in 1940, wrote about his feelings while at Oxford in public school:

> 'In a fighter plane, I believe, we have found a way to return to war as it ought to be, war which is individual combat between two people, in which one either kills or is killed. It's exciting, it's individual, and it's disinterested.'[2]

The Great War was perhaps the last time that such a romantic view of war, with its many chivalrous gestures, was a part of human history. There were several such incidents in World

War II, but their numbers appear small in comparison.

In WWI, Boelcke paved the way. He is not as famous as Manfred von Richthofen, the Red Baron, who shot down eighty opponents to become the "ace of aces". But von Richthofen owes much of his skill, record and fame to the lessons he learned from his instructor, Oswald Boelcke. Despite his unique contributions, Boelcke is a neglected agent in aviation history. He was an innovator, chivalrous and respected by friends and foes alike. He was the first German aviator to become an ace. He was the first to analyse the evolving air war and develop a set of fighter tactics. Boelcke and Max Immelmann were the first two pilots to be awarded the famous Blue Max, the *Pour le Mérite* (the German equivalent of the British Victoria Cross, the French *Légion d'honneur* and the US Medal of Honor).

Oswald Boelcke was a pioneer aviator and tactician whose character, vision and leadership had a dramatic effect on his colleagues, his squadron, the German air force, the public and his opponents. His legacy transcends his own time, influenced countless aviators in WWII and hovers over aviators of all nations. He overcame physical obstacles in his childhood and later life with a willpower and determination that is a model for modern man. He flew at a time when fighter tactics developed from lone wolf hunting to formation flying and teamwork, while the flying units grew from small sections to fighter squadrons and wings. Boelcke was the first pilot to effectively use this new weapon – the airplane. He was also the first to train and lead other pilots in the use of air-to-air fighter tactics. Moreover, he did not seek publicity. He was sceptical of the press. Yet he was noted for his several acts of chivalry that he extended to his victims. Boelcke's contributions to fighter aviation preceded Richthofen's and are more significant and enduring. Consider:

- Oswald Boelcke's character, his personal code of ethics, enabled him to be trusted and empowered to leadership by all he touched;
- Although he had whooping cough as a child and asthma throughout his life, he choose an adventurous life and overcame his adversities;
- He flew early in the Great War and matured his tactics in the Battle of the Somme, at a time when the tactics, techniques and procedures of aviation were not well known or non-existent;
- He was one of the first German pilots to shoot down an enemy aircraft in 1915;
- He was the first German ace with forty total victories, but he felt compassion and expressed concern and consideration for his victims;
- He taught Max Immelmann to fly the Fokker Eindecker;
- When Max Immelmann died in June 1916, Boelcke became the leading ace of the German air service and a national idol, whose reputation was enhanced and exploited for domestic political purposes to enhance public and military morale;
- The public and publicity side of Boelcke's and others' aerial exploits contributed inevitably to the mythology of military aviation – a new and powerful force in human affairs;
- Boelcke established one of the first forward operating bases of the German air service and connected his unit to the Verdun Front by a direct telephone line to reduce

response time in support of ground troops;

- He was never shot down;
- He recognised the tactical, technical, organisational and political potential of aviation and was the first aviator to develop, write down and teach fighter tactics. His principles of air-to-air engagements were the first air doctrine and tactics (the famous Boelcke's Dicta), which still have relevance today;
- He is one of the few German heroes of the Great War who was not tainted by later association with Nazism;
- He influenced the fledgling German air service to organise fighter squadrons, named Jagdstaffeln (literally "hunting squadrons" or Jastas) to specialise in the air-to-air mission, just in time for the Battle of the Somme;
- Boelcke's leadership as the first squadron commander of Jasta 2 enabled the Germans to wrest air superiority from the French and British during the Battle of the Somme;
- He led his squadron, flying the prototype of the Albatros D.II, which at that time was the fastest, most powerful, and heavily armed aircraft. He established in this squadron an unprecedented record of victories[3]. Jasta 2 became the second highest scoring unit in the German air service in WWI with a total of 336 victories and a casualty list of only forty-four. The squadron ended the war with twenty-five aces.
- Boelcke was so famous as a leader and so considerate of his opponents that upon his death in a midair collision, the Royal Flying Corps dropped a wreath on his funeral procession, and several of his victims sent another wreath from their German prisoner of war camp;
- Boelcke trained and mentored a generation of German fighter pilots and motivated countless generations to follow in all the nations of the world;
- Boelcke's legendary contributions are still commemorated in today's Luftwaffe designation of the Tactical Air Force Wing 31 Boelcke.
- Oswald Boelcke's name and legacy of leadership and inspiration live on.

CHAPTER I

FLYING IN WORLD WAR I

It is hard to imagine what it was like to fly aeroplanes in combat in WWI. The aeroplane was new. It had never been used as a weapon. It operated in the third dimension – vertical. Just as war at sea is conceptually, technologically and physically different from war on land, so the new war in the air could scarcely be imagined by sceptics who were trained in the conservative military and naval disciplines. The consequences of this innovation were felt by virtually everyone who participated in the air war, beginning with their initial training.

Pilot Training

There were no trained instructors – the only teachers were those few who learned to fly before the war, had been in the air service a few months longer or were withdrawn from combat. Frequently, there was no curriculum for the student to follow. The results have been described by the many memoirs of the survivors: inadequate classroom ground school; haphazard instruction; very little dual flying with an instructor; often premature and disastrous solo flights; high accident rates and extremely low experience for graduates. There was rarely any instruction in acrobatics, spins, spin recovery or combat tactics. Practice emergencies were limited to engine failure/forced landings.

British pilot training was probably the worst. Entry qualifications were based primarily on attendance at English public school. Some applicants were asked whether they could ride a horse, sail a boat or ride a motorcycle: those were the only "equivalent" skills to flying the recruiters could think of. Men who had done any of these "gentlemanly" things were reckoned to be able to go solo within two hours of instruction. The statistics are grisly: official British figures listed 14,166 pilots died during WWI. Of these, 8,000 died in pilot training (56 per cent).[1]

With this extremely high accident rate, one can ask why recruits continued to volunteer for flying training. We can only presume that the true numbers were not well known; the recruits were young and enthusiastic; there was a dread of the trenches; and they were drawn by the romanticism of flying. Individual deaths in training occurred on the average of one per every 90 hours flying time. One RFC Wing (the 23rd) averaged 110 crashes per month, with thirty-five fatalities and seventy-five minor crashes. One of the problems was simply that there was no overall plan for training. As mentioned, there was no special training for instructor pilots.

Most of the instructors had been withdrawn from active combat flying for exhaustion or mental breakdown. One official estimated that only 10 per cent were effective teachers. Training of pilots was completely haphazard. One flying training manual devoted only six of its 141 pages to the actual techniques of flying. One pilot's experience was that he had three instructors for the first four hours of flying. Then he was sent solo while they were all at lunch. The British Farman aircraft itself was part of the problem. Its top speed was only 40 mph, but if the pilot let it get below 35 mph, it would stall and most likely spin. This was much too small a margin for a normal student to handle. The great demand for pilots in France resulted in British pilots arriving at squadrons with as few as 15-20 hours of flying time. This was nonsense when compared to the training provided by the USAF today. USAF undergraduates receive approximately 200 hours of flying time with additional training in tactical aircraft before being awarded pilot's wings and assigned to an operational fighter squadron.[2]

The German accident rate in pilot training was only about one-quarter that of Britain's. French training was much more thorough and logical, based on what was known as the Blériot system. Student pilots spent the first two months in hands-on learning how to break down and maintain an engine. Then they were sent to an aerodrome and told to watch the flying machines and analyse the pilots' mistakes. The French flying programme was organised in sections, becoming more complex only when the student had mastered the basics. In contrast, the British aspirant's introduction to the RFC instruction by sergeants was on how to march.

Once the new British pilot was assigned to a combat squadron he was lucky if some more experienced pilot took it upon himself to provide some minimal orientation and aerial situation awareness. Most were just pointed to an airplane and told to stay with the flight that was taking off on a mission. Typical of the subjects neglected included: system engineering of their own aircraft; performance characteristics and limitations; emergency procedures; weapons capabilities and malfunctions; gunnery; formation flying; aircraft recognition; opposing aircraft performance and tactics. The lack of training in formation flying was especially critical because that is one skill that is essential for fighter flying, and it is the usual skill that differentiates the fighter-capable pilot from the rest of the student pilots. This would not change in Britain until late 1917, when the training system was overhauled, and pilots were not released to fly to France until they had 50 hours in the air.

The change occurred with the introduction of Robert Smith-Barry's Gosport flight school programme. Smith-Barry had experience as a pilot and commander of 60 Squadron in France. He developed a standardised training system that featured dual-place instruction as the norm, with the sequence of instruction strictly laid down. The programme was explained in a 42-page manual. The sequence of instruction can be described as briefing-demonstration-practice. Pupil questions were followed by the instructor's explanation. Then the sequence would begin again: practice-pupil questions-instructor explanation. After landing, the instructor would conduct a "debriefing" – a review of the student's performance and a critique intended to show the pupil how to improve. The goal was pupil confidence. The Smith-Barry system cut the accidental death rate in half, from one in 90 hours, to one in 192 hours[3]. The system was so effective at producing pilots and reducing accidents that it remained essentially the same through two world wars. Smith-Barry even got the prohibition against aerobatic flying lifted in August 1917.

Part of the problem with pilot selection in England was social class. The officers of all the English military services had traditionally come from the upper classes. It was not just a joking commentary that the first son inherited the estate, the second son went into the military, and the third son either went to India or joined the clergy. Thus, many officials in the Air Committee (the forerunner of the Air Ministry) thought the RFC should be limited to elite public school graduates. However, the actual pilot selection process resulted in an unexpected degree of social mobility. Working-class young men volunteered in droves and often turned out to be excellent pilots. Many without college degrees became non-commissioned officers (NCOs). Prejudice was common. One NCO pilot on leave from his combat squadron in France wrote of going to see a stage show in the Haymarket area of London, where he was literally kicked out by student officer cadets who insisted that 'all NCOs should use the side door'.[4] The snobbishness of the Royal Air Force, though not official policy, continued for many years. In 1940, a squadron commander in the novel, *Piece of Cake*, could still be heard to say, 'Time to bring some new blood, uncle,' Rex said. 'Breeding counts, you know.'[5] Even greater than the democratisation of the RFC was the "Dominion Intrusion". Of the 145 pilots listed in 24 Squadron history compiled after the war, thirty-one were from the British Empire and eight from the USA.[6]

Contrary to the Smith-Barry attempt at standardisation, it was still difficult to predict who would make a good pilot. Doctors were employed to screen applicants, initiating a practice that continues to this day – the medical examination. Included was a test of mental health, a 15-minute interview designed to identify three types of undesirable individuals: "impulsives, paranoids and psychopaths". Despite the best efforts of the medical professionals at the time, many applicants with these "undesirable" character traits survived the screening process and actually produced a disproportionate number of aces.[7]

In a summary of pilot-aspirant examinations, Sefton Bracher told the British Aeronautical Society in 1916:

> 'The most unexpected people make good pilots and very often the most promising ones never attain more than mediocrity in the air and for this reason it has always seemed to me undesirable to lay down a stereotyped process of training.'[8]

The pilots of all nations in WWI were overwhelmingly young. In the RFC, the age steadily decreased so that by 1918 the average age of pilots in 65 Squadron was only 20, and in 100 Squadron 22½.[9]

The Aircraft

The deficiencies in the training system were matched by the immaturity in aircraft manufacturing. Each aircraft was virtually handmade. The British Sopwith firm is an example. They were well-known and well-respected for their production of the Pup, Strutter, Camel and Snipe. Yet their building process was remarkably casual. Their objective was to design and construct a new fighter prototype in less than eight weeks. Sketches were transferred into chalk lines on the floor and walls of the shop with no thought to involve stress engineers. The resultant imprecision was so bad, that US firms building the aircraft parts under license found the plans completely unusable. Those few workmen who were engineers were civil engineers, which explains why most of the early airplanes looked like cross-braced bridges. Designers, whom we would now call aeronautical engineers, were by tradition "the lowest-paid skilled men in Edwardian industry".[10] The result was that major defects were built into the aircraft, many of which would not appear until the machines were flown in combat. Struts split, landing gear collapsed, fabric ripped, control lines separated, machine guns shot off propellers and wings flew off.

Engines were unreliable, and their manufacturing process was even less rigorous than the airframe. For example, the Avro 504 was a WWI biplane with a production run of more than 10,000 over a 20-year period. The original power was an 80 hp Gnome Lambda seven-cylinder rotary engine. Avro's manufacturing process for the crankcase began with a 100-lb block of steel, and over a series of fifty operations, ground it down to 28 lbs. Each cylinder surface was machined to a hundredth of a millimetre. "Even by the end of the war Rolls-Royce, makers of the only fully satisfactory British aero engines, had no machine tools or interchangeable parts."[11] It is a shame that Britain did not have Henry Ford who introduced mass production in the US in 1913.

Part of the problem in all of the participating countries was that there was no centralised, coordinated authority that could set standards and ensure quality control. Bureaus fought, ministers quarrelled, and the military services competed with each other. In Britain, there was an enormous debate about the best method of production: private industry or the government. The British Minister of Munitions is quoted as saying, that 'the chief impediment to large scale supply arose from the enormous multiplicity of types resulting from too much expert zeal unchecked by practical considerations.'[12]

Numbers confirm his point. In December 1916, the British Army, Royal Flying Corps and Royal Navy had on order 9,460 aircraft in seventy-six different types with 20,000 engines of fifty-seven kinds.[13]

The Physical Environment

The physical stresses on WWI pilots and observers are almost unimaginable today. The most obvious is the cold. Open cockpits were unheated. Its occupants were subject to propeller wash and an outside air temperature that grew colder with altitude. Using an average (adiabatic) lapse rate of 1.95 °C (35.5 °F) per 1,000 feet, a summer temperature of 24 °C (75 °F) on the surface would fall to 4.4 °C (40 °F) at 10,000 feet and -5 °C (22 °F) at 15,000 feet. Winter temperatures were abominable. A freezing temperature 0 °C (32 °F) at the airfield would mean -19 °C (-3 °F) at 10,000 feet and -29 °C (-21 °F) at 15,000 feet. As more powerful engines were developed, the fighters could climb to 20,000 feet to seek altitude advantage, where the temperature in still air would be -38 °C (-38 °F). Wind chill from 70-100 mph airflow would increase the effect even further.

British ace, James McCudden recorded a memorable description of the cold:

'The weather now became bitterly cold for us, and I have never experienced such cold as that which we went through on those de Havillands at 12,000 and 13,000 [feet] during December 1916. I remember that on one patrol I was so intensely cold and miserable that I did not trouble to look round at all to see whether any Huns were behind me or not; in fact, I did not care whether I was shot down or not. I was so utterly frozen. I cannot explain the intensity of the cold when high up on a pusher aeroplane, but it can be readily remembered by those who have experienced it.'[14]

Wolfgang Günther, Jasta 2, in flying suit. Flying at 15,000 feet, all the cockpits were bitterly cold. (Riseofflight.com)

British and American pilots often were required to fly in their dress uniforms, with high, stiff collars. German pilots wore more practical, full-length flying suits. Scarves, leather helmets, and heavy leather or fur coats were donned to keep out the cold, but they were only partially successful. Foul-smelling whale oil smeared on faces did not prevent frostbite or icicles. Rotary engines were worse. They spewed a constant stream of foul-smelling castor oil over the tiny windscreens and pilot's goggles.

There is a rhythm to fighter flying. In WWI there was a dawn patrol, followed by scheduled flights during the day and perhaps a patrol at dusk. There also were pairs of fighters that were stationed on the ground, on alert. They were readied to take off at a moment's notice and scramble in response to a telephoned order to intercept enemy fighters or bombers that had just been discovered.

Fighters did not fly at night unless they had a mandatory air defence mission (for example, protecting London). Drinks, dinner and relaxation were in the evening. However, two or three sorties a day were not uncommon. The English ace, Albert Ball was reported with as many as twelve flights in one day.[15] On the day Oswald Boelcke died, he was on his fifth sortie. No one flies that way anymore. The author was lucky to get two sorties in a day and was usually limited to a flight every other day. Only once in combat did I have two, five-hour flights over North Vietnam in one day.

Fighter/scout sorties varied in duration in a narrow range. Many were short, less than an hour's length, but others lasted two hours or more. Bomber and reconnaissance sorties were typically longer, although at lower altitudes. There was a typical routine: take-off on a grass or mud field; climb to altitude; cruise looking for the enemy; short, intense fighting; and glide back to base. As the war progressed, the cruising altitudes increased to 15,000 feet, then 20,000 feet and higher, all in debilitating cold. Most of the cruising flights never saw an enemy, and there was no action, only the cold. The manoeuvring fight, when encountered, could be a few seconds in a slashing attack, where the attacker was never seen, or it could be a turning, twisting, curving fight that lasted 30 minutes. The return to base could be a gentle glide over one's own lines or a frantic hunt for familiar landmarks and a long ordeal for the Allies against the west wind to a friendly field.

Another physical effect was altitude sickness caused by lack of oxygen (hypoxia). Modern aerospace medicine dictates the use of supplemental oxygen at all altitudes above 10,000 feet. Flight above 20,000 feet requires a pressurised cockpit. The "effective performance time" (also known as the "time of useful consciousness") is the best metric to indicate the ability of the body to operate at an optimum level of performance. USAF altitude chamber physiologists estimate that the effects of the lack of oxygen begin about 15,000 feet. At 18,000 feet the effective performance time in an open cockpit without supplemental oxygen is 20-30 minutes. Altitudes above 20,000 feet are exceptionally hazardous. At 25,000 feet the effective performance time is only 3-5 minutes.[16] Unconsciousness would follow quickly. Even before losing consciousness the body would feel disorientation, headache, fatigue, lethargy, dizziness, poor judgement, visual impairment, nausea and euphoria – just before passing out.

The flight surgeon profession had not yet been invented, so aircrews and mess hall cooks were only vaguely aware of the science of gas expansion. Certain foods cause excessive abdominal gas, which expands 100 per cent by volume at approximately 11,000 feet, and progressively more at higher altitudes. Descending at a great rate in a dive or even more slowly in a glide back to base, pilots and observers were subjected to increasing pressure that popped ear drums and caused other symptoms known previously only to mountain climbers, deep sea divers and workers in the caissons of bridge piers.

Noise Hazard

Noise was a constant hazard. Upon starting the engine, the crew would be subjected to noise levels of 120 decibels, with another 125 decibels emitting from the propeller tips whirling at about 30,000 feet per second. As a comparison, normal conversation is about 60-65 decibels. An unsilenced pneumatic drill at 3 feet makes about 110 decibels. Author Denis Winter cites that about ¼ of all WWI pilots suffered from marked permanent hearing loss.[17]

G-forces

Finally, pilots are subjected to G-forces when manoeuvring. (One G is the normal pull of gravity. Four Gs is four times gravity). Aerial manoeuvring required tight turns at G-levels that were not even measured. Positive Gs cause blood to be pulled from the brain and pooled in the stomach and lower legs. As the blood drains from the eyes, the pilot's vision begins to "greyout". With continued G-force, after about three seconds, the pilot suffers a "blackout". He can still hear, but he cannot see. With relaxation of the G-force, vision returns although there is a moment of uncertainty as he readjusts to the situation. The effects can be minimised if the pilot is in good physical condition and tightens his stomach muscles in advance of the onset of the G-forces. Loops, rapid climbs and tight turns were commonplace in the melee that was aerial combat. A normal over-the-top loop in peacetime is usually performed at 4 Gs. A loop in combat would probably be 5 Gs or more. The very tight, right turn generated by the rotary-engine-powered aircraft was said to produce 5 Gs. Seven and nine Gs were common in combat manoeuvres. The pilots did not wear G-suits and had to fight the symptoms of greyout, blackout and momentary unconsciousness as best they could. The effects are temporary, but they are exhausting. They are also hard on the airplane. Fabric ripped, struts collapsed, wires broke and propellers disintegrated.

What Did They Wear?

A British pilot, Bernard Rice related:

> 'Captains and majors favour the conventional service dress tunic with "pips" and crowns on the sleeves and not the epaulettes as today, breeches, leather leggings and puttees clothe the legs. The most popular at the time with lower commissioned ranks seems to be the "maternity jacket". A double-breasted garment buttoning right up to the neck and right across the chest thus giving two layers of very thick serge as protection against the elements. Even though a leather jacket, helmet and boots were necessary. Gloves of course and silk scarf. The scarf must be silk because moving the head all the time any other material would chafe badly. The goggles served more purposes than to keep out the slipstream. In those days the engine lubricating system was based on the "non-return" principle. In other words, the castor oil was burnt up in the cylinders and thrown out in the exhaust system, it was also known as the "total loss" principle. Modern internal combustion engines cool, clean and then re-use the oils, which are mineral and not vegetable in origin. Now, inhaling much of these exhaust gasses heavily laced with castor oil very often produced problems with the lower bowel.'[18]

The Stress Environment

Pilots new to combat did not immediately recognise the psychological effects it would have on them. Indeed, for some, the rhythm of living, flying and fighting were joyous. Kiffin Rockwell, a graduate of Virginia Military Institute and one of the youngest members of the Lafayette Escadrille, wrote to his mother in 1915:

> 'We are certainly living an incongruous life. We live like princes when we are not working. An auto comes to take us to the field; we climb into our machines – which the mechanics have taken care of – they fasten us in and fix us up snugly, put the motor en route, and away we go for two or three hours to prowl through the air, looking for an enemy machine to dive on and have it out with.'[19]

The psychological effects of stress were just as dangerous as the physical, but less well understood. The characteristics of fighter combat flying were isolation, high uncertainty, high accident rate, high loss rate due to enemy action and the consequent death of comrades. The title of Ian Mackersey's book, *No Empty Chairs*, is emblematic of the situation: there were *always* empty chairs in the mess, until a replacement arrived. The stress induced medical symptoms of stomach ulcers, insomnia, nightmares, and frayed nerves, not unlike post-traumatic stress disorder (PTSD), so prevalent in the Afghanistan and Iraq wars. Temporary and long-lasting nervous breakdowns were common in WWI.

Oswald Boelcke flew in the first half of WWI, August 1914-October 1916. He was exposed to all of these hazards, including psychological stress, which the German air service recognised and called "abgeflogen" (flown out). Boelcke's letters are virtually silent about stress or psychological effects affecting him or other German aviators, but he was grounded on several occasions to counter his attacks of asthma. On at least one occasion (February 1916) he was hospitalised with what he called 'stupid intestinal trouble'. Boelcke also was affected by the loss of Max Immelmann in what he referred to as a 'very sad affair'. In his letter of 4 July 1916 to his parents, he wrote:

> 'Immelmann lost his life by a silly chance. All that is written in the papers about a fight in the air, etc. is rot. A bit of his propeller flew off; the jarring tore the bracing wires connecting up to the fuselage, and then that broke away. Quite apart from the sad personal loss we have sustained, in my opinion we must not underestimate the moral effect on the enemy and the reaction of our own people.'[20]

Arch Whitehouse, American observer and pilot, ace with sixteen victories, and post-war author, maintains that Oswald, 'experienced another psychological disturbance' with the death of Max Immelmann, but the nature of the "disturbance" is not further described. We also have no confirmation of this from any other writing, and Whitehouse does not reveal his source for this judgement. Whitehouse himself suffered from the loss of his squadron mates. His British squadron lost three times the number of its pilots in 1917, which left him alone and desolate. He is reported to having gone on "long solitary walks". He lost weight to the point where his clothes hung loose and flapping.[21]

There are only three instances where Boelcke's letters touch on stress, nerves and his attitude toward shooting down other airmen. The first is when he engaged a French two-seater over the Meuse River in March 1916. He had fired at the Frenchman, hit him and thought he would fall, but:

> 'Then I saw to my astonishment that the machine was still flying level once more. I naturally went for it again – then I saw the most amazing sight. The [artillery] observer had climbed out of the machine and was sitting on the left wing, holding on to a strut. He stared up at me in terror and waved his hand. It was such a pitiful spectacle, and for a moment I hesitated to fire at him because he was completely defenceless. I must have shot away the controls and caused the machine to heel over; then the observer climbed out and sat on one of the wings to restore the balance. I sent just a few shots at the pilot so as to force him to go right down .... The machine then went down for a short stretch in a glide, but finally crashed from a low height.'[22]

The second incident is when he was grounded by the Crown Prince after the loss of Max Immelmann. Boelcke was then the leading German ace, and the Crown Prince and the Kaiser wanted him protected at all costs. Here the reference to stress is only by implication. Boelcke was ordered to report to the chief of the air service, and he received military orders that he was not to fly for the foreseeable future. Boelcke was stunned and furious:

'The chief made a long speech, the purpose of which was that I was to sit in a glass case in Charleville [the headquarters]; I was not to fly at all for the present, because my "nerves" must be rested, but I could organise a Fokker Staffel in Charleville. Well, you can just imagine my rage. I was to sit in a cold water sanatorium in Charleville, stare up at the sky and take over the job of leading a crowd of weak-nerved pilots in need of rest.'[23]

The third reference is less about stress than it sheds light on Boelcke's attitude toward the opponents he was fighting against. In a letter to his family on 17 September 1916, Oswald wrote:

'In view of the many "numbers" mother will be saying again that it is not right to number our victims in this unfeeling way. But we don't really do it – we do not number the victims who have fallen, but the machines we have brought down. That you can see from the fact that it only counts as one victory when two inmates are killed, but that it still remains a "number" when both the inmates escape unhurt. We have nothing against the individual; we only fight to prevent him from flying against us. So when we have eliminated an enemy force, we are pleased and book it as one up to us.'[24]

We should keep in mind when reading the letters of an aviator written 100 years ago and his biography written over eighty years ago, that they are edited records. They were unconsciously edited by Boelcke when he selected what to tell his parents or friends. They were also edited when his biographer, Johannes Werner, decided what to include and what to omit. Then they were edited again in the translation into English. German culture in the first quarter of the 20th century did not dwell on, explore or reward psychological feelings. The writings of Freud and Jung had not penetrated the world of the warrior. Werner was writing with the approval of the family, and he would not have been inclined to publish lengthy accounts of Boelcke's misgivings or brooding thoughts. Werner notes that, "it is quite comprehensible that Boelcke did not inform his parents about the losses these [September 1916] victories involved. Four pilots fell up to 1 October."[25] This is not to say that Oswald dwelled on or had misgivings over the stresses and fortunes of war. It is only to acknowledge that writings of the German air service aviators on psychological stresses are much rarer than in British or American memoirs.

That Boelcke was affected by combat stress is a matter of record. His batman, Ludwig Fischer, recorded: 'My captain kept on growing thinner and more serious. The superhuman burden of seven take-offs a day for fights and the worries about his Staffel weighed him down.'[26] He would not go on leave and was in a depressed mood the last week. He said he found an opponent that was a match for him and there was hard fighting.

The famous British ace, Albert Ball (forty-four victories), was candid about his misgivings in both private and official communications. On 16 July 1916, he wrote to his family that he was feeling poorly and his nerves needed a rest. But when he asked his commanding officer for a short period away from flying, he was reported to higher headquarters and banished from the squadron for several weeks, despite the fact that he was already an ace (See Chapter IX). He was lucky to be allowed to return, as the stigma of "fear of flying" was widespread, and some men's professional lives never recovered from it. To a degree this is still true.

Ball was described by his fellow pilots as possessing 'a natural lack of fear'. He neither smoked nor drank, was withdrawn, uncommunicative and unsociable. He was a loner on the ground and flew as a lone wolf. He returned to flying in September 1916 and flew furiously for a few weeks. But he soon informed his commanding officer that his nerves were again failing, 'causing him to take unnecessary chances'. He needed another rest and was sent home in October 1916 to a flying training billet. By that time, he had amassed thirty-one victories. In April 1917, Ball returned to France and continued to win victories – and be troubled. In one of his last letters he wrote, 'I hate this game. I do get tired of always living to kill and am really beginning to feel like a murderer.'[27]

German air service documents do not record a set number of weeks or months for aviators to serve in active combat units, but we know from memoirs that they had periodic home leaves. The British instituted home leave in November 1914, generally for seven days, awarded after the aviator had been actively flying for two or three months. By 1917, the period increased to fourteen days. Over a longer period, the British limited their crews to six months at a stretch, interspersed with three months home leave.[28] The squadron commander had a great deal of discretion. Some fliers were sent home and never returned to France. Ian Mackersey reported that many pilots were mentally traumatised by air combat in France and were reassigned as instructors in the flying schools with no additional training, where these 'war-shattered pilots' were reluctant to fly again.[29] The US Army Air Forces set a limit of twenty-five missions for bomber crews in Britain in WWII. The United States Army and Air Force assigned ground and air personnel to South Vietnam for a one-year period. Aircrew assigned to squadrons in Thailand were there until they flew 100 missions over North Vietnam.

The Royal Flying Corps used home leave and medical diagnosis to treat psychological problems. Being at home with family or in London with partygoers was a welcome tonic for many fliers. For more serious cases, the medical officer would be brought in. Denis Winter's research noted that the diagnosis was the important thing. Men with more than 100 hours flying time were most likely to make a recovery; bachelors did better than married men. The most serious cases were depressions and hysterics. Two types of pilots' previous occupations seemed to be of special concern: poorly-educated men and those who had been in clerical work. The worst combat-inflicted cases were those who suffered aerial fires or been subject to a direct hit by anti-aircraft shells. 'In the end, 48 per cent of those treated for what at that time was called either flying sickness D or aviators' neurasthenia were returned to full flying duty, 60 per cent to partial duty.'[30]

Fear of Fire
Pilots and observers in WWI were almost universally afraid of fire in the air. Every day they either sat on top of, or immediately behind a fuel tank containing highly flammable petrol.

In case of a puncture or a leak in the tank or a fuel line, the petrol often leaked down onto a hot engine, causing immediate ignition. The aircraft were built of wood and dope-covered fabric. British ace, Mick Mannock's last diary entry provides a description:

'To watch a machine burst into flames is a ghastly sight. At first a tiny flame peeps out of the tank as if almost ashamed at what it is about to do. Then it gets bigger as it licks its way along the length and breadth of the machine. Finally, all that can be seen is a large ball of fire enveloping in a terrifying embrace.'[31]

Mannock's aircraft was hit by ground fire on 26 July 1918, burst into flames and crashed. Fire had the most profound influence on the participants. One such record was written by German ace, Ernst Udet, upon the death of a comrade named Puz Hanisch. Udet had watched as his friend's aircraft caught fire and became enveloped in smoke and flames. Then it broke apart and 'fell like a flaming meteor.'[32] Udet described the scene upon landing:

'The others had already landed and I found them standing in a group on the flying ground, dejected and talking in low voices. Glinkermann [who had been flying with Hanisch] stood a little apart from the rest, immersed in thought and scribbling designs in the sand with the point of his walking stick. His dog was beside him, rubbing his nose against his master's knee. But Glinkermann was beyond taking notice of the animal. His thoughts were elsewhere. As I approached him, he lifted his head and looked at me. "You mustn't blame me, Knagges," [his nickname for Udet] he said. "I really couldn't prevent it. He came down at us straight-out of the sun and by the time I had realised what was happening it was all over." Pain had distorted his features. I knew him and realised that he would torture himself with reproaches and doubts for weeks to come. [Later] in the afternoon all the machines had gone up and towards evening they returned in two's and three's. Glinkermann had not come back. The two men who had been flying with him had lost sight of him. He had disappeared into the clouds and was last seen flying towards the west. The old story. The old, bitter story .... I had the greatest difficulty in concealing the despair which I felt. But Gontermann [the squadron commander] had handed over his Staffel to me and I was determined that no one should see me displaying signs of weakness.'[33]

Udet became the second highest-scoring ace in the German air service with sixty-two victories. He survived the war as the greatest living German ace and became a popular stunt pilot and a leading figure in the formation of the Luftwaffe in the 1930s. He became the director of research and development and was appointed colonel-general. Blamed by Hermann Goering for the failure to win the Battle of Britain, Udet committed suicide in 1941.

A similar fate fell to Raoul Lufbery, one of the most famous pilots in the American 94th Aero Squadron. He had flown with the Lafayette Escadrille and earned seventeen victories before transferring to the American air service. When his aircraft caught fire, he jumped to his death rather than be burned alive.

Captain Donald Hardman, RFC, was in a battle one day in early autumn 1918, when he shot down an aircraft that burst into flames. Seconds later, he was astonished to see the German pilot fall from the cockpit, suspended under a parachute.

Parachutes

Air Vice-Marshal Arthur Gould Lee began his flying career in WWI and was so disturbed by the RAF's failure to provide parachutes that he became passionate in researching the background of this issue. The following narrative is drawn from his book, *No Parachute* (Grub Street, London, 2013). Parachutes had been demonstrated in the US in 1908 and in Britain in 1912. The British event was at Hendon, a training base, the site of the current RAF Museum. Most of these life-saving inventions were from balloons and were not adopted for cockpit installation. But in the US, a successful jump from a Wright aeroplane was made in 1912. Their military adoption in Britain was forcefully, but unsuccessfully advocated by E.R. Calthrop, a retired engineer, to the British high command. Calthrop's proposals were repeatedly received and considered by the Air Ministry from 1914 to 1918. One such confirmed negative decision was by Major General Henderson, the commander-in-chief of the RFC. Upon being asked in a memorandum for his policy to permit the continued testing of parachutes by the Royal Aircraft Factory at Farnborough in late 1915, when he penned the order, 'No, certainly not!'[34]

In 1916, the Air Board officially decided the parachute was not ready, and that it should await further developments, but there was no one in the RFC developing it. Boer War generals did not see the need for them. There was an unconfirmed report that the high command believed that the presence of parachutes would cause pilots to abandon airplanes, by cowardice, that could otherwise be saved. This rumour was never confirmed. But one official, Major Baird who was the Secretary to the Air Board and also a Member of Parliament, said in the House of Commons, 'pilots did not desire parachutes for aeroplanes.'[35]

Parachutes began to be used in the German air force in the spring of 1918, but they were never issued or used in the Royal Flying Corps during the war. Air Vice-Marshal Arthur Gould Lee concludes that there was not one specific person, but rather a 'collective official mind actuated by intangible prejudice' that refused this life-saving device.

"Victories"

In the first year of the war, there was virtually no thought given to air superiority or control of the air, let alone any way to measure this aerial function. Even when pilots and gunners started shooting down enemy airplanes in what were to be proclaimed victories, there was little consideration to counting the successes for either statistical measurement or cumulative impact.[36] Thus, the rules of counting, however defined, had to be developed ad hoc by each belligerent. The French were the first to recognise and count success in aerial battle in the spring of 1915. The successes of Roland Garros and Adolphe Pégoud were noted, recorded, released by the French army and publicised by the French press. The news was instantly popular, and the victors became the rock stars of their day. Pilots' claims began to accumulate. Shortly, the army became concerned over the accuracy of the claims, and as bureaucracy does, it began to establish rules for counting, in order to substantiate legitimate claims as victories.

Issues abounded. For example:

- Does a victory only refer to aircraft being destroyed? What if it lands successfully?
- Does the destruction need to be caused by the act of a pilot? Does the aircraft destruction have to be in the air, or can it be an unmanned aircraft destroyed on the ground?
- What about airborne balloons used for artillery observation?
- What if the aircraft is not destroyed but only damaged?
- Do both crew members get credit if the opposing aircraft is destroyed by the gunner/observer?
- What information is required for a pilot to make a claim?
- What evidence is needed to verify a claim? Is an airborne witness sufficient, or must it be a disinterested ground party?
- What if two pilots damage the same aircraft? Is the victory shared?
- What if the opposing aircraft is hit, goes into a spin, but disappears into a cloud layer and is not seen to actually crash?

The administrative rules are not available, and each nation developed them differently, according to their own culture. Generally, the claim needed to be verified by a second party, and the armies' preference was for ground confirmation – someone who saw the plane fall, land or crash. Complete destruction was not required, but only removal from the fight by explosion, crash or landing. Usually the victim needed to be flying, but in WWII, a grounded aircraft could be counted if it was destroyed by machine-gun fire. Balloons counted the same as aircraft as the risk to the attacking crew was the same, if not higher than in aerial combat.

The answers to these questions were difficult and sometimes controversial in the early days of flying. They were complicated by the heat of battle, multiple viewpoints and the fleeting nature of data in a whirling melee of aircraft. For instance, Norman Franks points out that German pilots were accustomed to identifying opposing aircraft by type rather than a specific name (e.g., a Vickers could have been any of the British pusher types: F.B.5, F.E.2, F.E.8 or D.H.2). Franks has this wonderful description: 'However professional these various airmen were, and in whatever war, they were still comparative youngsters, filled with enthusiasm and fear, optimism and a full measure of adrenalin.'[37] Overclaims were common, but the degree of the practice differed among the belligerents.

For the nations fighting in WWI, historians generally agree that the Germans developed the most rigorous procedures for investigating claims. Their process was to start with the information provided by the pilot, which needed to include date, time, circumstances, type of enemy aircraft, damage inflicted and location of the downed aircraft. This was facilitated by the geographical fact that German fighter squadrons generally fought on their side of the front lines, and most of their victims fell within sight of German troops. Thus, most of the downed aircraft were in the possession of German soldiers and could be seen, inspected and verified by the army. Infantry were glad to participate, and they would often report by telephone up their chain of command and to the local flying unit. Sometimes, the report of a downed enemy would reach the squadron before the pilots landed. The process was designed to be thorough, and confirmations frequently would take several days or weeks. The German records were printed in an official document called the *Nachrichtenblatt der Luftfahrtruppen,* some of which are in the possession of the author. The confirmation process was less accurate in the first years and the last hectic weeks of the war. Aircraft forced down were also counted as victories because this usually resulted in the death or capture of the enemy aircrew.

British generals officially discouraged the counting of victories because the high command wanted to retain the communal value of fighting for "king and country". Also, they did not want to sponsor a system that glorified individual pilots over those hard-working ranks who did their work in obscurity. Thus, the RFC confirmation system was rather more casual, sometimes even relying solely on the pilot's word as being sufficient for confirmation of a claim as a victory. France and Italy developed verification processes that were in between the strict German and casual British ones in their rigour. The American Army Air Service adopted French standards, except for those units flying under operational control of the British.

Aces

The ace is the top card in a deck. The aviator ace was intended to denote the top fighter pilots. The first ace was French Second Lieutenant Adolphe Pégoud. Pégoud had been a pre-war daredevil pilot and a publicist of his own efforts to demonstrate aviation to the public. After he gained his fifth victory on 3 April 1915, the French newspapers described him as a "Volant l'As" (flying ace). The actual number of victories required varied among the belligerents, especially in the early years of the war, but the consensus has settled on five as the requirement for this status.

The British used the phrase "star-turns", which was a show business term. German usage sometimes designated pilots with four victories as "Kanone" ("cannon"). More figuratively, the term could be translated as "gun" or "gunner" with "uberkanone" translating as "top gun", well known in the United States. Kanone is still used in Germany as an accolade for top performers like "sportskanone". Germany began using ten as the requirement but later adopted the five-victory norm for designating an "ace".

Aces as National Heroes

In the opening of the 20th century, famous aviators were publicised by the press and admired by the public. The Wright Brothers, Louis Blériot, Alberto Santos-Dumont, Harriet Quimby and Glenn Curtiss are only a few examples. The historian John Cuneo noted that 'a threatening danger from the skies produces a far greater impact on the morale of an earthbound foe than the same danger on his own level.'[38] World War I did not invent the aviation hero – they were created by public adulation ten years earlier – but it accelerated the use of aviators as symbols of national virtue and success. France led the way. As just mentioned, Adolphe Pégoud was a national figure well before the war, and his exploits were broadcast internationally. When he and Roland Garros shot down aircraft in the spring of 1915, French army officers recognised an opportunity for publicity, and they issued public releases that characterised their exploits. There is no doubt that this policy decision was not for altruistic reasons or even primarily to reward the pilots. There were most likely multiple motivations: 1) to broadcast national aviation success in order to increase public confidence and morale; 2) to distract the press and the public from the hardships and thousands of casualties in the ground war with little discernible progress; 3) to motivate young men to join the military; 4) to incentivise pilots to higher performance; and lastly 5) to reward aviators for their actions so they would continue to be models of national virtue.

With the determination and efficiency of the German/Prussian general staff, the German air service was quick to exploit the victories of its aviators in the service of the state. Press releases of Wintgens, Boelcke and Immelmann supplied the newspapers with frequent news of their fighter pilots' successes. To the public this became known as the "ace race". Understanding the proclivities of civilians, and especially children, to collect cards, the Germans sponsored the distribution of Sanke cards with portraits of famous war heroes. Interestingly, in a society that still respected and revered royalty and social class, the adoration of combat heroes was a democratising element. Some of the aviation heroes were royalty, but most were middle or lower class – officers and enlisted.

England was the outlier. There, as mentioned, official army and navy policy was not to publicise individual accomplishments in order to maintain the fiction that all soldiers and aviators were serving to preserve the nation. The clearest statement of this policy was an anonymous article published in the magazine, *Flying*, in 1917, under the title, "The Flying Corps Spirit":

'The Royal Flying Corps is coldly impersonal on its official reports. It is in this aspect splendidly unique. It alone among the belligerents steadily refuses the limelight so far as its personnel are concerned. In its bulletins, airplanes, not men, are mentioned. The names of its flying officers and observers are recorded only on the Roll of Honour [of the dead] or on the list of awards.

'On the whole, our policy is peculiarly British and it is based on British traditions. It springs partly from the regimental spirit, partly from the public school spirit, and partly from the sporting spirit which is found in the British wherever they are....'[39]

This has always appeared to the author to be ironic, that the British nation, a constitutional democracy, was the most undemocratic in its treatment of famous aviators.

The Military Contribution of Aces

In post-WWI analysis, it has become apparent that the identification of aces had a more practical use than just making heroes. Lieutenant General Jack Merritt and Pierre Sprey, in their article, "Negative Marginal Returns in Weapons Acquisition", concluded that a very small number of pilots (aces) dominate the air-to-air fight. Less than four per cent of the pilots in WWI contributed about forty per cent of the air-to-air victories.[40] (See the concluding chapter in this volume for observations about aces in Jasta Boelcke, which confirms this finding.)

CHAPTER II

Short History of the German Air Service

Differing Strategies

Military arms exist to implement political/military strategies of the nation state. The development and capability of Germany's air service needs to be understood in the context of its overall strategy, what could be called its system of warfare. Since at least the writing of Karl von Clausewitz, in his classic *On War* (Fernand Duemmler, Berlin, 1832) German military thought was dominated by the belief that the "fog of war" would cloud the implementation of all war plans. Therefore, all campaign planning embodied three features: 1) a bold offensive advance; 2) an enveloping attack of the enemy's ground forces; and 3) emphasising full initiative in the lower-level commanders.[1] The assumption behind this thinking was that information from the rapidly advancing front would be slow, unconfirmed and of little value. The natural result of that assumption was that tactical reconnaissance (cavalry and aircraft) would be less important than infantry and artillery.

Therefore, most German military strategists in the Second Empire, which was inaugurated in 1871, did not envision a role for aircraft to perform reconnaissance or artillery spotting. That belief led to underfunding by the war ministry of aircraft development. This mistake was compounded by the Germans' feeling of superiority in military arms that led them to neglect the impact of foreign aviation developments that would have challenged their assumptions.

In contrast, French military strategy following the Franco-Prussian War (1870-1871) was based initially on defence. The belief was that French intelligence and reconnaissance would warn of an attack and its disposition, and this information would be transmitted accurately and rapidly to the higher command. Thus, an active defence would be possible. However, when General Joffre became chief of the French general staff in July 1911, he turned the strategy upside down, into a vigorous offence. The change in the belief system that supported this radical change of strategy was the adoption of the "fog of war" theory – that the information gathered by the immature aircraft of the time would be late, inaccurate and contradictory.[2]

Airships

The German general staff and its officers were not so much impressed by the Wright Brothers' invention as they were by Count Ferdinand von Zeppelin's airships. However, Germany became one of the nations negotiating with the Wrights for the production of a military flying machine. The US Department of War's Ordnance and Fortifications Department had rejected the Wrights' offer of their "Flyer". This led the brothers to negotiate with the British, French and German armies between 1905 and 1908. All of the negotiations foundered, each on different issues. Prussian general staff officer Hermann von der Lieth-Thomson in 1907 was assigned to survey and report on foreign aviation developments.[3] In a prescient action, he advised his superiors that they should not rely on the observation of foreign aircraft, but should develop their own domestic aviation capability.

The German airship lobby was not deterred, and it was domestic. The airship's lighter-than-air feature and its abilities to lift heavy payloads and fly long distances seemed to offer the best prospects for military applications. Germany's leaders recognised that France had invested heavily in fixed-wing aircraft, and many believed that Germany needed to preserve its advantage in airships as a symbol of German air superiority.

At this point, a review of German bureaucratic politics is helpful to sort out the issues, proponents, and results of an inter-governmental battle. The Prussian war ministry was established during the Napoleonic Wars to bring the army under constitutional (civilian) control through administration and authority over the budget. The German general staff was organised primarily as a planning agency to command the German army. It is not wide-ly recognised that the German general staff was a democratising element of the German government. Staff members were recruited from junior officers on the basis of merit alone. One of the responsibilities of general staff officers was to appeal the decisions of line army commanders, and this provided a check on the follies of the nobility, whose positions were derived more from aristocratic connections, than merit.

General von Heeringen became the minister for war in 1909, and General Helmuth Graf von Moltke ("von Moltke the younger") was chief of the German general staff from 1906 to 1916. They were bitter opponents. Von Heeringen doubted the value of airplanes and supported the development of lighter-than-air craft, and in this fight he gained support of the army. Part of the army's dislike of the airplane was tied to the offensive strategy, which envisioned a campaign army that would advance in lines of march. Army officers demanded that all arms accompanying its divisions be capable of being broken down for transpor-tation on wagons pulled by horses. There are videos of early German aircraft with wings folded, awkwardly being readied for a field march.

The principal general staff officer who supported von Moltke was Oberst (Colonel) Erich von Ludendorff, a brilliant and hard-working officer in the mobility department. Luden-dorff had learned to fly and was known as the leading advocate of aircraft on the general staff. Ludendorff, in turn, was supported by his "action officer", Major Hermann von der Li-eth-Thomsen. Lieth-Thomsen published an article in the general staff-sponsored periodical of 1911 that advocated aircraft over dirigibles for the mission of reconnaissance. Von Molt-ke was not yet convinced, and in his input to the 1911-1912 budget, he urged full funding for dirigibles but was silent on the need for airplanes.[4]

Heavier-than-air machines were often called "flying contraptions" and were having many accidents at the time. The German people became apathetic about airplanes. Also, German engine manufacturers neglected the development of aircraft engines, and by 1911, the German military had only procured twenty-eight airplanes.

Another development in 1911 should have been noticed, but seems to have been neglected by the leaders. The army put out a call to recruit officers to transfer from other branches to aviation to man the small number of dirigibles and airplanes; 900 officers responded. In 1912, a group of German citizens became advocates for aviation and created a national aviation fund that raised $1,785,000 to support aircraft, pilots and record-breaking flights.[5] The national apathy had been broken.

Organisational Changes

Despite his earlier neglect of heavier-than-air aircraft, General von Moltke expressed concern about the size of the French air service as early as 1912. With the added support of the public, von Moltke submitted his programme for a large air force on 26 September 1912.[6] The essentially Prussian organisation incorporated contingents from the German kingdoms of Saxony and Württemberg, but the kingdom of Bavaria maintained its own air section.[7] The von Moltke programme had some effect, but when the German flying force (Fliegertruppe) was established on 1 October 1912, it was not nearly as large as Ludendorff and von Moltke wanted. Accordingly, von Moltke on 21 December 1912, submitted a report to the German Imperial Chancellor Bethmann-Hollweg, that advocated a separate air service. This, too, was not implemented.

One year later, 1 October 1913, the inspectorate of the flying troops (Idflieg – Inspektion der Fliegertruppe) was formed, with a comparable organisation for the airships. Oberst Walter von Eberhardt was selected to head the new office.

The Moroccan and Balkan crises of 1911 and 1912 spurred the Prussian war ministry to multiply its aircraft orders and to think about using aircraft to support the army. Industry responded, and production increased to 139 aircraft in 1912 and 461 in 1913. By February 1914, there were eleven manufacturers producing airplanes. The army estimated that this industrial base could produce over 100 aircraft per month. Operationally, in 1912, the German war ministry created three bases ("stations") for aeroplanes. The following year the army bill of 1913 transformed the "flying stations" into "flying battalions" under the inspectorate of flying troops. The organisation of the German air service in 1914 is shown in the figure below.

The organisation of the Prussian flying troops aircraft before March 11, 1915. (Reproduced from *German Air Power in World War I* by John H. Morrow, Jr. by permission of the University of Nebraska Press. Copyright 1982 by the University of Nebraska Press.)

This organisational structure recognised the rising role of aircraft, but it placed the inspectorate of flying troops under military transportation, which was primarily a procurement agency, not an operational organisation. This chain of command was deliberate as it kept the new aviation elements under the authority of the war ministry and its control of the budget. While appropriate during peacetime, especially for a fledgling organisation with no historical, doctrinal, or operational sponsor, it would prove to be completely wrong for wartime. The German high command (OHL) that controlled the army was not even in the aviation chain of command. The result was when the German army went to war in mid-1914, 'the picture on the ground was one of incompetence and inadequacy ....'[8]

German aviation sections (abteilungen) were assigned to army corps with the mission of strategic aerial reconnaissance. Their full name would become flying field sections (Feld-Flieger-Abteilungen – FFAs) Each section was assigned six aircraft and attached to a specific army unit, but aircraft were in short supply, and most sections had fewer. This piecemeal assignment of aircraft ensured that the rank of the aviation section commander was subordinate to that of his ground commander. In addition, the six aircraft were of different types, which made the job of resupply of parts much more complicated. Even there, aircraft were considered inferior to horses because cavalrymen were not limited by night and fog.[9] This argument is an example of the problems raised by new weapons. Moreover, these problems are broadly intellectual rather than narrowly technical.[10] The fact that the clip-fed, repeating, semi-automatic rifle and the machine gun were in the hands of front-line infantry was conveniently overlooked as devastating threats to the horse, let alone the viability of the massed cavalry charge.

In August 1914, when Germany went to war, it had ten first-rate dirigibles, but no plans for their use. In contrast, France had plans for its dirigibles to conduct strategic reconnaissance, but it had not developed the dirigibles' capabilities to accomplish the mission. The German army fielded forty-one flying sections of about 245 two-seat reconnaissance aircraft, with 254 pilots and 271 observers.[11] Eight of the aviation sections were assigned to fortress defence, and three of the field sections were assigned to the east. Thus, there were about 180 aircraft in thirty field sections on the Western Front.

France had twenty-one army and two cavalry escadrilles with about 140 aircraft. The British Expeditionary Force deployed four squadrons with twelve aircraft each, for a total of forty-eight aircraft. The Allied total was approximately 184 airplanes. Thus, the air forces opposing one another across the Rhine were about equal. However, as John Cuneo pointed out, no nation regarded the airplane as anything more than an auxiliary to the cavalry.

The German Offensive in the West

The rapid advance of the German army across Belgium and northern France gave the cavalry a prominent role, and the aircraft only assisted. However, when German General Kluck changed direction in his march to encircle Paris, French General Joffe began receiving rapid reports from his aircraft, and he became well informed of his enemy's intentions. He was able to blunt the Germans at the Battle of the Marne, causing the German army to retreat to the Aisne river.

Both sides began to dig in, and the front became defined by trenches. As the "race to the sea" began, aerial reconnaissance reports came in more rapidly than cavalry reports. The result was that each of the antagonists' air services denied the flanking armies tactical surprise. Commanders could know their opponents' intentions within an hour or two. With the front becoming stabilised, infantry troops dug in with machine guns strategically placed. Cavalry attacks against dug-in infantry with machine guns were disastrous. As the artillery moved up to support both defensive and offensive ground operations, the aircraft became indispensable in pinpointing and communicating artillery battery locations. The airplane became the primary reconnaissance arm by both merit and default.

Colonel Eberhardt tried hard to convince the general staff that the aviation units needed to be organised in their own, independent arm, but he was unsuccessful. Eberhardt was replaced by another aviation supporter, Major Roethe, but he too, was unable to provide the leadership needed to manage the Fliegertruppe in the midst of its multiple adversaries.[12]

As the war progressed, it became apparent that the placement of the Inspectorate of Aviation under the war ministry and the general inspectorate of military transportation was a problem. For example, the aviation section had almost no relationship to the group of transport units (railwaymen, motor transport, etc.). This alignment made the aviation leadership remote from the flying units at the front. Finally, in March 1915, eight months into the war, the German cabinet ordered the creation of the "chief of war aviation" (Feldflugchef) and placed him directly under the OHL. The man chosen to head this new organisation was Major Lieth-Thomsen, a protégé of General Ludendorff. He was promoted to oberstleutnant and given two broad sets of responsibilities. First, the acceptance of aircraft from the factories, their testing, and base construction was organised under the Inspectorate of Flying Troops. Second, operational activities at the airfields and army units were under staff officers of aviation. Lieth-Thomsen was assigned a most capable and innovative assistant, Major Wilhelm Siegert. Siegert had taken flying lessons in 1910 and commanded a group of three stations studying reconnaissance problems in 1912. He too was a passionate advocate of airpower. The resulting reorganisation of the German air service in 1915 is shown below.

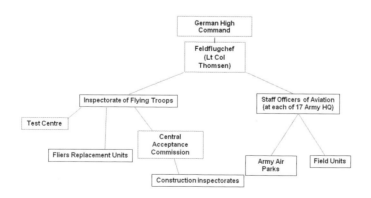

Organisation of the German air service, May 1915. (Reproduced from *German Air Power in World War I* by John H. Morrow, Jr. by permission of the University of Nebraska Press Copyright 1982, the University of Nebraska Press.)

Single-seat aircraft were at first dispersed, with one or two unarmed Taube, Fokker Ms or unarmed Fokker Eindeckers (all monoplanes) being assigned to each reconnaissance or bomber section. These single-seat units were called Feldflieger Abteilung (field flying sections). They supported the army corps-level missions of reconnaissance, photography, artillery-ranging and some bombing. The low-altitude ceiling of the Taube (about 6,000 feet) soon resulted in its being withdrawn from front-line units, leaving the Eindecker as the primary operational aircraft. Oswald Boelcke was one of the first of these pilots. As his reputation grew with the Fokker, his advice started to influence the infant service's further organisational and technical development.

The French were the first to recognise the fighting potential of specialised fighter aircraft. Since Louis Blériot's flight across the English Channel, France had invested heavily in military aircraft and led the world in the development of higher performance engines and an aerial-reconnaissance system. With the onset of war in August 1914, the French air service had 141 airplanes in twenty-one squadrons, with another 126 in reserve and fifty more in flight schools.[13] In September 1915, the high command designated squadron N12 as escadrille de chasseur, (hunting or pursuit squadron). This was the first unit on either side to be so specifically identified.

The German air service was inching toward the same conclusion. Major Siegert recommended the organisation of "carrier pigeon" units as a code name for Kampfgeschwader ("combat wings") that included combat single-seater detachments (Kampfeinsitzer Kommandos or KEKs). Some of the single-seat units became more permanent and were redesignated Fokker Staffeln. Their mission was "aerial guard duty" what we today would call "defensive counter-air". This was consistent with the Clausewitz theory that the defence was the stronger posture. However, the staff also dictated that the tactic to be used at Verdun was Sperre or "blockade", a passive and ineffectual use of airpower. Oswald Boelcke, flying Fokker Eindeckers, was assigned to command one of these temporary KEKs on the Verdun Front, and he promptly requested to be allowed to take his unit to Sivry, only 11 km from the front north of Verdun. Boelcke's unit was given the designation KEK Sivry-sur-Meuse (Sivry on the Meuse).

Boelcke defied the blockade directive and arranged instead a direct telephone line to a forward-observation post, which would phone him whenever French aircraft were spotted heading toward the front line. Boelcke's unit had such success with this tactic that it was adopted as German tactical doctrine for the rest of the war.[14]

Although there were only one or two Eindeckers in these temporary units, Boelcke and the other scout pilots occasionally flew together. Slowly they were practising and learning the value of the protection provided when more than one set of eyes was searching the sky for opponents, especially those who might attempt a surprise attack. With several more Fokkers assigned to his Verdun unit, these opportunities increased. Thus, the tactical formation of "leader" and "wingman" emerged. The task of the leader was to search for victims and be the "shooter"; the task of the wingman was to search for enemy aircraft and protect the leader. If the leader's guns jammed or if he ran out of ammunition, the wingman would be cleared to fire. With Boelcke's increased number of aircraft at Verdun, he had more opportunities to use this practice. Increasingly, he became an advocate of assembling yet a larger number of fighters into a Staffel, employing the principle of mass. With his increased professional prestige, his recommendations were given serious consideration at higher command levels.

In late 1915 or early 1916, Field Aviation Chief Lieth-Thomsen recommended the flying units be removed from lower-level corps headquarters control and placed under each of the seventeen higher-level army headquarters, where there were aviation staff officers who had flying experience and could better manage the flying sections. The high command rejected this proposal[15], but Lieth-Thomsen was not deterred. In fact, he had already strengthened the forces gathering for Verdun by concentrating fighter sections and scheduling reconnaissance sorties. German ground-support units were called Kagohls, flying two-seat C-type planes for bombing enemy targets in what we today would call interdiction missions. Lieth-Thomsen deployed two Kagohls of bombers and three units of fighters (KEKs) to the Verdun sector to support the offensive.

By 1 April 1916, the number of German combat aviation units had expanded to 163: 155 on the Eastern and Western Fronts, with six in the Middle East, Bulgaria and Turkey, and two in training. Of these, eighty-one were field flying sections.[16]

Despite the popular impression that German officers only followed orders and did not initiate actions, the actual German command practice was to delegate a great deal of authority to far more junior hands than the English or French. This practice has a formal German name, "Auftragstaktik". This cultural practice was one of the essential three features of the German grand strategy. Thus, Oberstleutnant Lieth-Thomsen held virtual sway over the entire front-line German sections, while in the French air service the position was held by a commandant and in the English, a brigadier general.

Even with an increasing numbers of German fighter and bomber units and the effectiveness of the Fokker Scourge, Germany suffered extremely large losses at Verdun. With the offensive judged a failure, the high command dismissed its architect, General Staff Chief Erich von Falkenhayn, and replaced him with Field Marshal Paul von Hindenburg, who had been the victorious commander on the Eastern Front.[17]

With the entire army at his disposal, von Hindenburg ordered a reorganisation of the Fliegertruppe. On 8 October 1916, the German high command redesignated the German air service as the German air force, elevating it within the Imperial German Army. The British were to create the Royal Air Force as an independent service, but not until eighteen months later. Lieutenant General Ernst von Hoeppner was appointed Kommandierende General der Luftstreitkräfte, abbreviated to Kogenluft, (commanding general of the German air force). After the appointment of Lieth-Thomsen as deputy to Lieutenant General von Hoeppner, the colonel continued to make decisions and direct the German air service forces at the operational level. The performance of this organisation and its star pilot is the rest of this story.

CHAPTER III

BOELCKE'S EARLY LIFE AND ENTRY INTO THE ARMY

Oswald Max Boelcke was born on 19 May 1891, in Giebichenstein, Germany, a suburb of Halle, a small town of Saxony-Anhalt about ninety miles south-west of Berlin. He was the son of a schoolmaster, the fourth child of six – five sons and a daughter. He was destined to become the most famous of his family, even though he had none of the advantages of being first born or wealthy. His parents had only returned to Germany from Argentina six months before his birth. His father, Hermann, had been the headmaster and rector of the German Protestant school in Buenos Aires for six years. His new position was as the senior assistant master in the higher modern school in Halle.

The Boelcke family house in Dessau. (Walter Waiss)

Oswald was troubled with adversity as a toddler. When he was three years old, he became sick with a severe attack of whooping cough. As a result, he was afflicted with a strong tendency to asthma that plagued him with continual colds throughout his life. When Oswald was four-and-a-half, the family moved a distance of about 30 miles north-east to Dessau, a small town located closer to Berlin. There, (*Herr Doctor*) Hermann Bölcke had transferred to the Antoinette School, where he was awarded the title of professor. Oswald's character thus started with educated parents in a small town where he was physically challenged. Dessau became Oswald's real home, which was near the Junkers aircraft factory and within hearing distance of the aircraft that flew overhead.

Oswald was challenged from birth with a universal question; how could he measure up to his older brothers? While he was still young, Oswald and his oldest brother Wilhelm changed the spelling of the family name from Bölcke to Boelcke, removing the umlaut and reverting to the Latin spelling.

Dessau lies on the Mulde River at its confluence with the Elbe. The town, which developed from a Sorbian settlement, was first mentioned in history books in 1213, and from 1603 it was the residence of the counts, princes, and dukes of Anhalt. The young Oswald pedalled his bicycle around this scenic town and often visited its 18th century castle. To counter his bouts of asthma and improve his breathing, he practised long walks, bicycle riding and long-distance running. He learned to swim at an early age from the hands of his father. Spectators were amazed when, after only a few minutes, he was paddling around solo in the cold Mulde River.

Oswald Boelcke in 1901 when he was 10 years old. (Walter Waiss)

The young Boelcke was called to the adventure of the military profession at an early age. He already knew that the positions in the officer corps were usually reserved for families of the nobility or sons of military officers. When he was still in elementary school (the third form) about 10 years old, he took a bold move and (without telling his parents) wrote directly to Emperor Wilhelm, requesting a cadetship in the army. Many months later, the family was shocked when they received a letter from Lieutenant General von Schwartzkoppen, the commander of the cadet corps at Metz, the military academy, telling them that the emperor had granted Oswald's request. His parents were elated, but became concerned over his education. In a sense, they denied his call to adventure as they kept him in school until he completed the gymnasium (high school) curriculum.

Oswald thus started life with an ordinary middle-class background in a society where class distinctions were important. Moreover, he had neither an imposing physical stature – standing only about 5 feet 7 inches – nor robust health. His tendency toward asthma interfered with his activities on several occasions in later life.

His character responded to this physical challenge. He compensated for his chronic condition by concentrating on rigorous sports of swimming, diving, tennis, rowing, gymnastics and soccer. Shortly after his seventeenth birthday, his father took him on a mountain climbing expedition to the Austrian Alps. He loved the sport and quickly became a 'skilled and fearless climber', excelling far beyond his father and brother Martin.[1] He felt he had finally made his father proud of him.

While in high school he studied history, mathematics and physics but he excelled in sports. His high school principal, Dr. Wiehmann, later described a youthful character:

'He had no mind for books or things studious; in him there burned the desire for action. He was energetic, dynamic, and needed to use his bodily vigour. Rowing, swimming, diving (in which he won prizes as a schoolboy), ball games of all kinds, and gymnastics, he choose as his favourite occupations before he entered his profession as a soldier.'[2]

Through his youth and subsequent adulthood, he maintained a positive attitude and tremendous will power. His systematic physical training was evidence of his will and determination to succeed. Reportedly, he was a born leader. Other boys called him 'a real good sport.' They admired him as the best athlete in gymnastics, and they submitted willingly to his leadership.

Oswald Boelcke at age 19, after receiving his high school (gymnasium) certificate and abitur in Dessau, 2 February 1911. (Walter Waiss)

There were also indications of his aspirations in his written and spoken work. His favourite books were of the works of Heinrich von Treitschke and the reports of the general staff. Von Trietschke (15 September 1834 – 28 April 1896), was a German nationalist professor, historian, political writer and National Liberal member of the Reichstag.[3] He was an advocate of Prussian destiny and became the official historiographer of Prussia. In 1895, he became editor of the *Historische Zeitschrift* (Historical Journal).

When he was 17 years old, Oswald chose three subjects for his elocution class and revealed a remarkable interest in aviation. His three themes were: "General Scharnhorst and his army reforms", "The first airship flights" and a 12-page essay, "Count Zeppelin's life before his earliest experiments in aeronautics". For his matriculation in 1910, he wrote in an essay that his favourite author was Homer, 'who took me back to the wonderful heroic age of Greece'. In the empire period of Wilhelm II, it was well accorded to be a member of the nobility or a military officer. Oswald grew up in awe of the upper classes because Dessau had its own noble families. Officers in Prussia also had a special distinction and an elevated life style. The class system in Europe tended to operate against the possibility of social mobility, but the class system in Germany was never as strong or rigid as in Britain or France. Unlike some trades and professions, the military offered the opportunity for social mobility based on merit. It is no accident that the military profession worldwide tends to attract lower-middle-class youth, many of whom achieve high positions of military and political leadership.

Meanwhile, the family continued to nurture the young Oswald. He was confirmed in St. Johns Church, Dessau, on 5 April 1908, at age 17. The motto of the church was, "I am not ashamed of the gospel, because it is the power of God for the salvation of everyone who believes". He drove himself to prove that he was capable and worthy.

Oswald Boelcke passed his matriculation exam with high marks and became abitur (from the Latin abire "leave, go off") with distinction. Abitur can be compared to A level exams. He graduated from the gymnasium just before Easter 1911, at age 19. On 11 March 1911, he left home and joined the Prussian cadet corps as an aspirant (a cadet in training to become a commissioned officer).

What can we say about his character at this early point? Six observations: 1) he was faced with adversity in health, but overcame it with vigorous athletics; 2) he was the fourth of six children, and it would have been perfectly natural for him to seek a distinctive role for himself and to strive for his father's recognition and approval; 3) he developed an adventurous spirit (he wanted to leave home, join the army and fly); 4) he showed initiative by writing to the Emperor; 5) he chose a profession of public service (service above self) and 6) he was well rounded, with social skills as well as enough academic preparation. His father, Herr Professor Bölcke, was most likely his first mentor.

Early Military Career

Boelcke crossed the threshold into the military profession on 15 March 1911. He was assigned to the No. 3 Telegrapher's Battalion at Koblenz. He wrote a letter four days later, which started his frequent correspondence with his family.

He wrote hundreds of letters, all of which the family retained. The letters he wrote during the war, after 3 August 1914, form the basis of the book, *Captain Boelcke's Fieldbook*, which his father published shortly after his death.[4] However, the earlier letters were available to his biographer, Professor Johannes Werner, who was given full access to the family and Oswald's letters. Their contents were not available to the public until Werner published Boelcke's biography in 1932.[5]

The city of Koblenz sits at a beautiful conjunction where the Moselle flows into the Rhine. There aspirants were under the command of an ensign, who supervised their scheduled activities: reveille at 5:00 am, stable clean-

The Bölcke family in Dessau, Standing from left: Martin, Oswald, and Wilhelm. Seated from left: Max, mother Mathilde and father Hermann Bölcke. (Walter Waiss)

ing, riding, inspections and field training that included telegraph cable laying. If Oswald had seen an occasional airplane at his home in Dessau, he saw many more on the parade grounds at Koblenz. He longed to join them. He also enjoyed the walks he and his comrades took to the "Deutsches Eck", the corner where stood a giant statue of Emperor Wilhelm I. Examinations at the telegraph battalion consisted of preliminary and final riding inspections and a set of imperial manoeuvres, which took him to Strasburg. There he saw large numbers of airships, monoplanes and biplanes. 'Flying is a fine game', he wrote. Graduation followed with the aspirants getting Christmas leave on 23 December 1911. Boelcke spent the holiday in happy days with his family in Dessau.

In January 1912, he was admitted into the Kriegschule (military academy) in Metz, Alsace-Lorraine (then a part of Germany) with a class of about 100. The curriculum was balanced between classroom lectures and practical fieldwork. The latter included infantry tactics, the art of fortifications, scouting, map reading and map drawing. Drill and gymnastics were also included daily. He even received personal instruction in penmanship. On 22 February 1912, he wrote to his parents, 'Aren't you surprised to find how nicely I have written this letter? I have been told in most forcible language that as a future officer I must acquire handwriting because my old one looked like a specimen from an infant's school. Father always used to say the same thing.'[6]

In March, he participated in "officers' patrols" on horseback, which he loved. Having come from the telegraph battalion where the aspirant's normal position was astride a fine stallion, he was at home in the saddle. In a rare expression of hubris, he wrote, 'I cannot understand why so many fellows grumble at the practical course as being too strenuous .... It is funny to see the infantrymen when they get off their horses; they can hardly walk a step.'

During the late spring, classes ended at 4:30 pm, which gave Boelcke some free time to play tennis and explore a new venture.

'Generally I go out to the big parade ground at Frescaty, where there are several monoplanes and biplanes flying every evening. One monoplane makes particularly fine flights (glides, etc.). I never get tired of watching and always stare at them with eyes of longing. It must be a wonderful sport – more beautiful even than riding! They are expecting more aviators here; there are to be fifteen of them when the emperor visits us on 15 May, as well as a Zeppelin, a Parseval [another dirigible type] and several captive balloons.'[7]

This longing to fly, the beauty of being free from the bonds of the earth, is a feeling that every pilot dreams about. The spring continued with lots of field manoeuvres and parades. Some were even attended by the emperor. The official examinations were in June and consisted of tactics, reconnaissance, fortifications, arms, military correspondence and more map drawing. An oral examination followed in each of the subjects in front of the higher military examining commission from Berlin. Boelcke scored "fair" in some of the written exams, but "good" or "very good" in all of the orals. His overall grade was "good" with an "excellent" in leadership. Graduation was in July 1912, and Boelcke was commissioned as an ensign in the telegraph battalion, Prussian army. Because he had abitur, his commission was pre-dated to 23 August 1910, making him senior to the other new ensigns in his battalion.

Promotions came rapidly. On 2 August 1912, he was promoted to "swordknot ensign" and transferred to the wireless company. Three weeks later he was promoted again and sent a proud telegram to his parents: 'Leutnant Boelcke presents his compliments to Herr and Frau Professor Boelcke.'[8]

The next two years went by quickly as Boelcke learned his trade as a wireless officer. His principal duties in Koblenz were training telegraph and wireless recruits, a job he thoroughly enjoyed. He had extensive field training, on horseback, but always accompanied by his dog, "Ibi".

Oswald Boelcke as an ensign in 1912. (Walter Waiss)

He also had lots of free time. He joined a reading group (which met at ladies' houses), a dancing group and a hiking club. In his words, he had a 'lovely, gay, active life'. His letter to his parents of 31 August 1913 is most interesting as it shows another aspect of his young life:

Boelcke with two of his horses and his dog "Ibi" in the wireless battalion. (Walter Waiss)

'I am sure you will have been surprised to get my letter from Baden-Baden. It happened like this: several ladies and gentlemen from our dancing circle wanted to go to Baden, because the race week and the dancing tournament for the world's championship were on there at the same time. It sounded most enticing, and as I had nothing particularly on in the service line, I suddenly decided to join their party.

'The dancing tournament was the principal attraction for me. It was just what I wanted to see; I have never come across such perfect dancing before. They only did the very latest dances, such as the Boston, One Step and Tango. I only wished that all the philistines could have been there who write and preach so narrow-mindedly about the licentiousness of modern dancing – they would have seen what nonsense they talk. Everything about these new dances was full of beauty, grace and harmony – the perfection of an art. Certainly these dances are so difficult that anyone who has no gift for dancing ought to keep his fingers – or rather, his feet – off them. It merely depends who is dancing these steps and how – some people can dance every waltz vulgarly.

'I was there every evening from Sunday to Tuesday and learnt a lot, first by looking on and then by dancing myself."[9]

In October 1913, he was transferred to Darmstadt where the country was one large riding ground. On a visit to Frankfurt, he witnessed a French flyer, Adolphe Pégoud, conduct an air show of aerobatics, which made a big impression on the young Boelcke. He was now 22 years old. February 1914 found him trying out for the officers' pentathlon for the 1916 Olympics to be held in Berlin. The five events in which he competed were: 4,000-metre cross-country; 300-metre swimming; pistol shooting; fencing and 5,000-metre obstacle race. Boelcke took first in swimming, second in cross-country, but sixth and seventh in fencing and shooting. He was third overall. With this position he qualified for the German Olympic team and would have competed in 1916. For one of his events he received a bronze medal, dated 9 May 1914, emblazoned with a raised eagle and the phrase, "From the Mayor of Frankfurt am Main", in a rectangular leather case with a gold-plated cover. The games were soon cancelled because of the war.

In April 1914, Boelcke applied to transfer to flight school. Unknown to his parents, Boelcke had become even more passionate about flying. While on a temporary assignment to Metz in 1913, he and his friend Walter Baltzer had the opportunity to fly frequently as passengers with the 3rd Air Battalion. He secretly planned at that time to initiate a transfer, but the two lieutenants conspired to not tell their parents for fear of their worrying about their sons in this "dangerous sport".

Pilot Training

Oswald Boelcke was accepted for pilot training on 29 May 1914. He began at the Halberstädter Fliegerschule (Halberstadt Flying School), Saxony, on 2 June. Government flight training in the fledging Fliegertruppe (flying troops) was contracted to civilian companies and only six weeks in length. He could continue the deception of his parents from June to August because he visited them in Dessau on his motorcycle every weekend and did not write letters. He recorded his experiences as a student pilot only in letters to his friend, Walter Baltzer.

If the weather was good they were awakened every day at 3:30 am to start training at 4:00. There were only four instructors and four dual-controlled flying machines – three 70 hp Bristol Taube and one 100 hp version. The Taube was the first aeroplane to be mass-produced in Germany and Boelcke's first trainer.

Boelcke's training aircraft, the Taube ("Dove"). (WWI Aircraft Models)

The school was only allocated two single-seat machines for solos. It is an interesting aside that the European airplane designers and manufacturers in 1914 were a close-knit group, exchanging information and sharing techniques across national boundaries. In a sense, they had a shared purpose: to convince their governments and their people that aeroplanes were important and reliable. Thus, the Halberstadt firm in Germany was affiliated with the Bristol works in England. Boelcke soloed in a British-made Taube aircraft.[10]

Each instructor had three pupils. The aeroplanes were exceedingly slow and so under-powered they often could not rise above 15-30 feet off the ground. This resulted in a lot of taxiing practice. Worse, if the instructor got fed up with the lack of progress of one student, he might stomp off and leave the other two standing around.

One might have predicted that Oswald Boelcke – the asthmatic child who loved and excelled at vigorous and dangerous sports – might be a little put off and impatient with a training curriculum that stressed slow airplanes and dogmatic instruction. In his letter, not to his parents, but to Walter Baltzer, of 16 June 1914, he wrote:

> 'Our machines are 70 hp Bristol Taube, which possess one excellent quality for instructional purposes, i.e., slowness, but often, however, they also have the vice of refusing to do anything at all; if the weather is a bit warm or the engine not quite at its best, the brutes cannot get higher than five to ten metres when carrying two men, with the result that we do nothing but taxiing, and so one learns nothing. It often happens that the pilot is fed up when he has finished instructing one pupil; consequently one can hang around for four hours and hardly get a turn – that always makes me wild.'[11]

When they did get airborne, the usual routine was one six-minute pattern and one landing from about 300 feet. Finally, Boelcke got a flight on the 100 hp machine and stayed airborne for 40 minutes, with an altitude record of 4,500 feet. By 3 July, he had logged 3 hours, 51 minutes on thirty flights (an incredibly low average of less than 8 minutes each). His instructor then sent him off to solo. His solo flight was even more eventful. The engine did the required 1,400 rpm on take-off, but slowly lost power 'with consistent malice'. At 50 feet altitude he had no chance to turn back, but landed straight ahead into a corn field.[12] [In over 100 years, that piece of flying advice has remained constant. 'If the engine fails on take-off, never turn back; you do not have enough altitude to make the turn safely.']

Further training consisted of "altitude flights", where he climbed to 1,000 feet and performed figure eights over two fixed points on the ground. The altitude was not high, although it caused his asthma to act up, and he suffered a shortness of breath. Thrilled with the flying, Boelcke was disappointed and more than a little upset that the students received so little actual time in the air. He recorded in his letters that he was allowed only four solo flights in the entire curriculum. His skill as a pilot was demonstrated when he was able to make two good landings in front of the commanding officer. On 31 July 1914, Boelcke passed his second test – an hour and eight-minute cross-country flight with a maximum altitude of 4,000 feet. He was scheduled to graduate in two weeks with his pilots' wings.

Pre-War Military Doctrine

Military doctrine can be described as fundamental principles, a 'set of shared values that give direction and purpose to organisational activity'.[13] It can be more informally described as a set of lessons learned from past experience. Thus, it is inherently a traditional value. Though the military profession is not as conservative as many people think, it is true that the traditional values of discipline and reliability are inculcated in both the training of pilots and the selection of aircraft. Moreover, the dominant military service before WWI in all the western countries (except England) was the army. This was especially true in France, Russia, Germany and the United States. These military professionals tended to view the airplane either as a nuisance or as an extension of the cavalry – good only for reconnaissance. Even the single mission of reconnaissance was suspect. A prime example of pre-war military thinking was enunciated by General Sir Douglas Haig, commander-in-chief, Aldershot Military Command, south-west of London, who said in a speech to army cadets in July 1914:

> 'I hope none of you gentlemen are so foolish as to think that aeroplanes will be able to be usefully employed for reconnaissance in the air. There is only one way for a commander to get information by reconnaissance and that is by the use of cavalry.'[14]

In using aircraft for the reconnaissance mission, the German and British armies preferred slow, stable two-seaters. Slow because speed was not needed, and slow provided more time for observation; and stable to facilitate accurate viewing and mapping of ground locations. The military procurement agencies of the time also preferred standardised production over innovation – quantity over quality. The British exhibited the same preference and assigned the mission to the venerable B.E.2C, which had been built for stability and deployed in the Royal Flying Corps since 1912. It was a solid, reliable platform with a speed of only 62 mph. This was far below the world speed record of 126 mph set in 1913 by a French Deperdussin sport monoplane.

The Germans used the Albatros B. II unarmed reconnaissance biplane (top speed 65 mph) and the Aviatik B. I (62 mph). The French used the Caudron G.3 with a top speed of 68 mph. All of these aircraft were biplanes because there was some prejudice against monoplanes for their alleged instability.

The training of pilots and observers was similarly conservative – stressing basic flying skills and safety over sporting acrobatics and innovative tactics. As the military historian and student of German aviation, John H. Morrow, Jr., described in his excellent study, *The Great War in the Air: Military Aviation from 1909 to 1921*:

> 'Armies clearly distinguished between sport and military aviation in airplane type and pilot training, and the untrammelled individualism and daredevilry associated with aviation sport were anathema to the military's emphasis in the disciplined fulfilment of one's mission as part of a unit. Pre-war military aviation agencies had sought to minimise flight risks [which were many] through standardisation of aircraft controls, installation of instruments, surveillance of construction, and the introduction of safety standards and stress tests. Ultimately the military sought to acquire slow stable planes for average pilots, not the great and gifted sport fliers whom some officers regarded as acrobats[and daredevils].'[15]

The role of the airplane in the years leading up to WWI was not well understood and subject to multiple speculation. Although many professionals were attracted by the possibilities of the technology, they tended to view it in the narrow terms of their own experience. The Wright brothers had demonstrated that heavier-than-air craft could fly for some hours and cover relatively short distances. However, they preferred to keep their invention away from public view. European pilots were more adventuresome, but few of them thought in larger terms.

Thus, at the Great War's beginning, there was a force of inadequately-trained pilots operating largely under traditional army rules, with a restricted view of their role. They did, however, all share a feeling: that they were different; they had a special skill in a unique venue. US General Carl Spaatz, Army Air Corps, said it best: "I guess we considered ourselves a different breed of cat, right in the beginning. We flew through the air and the other people walked on the ground; it was as simple as that."[16] The role of aviators was all to change, and Oswald Boelcke was one of the people who made it happen.

CHAPTER IV

World War I Begins – 1914

The German army mobilised on 1 August 1914 and activated its aviation elements, the Fliegertruppe, on 2 August. The Fliegertruppe was organised into fifty-five sections, the most numerous of which were the thirty field flying sections, which were supposed to have six aircraft each, but lacked these numbers.[1] Each of the eight German armies was assigned one airship and one aircraft Abteilung (section) of less than a dozen reconnaissance aircraft. Each of the twenty-five army corps headquarters was allotted an aeroplane section. Ten fortresses were each provided four airplanes. The OHL retained lighter-than-air airships under its own command but had not provided itself any airplanes.

The strategy of the German army was to fight a defensive campaign in the east, against Russia, and take the offensive on the Western Front. In the west, the operational plans called for a holding action in the south, opposite Verdun, and launch a massive offensive in the north, through Belgium and into northern France to capture Paris. This was called the Schlieffen Plan.

The cavalry was given the primary mission of reconnaissance in the initial offensive across Belgium and into north-eastern France. When General Kluck on the extreme right wing of the German army turned south-east, the move was detected and reported by French aerial reconnaissance. The French rushed troops to the critical point and won the Battle of the Marne. The Germans retreated eastward to the Aisne river, but the rapidly moving troops opened a gap between the German 1st and 2nd Armies. However, German reconnaissance aircraft spotted and reported the gap before the French could take advantage of the mistake. German commanders reacted quickly to their own missteps and changed what could have been a rout into an orderly retreat. Again during the northward "race to the sea" reconnaissance aircraft kept their respective commands informed on the positions of enemy troops and were recognised for their contribution. When the troops settled into static trenches, the front line reached from the English Channel through north-eastern France to the Swiss border. At its deepest point, the German lines were some 130 miles inside France. Thus, the overwhelming portion of the fighting on the Western Front in WWI was on French soil. The vaunted cavalry lost their effectiveness against the opposing trench lines, defended with dug-in infantry and machine guns, and virtually all reconnaissance fell to aviation. One of the results of this impasse was that a large number of cavalry officers applied for transfer to the air services, including Manfred von Richthofen later in the year.

Boelcke Gets His Wings
Oswald Boelcke passed his final pilot's exam on 15 August 1914, twelve days after Germany

declared war on France and Russia. The seal of graduation and his new status was a set of Prussian pilot's wings. This was not considered unusual since Prussia had been the leader of the German Second Empire since 1871. What was unusual was the oval shape of the badge itself and its use of the imperial crown and the embossed figure of an early German aircraft, the Etrich-Rumpler Taube (Dove). Other nations' air services badges resembled actual bird wings. This badge was the outward symbol of his entry into the special world of military pilots.

Boelcke had always been a prodigious letter writer, primarily to his family. The first letter after the war began was written at his pilot training base, Halberstadt, and is dated 1 August 1914:

'Where I will be sent from here, I cannot say as yet. My old mobilisation orders commanded me to report to a reconnoitering squadron in the first line, as commander. But these have been countermanded, and I do not know anything about my destination. I expect to get telegraphic orders to-day or to-morrow.'[2]

The new pilot was not assigned back to the telegraph battalion in a reconnaissance squadron, as he had wished, but instead to a replacement section at Darmstadt. There he helped

Prussian pilot's wings.
(Walter Waiss)

train fifty new student pilots, flying an Aviatik B.I biplane. Like so many young men, he was impatient to get into action. He was active socially, but that was not enough. He soon wrote, 'All acquaintances here – especially the ladies – pet and spoil me, but what is the good of that if the war is over before I get out to the front!'[3] The ladies of Koblenz called him their 'golden lad'.

Meanwhile his oldest brother Wilhelm also had entered the German air service. He was a leutnant stationed as an observer with a biplane unit, Fliegerabteilung 13 at Montmédy. On 1 September 1914, Boelcke was ordered to fly from Trier to Sedan with an observer. On the way, he 'inadvertently' landed in Montmédy, and the two brothers had a reunion. One might observe that this deliberate act was an early indication that Boelcke preferred "daring" over "reliability". Due to Wilhelm's influence (and the commander's acquiescence) Oswald was transferred into the unit, and they began to fly together. In a letter to his parents on 4 September 1914, the younger Boelcke wrote,

'Have been here with the division for two days. As I had no observer along, Wilhelm has commandeered me. Of course, I like to fly best with Wilhelm, since he has the best judgement and practical experience. As he already knows the country fairly well, he doesn't need a map at all to set his course. We flew over the enemy's positions for about an hour and a half at a height of 2,800 metres

Oswald Boelcke just after graduation from pilot training, 1914. (Andreas Thies)

(9,200 feet) till Wilhelm had spotted everything. Then we made a quick return. He had found the position of all the enemy's artillery. As a result of his reports, the first shots fired struck home.'[4]

It was ironic that as his father had been his first mentor in seeking an adventurous life, and now his older brother was his second. Wilhelm taught Oswald the skills of artillery spotting, the professional values of the military officer and culture of the military aviator. The younger Boelcke learned eagerly.

In 1914, there was no thought that there would be any air combat. The French air force owned only two machine guns; the British and the German air service had none. The aerial convention of the time was that since the primary mission of the unarmed aeroplane was to observe enemy movements and artillery positions, the most important crew member was the observer. This crew position was almost always filled by a commissioned officer, usually an artillery lieutenant or captain who was in current terms the "aircraft commander". Pilots in the German air service and the RFC were frequently enlisted men, and the pilot was considered a chauffeur. In Germany, the observer was euphemistically called "Franz" and the pilot was "Emil". The connection between the two was humorously characterised by an unknown German airman: 'Like Max and Maurice, like wind and storm, like whisky and soda, so do "Emil" and "Franz" belong together. They animate the dead material with human spirit, form the airplane crew and make it the important implement of military reconnaissance.'[5] There is still in Germany today, a colloquialism, if you guide someone in the wrong direction or you drive the wrong way, you can say, 'Ich habe mich verfranzt'. ('I have verfranzt myself.')

Manfred von Richthofen told a funny story from his own experience. It seems he was engaged in a fight in March 1917, when an English pilot put several bullets through his fuel tank. Forced to land, he was soon surrounded by a large crowd, when a German engineering officer ran up, all out of breath and excited. Von Richthofen introduced himself, and the officer invited him to ride in his car. Suddenly, the officer jumped up and exclaimed, 'Good Lord, where is your chauffeur?'[6]

Oswald and his brother Wilhelm at Pontfaverger, autumn 1914, in front of a modified Albatros B.I at Fliegerabteilung 13 The aircraft identification "Iron Cross" is not yet standardised. Note the break in the centre of the top wing that allows it to be folded back for transportation on roads. (Walter Waiss)

The two brothers flew together in an early two-seat Albatros B.I biplane, Oswald as pilot, Wilhelm as observer. (The Albatros company constructed many reconnaissance, light-bomber and fighter biplanes during WWI.) The two brothers flew numerous reconnaissance missions to report the locations of French artillery as the German divisions advanced rapidly. General von Pritzelwitz awarded Wilhelm the Iron Cross for his observation work. Six weeks of offensive attack took the German army within miles of Paris. But then in mid-September the tide changed, and the brothers witnessed the retreat of the 1st and 2nd Armies to the Marne and then the Aisne river. By the end of September 1914, flying out of Buzancy, the two flyers were already observing the two armies facing each other in trenches. High winds, rain and the lack of infantry activity led to aerial inactivity; Boelcke frankly admitted to being bored, and the wet weather affected his asthma. When the weather cleared he was up flying artillery-spotting missions in the Argonne Forest region of France.

Boelcke was awarded the Iron Cross Second Class on 12 October, reportedly for flying fifty combat missions.[7] The actual medal was only to be worn on the day of award; subsequently, the ribbon was folded and inserted into the second buttonhole on the right of the blouse. Even at this early stage in the evolution of aviation, the significance of the number of combat missions must have been recognised.

Later that month, Boelcke recorded his anticipation of getting a new airplane. He wrote in his *Fieldbook* on 30 November, 'I did not get the Fokker as yet. I was to get it at R[ethel], Thursday. Too bad. To fly for the artillery, which is our main work just now, the Fokker is very excellent, because of its speed, stability and ease of control. A new machine has been ordered for me at the factory, but I cannot say if I am going to get it, and when.'[8] Ten days later an unarmed Fokker M8 arrived for his use.

Iron Cross Second Class medal. (Walter Waiss)

'Yesterday I was in R[ethel] and got my Fokker, which had arrived in the meantime. It is a small monoplane, with a French rotary engine in front; it is about half as large as a Taube. This is the last modern machine which I have learned to fly; now I can fly all the types we make in .Germany. The Fokker was my big Christmas present. I now have two machines: the large biplane for long flights and the small Fokker for range finding. This 'plane flies wonderfully and is very easy to handle. Now my two children are resting together in a tent, the little one in a hollow, with its tail under the plane of the big one.

Ltn Oswald Boelcke'[9]

Boelcke loved the Fokker M8. Its light weight and powerful engine gave it good speed, a high climb rate, and its design gave it manoeuvrability – all excellent qualities for the mission of artillery spotting. However, the craft developed a rep-

Unarmed Fokker M8. (William Whitson)

utation for unserviceability. The Prussian inspectorate of aviation sent a commission to the Fokker factory and focused on the welding of the steel tubes that framed the fuselage. The inspectorate's regulations were over-specified; they only recognised wood and fabric construction; they did not allow for welded steel tubing. Fokker's chief technician, Reinhold Platz, convinced the sceptical engineers that the steel structure surpassed their requirements.[10]

On 16 November 1914, the German war ministry (inspectorate) made one of the worst decisions of the war. It decided to limit the development of aircraft engines to those with less than 150 horsepower in order to concentrate on mass production. This could have been with the expectation that the war would be a short one, despite information from the front that there was no end in sight. In any case, this essentially froze research and development on engine power and inhibited the development of heavier and faster aircraft, which would have needed a more powerful engine. It is ironic that the Luftwaffe would make exactly the same mistake in the late 1930s when it concentrated production of the Bf-109 and retarded the conceptual and engineering development of faster and longer-ranged fighters.

The Prussian inspectorate made a decision in December 1914 that seemed to ignore the November decision on engines. The decree increased the performance requirements for aircraft – higher, faster, and farther. How did it not occur to them that these requirements would require more powerful engines? The big three manufacturers, LVG, Albatros and Rumpler, met with inspectorate personnel and objected strenuously to the revisions. They argued that the changes would slow production and require the development of new tools, techniques and prototypes. Thus, they were being asked to institute research and development, which would interfere with their profitable serial production. Further, they were all working on fixed-price contracts, that specified production output at a set schedule. Who would pay for this diversion? In addition, the task of research, development, test and evaluation was inherently fraught with delay and risk, which are not appropriate for fixed-price contracts. (This tension between quantity and quality is a fundamental component of aircraft procurement that remains today.) What the manufacturers were responding to was the eternal industrial dilemma of the triangular relationship among "performance-schedule-price" where changes in one desirable feature inevitably mean changes in the other two. The result of this early debate was a compromise. The inspectorate insisted on a reduced set of performance improvements, gave in on schedule, but held the line on prices. The manufacturers agreed to make the incremental performance enhancements and argued hard and complained bitterly about the prices. The inspectorate of aviation did not agree to increase prices until February 1915 and then only by three per cent.[11]

Bavarian Independence

Another organisational factor that limited the effectiveness of the German air service was the semi-autonomy of the Bavarian regional government and its aviation manufacturers. The proud Bavarian authorities decided to continue their pre-war policy of restricting the invasion of Prussian manufacturers by buying only from the local factories of Otto and LVG. They even rejected an offer from Albatros in Berlin to build airplanes for Bavaria. They were trying to protect Bavarian industries from Prussian competition. As late as November

1914, two months after the Battle of the Marne, when Albatros proposed to produce aeroplanes for Bavaria from a subsidiary in Augsburg Nürnberg, the Bavarian war ministry again rejected the offer with the argument that their small government would never be capable of funding *three* factories after the war.[12]

In conclusion, the strategic and tactical situations in late 1914 did not demand industrial efficiency or performance increases that would become apparent in 1915 and thereafter. The front lines were relatively stagnant, and the aerial tasks were well identified as unarmed reconnaissance, artillery spotting and communications. There was no air combat threat to speak of, and the slow, stable aircraft of the period on both sides were adequate for the missions at hand. There was very little thought given to arming the aircraft. An RFC staff officer is quoted as saying at the start of the war, 'There should be no attempt at aerial conflict'.[13] Seeing, not fighting, was to be the role of the airplane.

At this early point in his career, we can witness that Boelcke is evolving from the romantic youth to the young professional, still adventurous, serving in an assigned position, and gaining expertise in flying, and flying in combat. By the end of 1914, Wilhelm Boelcke had logged sixty-one combat missions and Oswald had forty-two. All this was to accelerate in 1915 and even more dramatically in 1916.

CHAPTER V

Fighter Aviation Begins – 1915

As the year 1915 dawned, and it became obvious that the war had not ended by Christmas, the belligerency of the participants increased. In the air no one knew what to call the aeroplanes that were to conduct the new mission of "air superiority". Several terms were coined and evolved with usage: "scouts", "chase", "pursuit" and eventually in the 1940s, "fighter". These terms are essentially synonymous.

On 27 January 1915, Boelcke was awarded the Iron Cross of the First Class, which his brother Wilhelm had received in November 1914.[1] Unlike the Iron Cross of the Second Class, this medal is worn on the left breast. On the occasion of his brother's award the previous October, Oswald noted that Wilhelm 'has covered a total distance of 6,500 kilometres over the enemy's soil, while I have covered 3,400'.[2] This statement is interesting as it reveals the search for common statistical reference points to gauge "flying experience". Distance behind enemy lines may have been an accepted measure of merit for cavalrymen, to which the early aviators were likened, but it is less relevant for aviators. Part of the reason is that it rewards those who fly the faster aircraft, and diminishes the contribution of crewmembers who fly slower aircraft. Thus, a pilot or observer in a faster airplane would earn a higher rating (i.e., longer distance flown) than one in a slower plane. "Behind enemy lines" also emphasises the offensive and neglects sorties flown in air defence, behind one's own lines. Sometime in WWI, as aviators took more command of their own profession, this practice evolved, and "flying hours" replaced "distance flown" as the general metric to rate experience.

Boelcke and Nurse Klara. (Walter Waiss)

Early in 1915, Boelcke's bronchial trouble flared up, and he was hospitalised. The cold, wet, winter weather affected his lungs, and he found it difficult to breath. Again, his willpower and good medicine overcame the illness. Following his medical stay at Rethel he was reassigned to the German air service's inspectorate division. After two weeks of boring routine on a desk, he was again assigned to Fliegerabteilung 13 with his brother. Showing his playful side, the young Boelcke gave two nurses a ride in his aircraft and was resoundingly chewed out by his commander. The nurses were sisters: Blanka and Klara. We do not know if any romantic attachment resulted.

Combat Experience Metrics

The Germans recognised the importance of experience in operational flying early in the war. Their first innovation was to provide initial combat experience by assigning new pilots first to two-seater aircraft. These aircraft were slower, somewhat safer and had the advantage of two crewmembers. After a period of time (usually six months) and upon gaining a certain amount of "situation awareness" in the combat theatre, they transferred the most aggressive and most promising pilots to single-seater sections. Much later, in 1916-1917, they organised advanced training units called Jastaschulen (tactical schools) that provided instruction in operational and combat tactics. These two policies were valuable in reducing combat losses by providing combat experience and tactical lessons in relative safety.

The importance of pilot experience in combat cannot be overrated. There are four metrics that pilots and other aircrew members use to rate themselves and their compatriots today:

- total flying time (in hours);
- time in a geographic theatre (in months);
- flying time in a particular aircraft type; and
- number of combat missions. The navy adds a fifth metric: the number of aircraft carrier landings ("traps").

These metrics can be explained in more detail. *Total flying time* begins with pilot training and continues through an aircrew member's life. Fighter pilots with less than 400 hours today are novices and usually fly with supervision. In modern combat, they would usually fly as "wingmen" or simply "wing". Those with 400-1,000 hours are young but moderately experienced. They would usually fly as "element leaders" or flight leaders in charge of a two-ship formation. Those with over 1,000 hours are flight leaders, capable of leading a flight of three or four aircraft. Pilots with over 1,500 are veterans and instructors; they can perform any of the above roles.

Time in theatre relates to flying time in a region of operations. In World Wars I and II, there were distinctions among the theatres of operations: Western Front, Eastern Front, Italian Front, Middle East, and Pacific. This criterion becomes more important if it is the second or more time in the same area. This criterion is also relevant to ground forces as multiple tours for US troops in South West Asia were common. In the Great War, the nature of aerial combat between the Eastern and Western Fronts was dynamically different (the Eastern Front being less dangerous) so the theatre time was an important distinction.

Flying time in an aircraft type is also vital, especially in combat. The skill and leadership of a junior officer with high aircraft time can be recognised and rewarded in a squadron setting. This is truer in combat than in peacetime flying because of the informality that combat brings. Skill is more important than rank. Analysis has shown that the total number of flying hours is less relevant than the time in a given aircraft. Thus, a young captain or lieutenant in combat with 1,000 hours in a particular aircraft would be accorded more "experience" because his aircraft experience was more relevant to the mission at hand than a more senior officer with most of his flying time in other aircraft. Top-scoring aces in WWI, WWII, Korea and Vietnam tended to have high time in the aircraft they were flying.

Number of combat missions is the best indicator of aircrew survival in wartime because it combines flying time with local time in theatre, and gives credit for time in a specific aircraft. The combination is a measure of personal flying skill, combat situation awareness, experience with the current enemy threat and better knowledge of friendly capabilities.

The First Five Engagements

Pilots new to a theatre of operations with no combat missions are notoriously likely to be shot down. H.K. Weiss published a remarkably innovative analysis in 1965 of survival rates versus *decisive* air battles. His data showed that a pilot who survives the first five decisive engagements is more than *twenty times* more likely to survive their next one.[3] The main reasons are:

- Less capable pilots and crews do not look around enough and are surprised by enemy aircraft. They are quickly killed off;
- Many Allied pilots in WWI were flying their first combat mission in an airplane they had never flown before;
- Those with poor prior training are shot down quickly. There are numerous anecdotal accounts of pilots being so overwhelmed by the onrush of physical and mental sensations on the first and early combat missions in WWI that they get lost from their own formations and become "sitting ducks". Many didn't even see the enemy aircraft in the sky and didn't realise they were being attacked until they heard bullets flying past their cockpit;
- The incremental development of flying skills and situation awareness need time and experience to mature;
- Situation awareness is vital – one needs to know the full environment surrounding the aircraft; the ability to see and understand the many inputs that are being received; the big picture; knowing where one's comrades are, where to look for the enemy and what to do in case of an emergency.
- "Thinking behind of the aircraft". Events in the air tend to happen quickly, faster than anticipated. A pilot with low situation awareness is often thinking "behind" the aircraft (i.e., they are surprised by events and react slowly). Good pilots learn to think ahead and anticipate what the next action will be. They control the situation.

The aircraft is a machine, and the pilot's connection to the machine is through the cockpit. The cockpit of WWI aircraft contained several primitive instruments, sometimes a large number of levers to control fuel flow, fuel mixture, gas tank selection, compression ratio, engine speed and triggers for one or two machine guns. These were in addition to the main flight controls of stick and rudder. New pilots routinely get preoccupied and spend excessive time looking for a particular switch or instrument within the cockpit, which limits their ability to look outside for enemy threats.

Weiss' attrition curve begins with a probability of loss of about 40 per cent in a pilot's first decisive encounter, which drops to less than five per cent by the tenth mission. This data was portrayed on a graph. Similar British documentation of the high loss rate of pilots new to combat states that 80 per cent of casualties in the RFC were with pilots with fewer than twenty combat missions.[4]

Air Superiority

World War I began with little strategy for the use of aviation in combat, no concept of fighter aircraft and no mission of air superiority. Existing doctrine in most countries tied the air machine to the missions of the army – primarily reconnaissance and artillery spotting. From 1910 on, the French army developed this into a very intricate system. It is one reason French aviation was so responsive from the First Battle of the Marne through the race to the sea. It was not until the war began, and the armies found themselves being observed by the enemy, did it occur to assign some kind offensive (bombing) or "denial" mission to the aeroplane. Thus, the concept of "air superiority" evolved slowly, with a mission that we can currently define as *'dominating the air battle by one force to permit the conduct of its own operations at a given time and place and denying this capability to the opponent'.*[5]

In the years of 1914 and early 1915, many unarmed pilots and observers from England, France and Germany waved to each other as they passed in the air. It seemed as if a new era of chivalry had dawned. Soon all that changed. Different countries adapted in distinctive ways.

The British Empire: The Doctrine of the Offensive Spirit

The dominant force in Great Britain had always been the Royal Navy. The army was kept small and mainly used for colonial insurrections. (Recall the rebellion of the American colonies and Victorian India. After all, it was the army under Cromwell that had beheaded a king.) The Royal Flying Corps (RFC) had been formed in 1912 and deployed its part of the small British Expeditionary Force to France in August 1914. The RFC field commander was Brigadier General Sir David Henderson. He was a decorated veteran of the Boer War and had learned to fly in his fifties. The most prominent officer in the RFC was Lieutenant Colonel Hugh Trenchard. He had learned to fly at age 39 in 1912. In September of that year, he was the observer in the single-reconnaissance aircraft to spot the opposing forces in the annual military war games held in East Anglia. He had his pilot land at Blue Force headquarters and delivered his spotting report to Blue Force commander, General Grierson. Trenchard then volunteered to carry the general's revised war plan to his cavalry commander, an action that provided the victory to the Blue Forces. As a captain in 1913, he was an instructor at the Central Flying School. In 1915, as a lieutenant colonel he became the commander of the First Wing, RFC, in France.

The RFC was the first air service to win an aerial victory on the Western Front. On 26 August 1914, several British machines pursued a German Taube and drove it down to the ground. Three days later another British pilot did the same.

The RFC had between eighty-five to ninety aircraft at the Western Front in March 1915, 106 in June and 153 in September. These numbers were small when compared to the French and German aircraft. Still, Lieutenant Colonel Trenchard insisted his First Wing conduct relentless, offensive action, which became known as the "offensive spirit". This included high sortie rates by each squadron and fighters attacking every suspected enemy plane, regardless of location, weather, numbers or condition. Yet the RFC high command provided no tactical doctrine, no tactics and no techniques. The de facto employment doctrine was direct and aggressive. Major Lanoe Hawker, commander of 24 Squadron, ordered, 'Attack everything'. This British doctrine of seeking combat regardless of time or location could have been derived from Royal Navy doctrine, but it was alien to evolving French and German fighter tactics. One critical contemporary commented that Trenchard pressed the RFC so hard that 'it suffered losses wholly disproportionate to any good achieved'.[6]

As an example, German Leutnant Baldamus was shot down by the RFC on 11 December 1916, and became a prisoner of war. From this vantage point he observed British pilots and commented on the contrast between the British and German tactics:

> 'You [RFC pilots] seem to be magnetically attracted to any German aeroplane you see, and never weigh the situation. I saw one of your machines take on one Fokker, then two Fokkers, then three Fokkers, before being shot down at Lille. We do not look for fights unless it is our duty. With us a machine should return without a fight, unless it is specifically sent up to fight. To return without a fight and with our work done, is the task with us.'[7]

In what some might call typical British fashion, some in the RFC interpreted the German tactics as a lack of courage.[8]

France

Among the Allied Powers, the French were the most aggressive in recognising and adapting the air arm for war. They had conducted numerous experiments to this end before the war. On 5 October 1914, Sergeant Joseph Frantz and Corporal Louis Quenault, flying a Voisin III of French Escadrille VB24 were the first aviators in history to shoot down another aircraft with machine-gun fire, downing a German Aviatik B.II. By 1915, the French had multiple observers and pilots firing carbines at opposing aircraft.[9] One of the most famous pilots was Adolphe Pégoud.

Pégoud earned his pilot's rating in 1913, was the first person to make a parachute jump, the first to perform an intentional acrobatic loop and the first to fly inverted. He was also an instructor pilot and the chief test pilot for Louis Blériot. At the beginning of WWI, he volunteered his services as a pilot in the *Aéronautique Militaire*, which had been created as a branch of the French army on 22 October 1910. With their early victories obtained by the use of firearms in the air, the French can be said to be the first holders of air superiority. But they neither sought it, nor exploited it. Its meaning and value were not understood. Ironically, the German air service elevated the French superiority to superhuman proportions, and its pilots spread the fiction that all French aircraft carried machine guns.

Flying a Maurice Farman on 5 February 1915, Second Lieutenant Pégoud and his observer/gunner shot down two German aircraft (a Taube and an Aviatik C) and forced another to land (a second Aviatik C). On 3 April, he followed up this hat-trick by downing a German two-seater and another Aviatik, making a total of five. This made him officially an ace. In late spring 1915, the French fielded three single-seat squadrons flying Morane-Saulnier monoplanes, and Pégoud was transferred to Escadrille 49. A sixth victory followed on

11 July 1915. The next month, on 31 August 1915, Pégoud was flying a new Nieuport Bébé when he encountered one of his own German students that he had instructed before the war. Unteroffizier (Corporal) Walter Kandulski shot down and killed his instructor, Pégoud, who was 26 years old. Kandulski survived the war.

By the end of March 1915, barely nine months into the war, the French had fifty-one squadrons flying on the Western Front, two more in Serbia and 390 aircraft in the Near East.[10] However, French emphasis in 1915 was on bomber production and employment – not fighters. French factories were also working hard on increasing the horsepower of aircraft engines, both rotary and in-line. For example, the 90 hp Gnome was increased to 130 hp, and the Hispano-Suiza firm produced a 150 hp V8 engine.

Roland Garros, Escadrille 26, mounted a fixed machine gun to the forward fuselage of his Morane-Saulnier monoplane, firing through the propeller arc. His ingenious method to avoiding damage to his own prop was to affix triangular steel wedges onto the rear of the propeller, which would deflect bullets that would otherwise penetrate the wooden thruster. Sometimes the device worked; sometimes it did not. Garros' accomplishments with this haphazard device led to a low point in German air morale.

German Military Initiative

Despite the popular conception that German military operations are dictated from the top, German tactical doctrine delegates considerable decision-making to junior officers. Those on the scene were allowed and encouraged to take the initiative and not to delay, waiting for higher headquarters approval. This concept is embedded in German culture and is called, "Auftragstaktik" (mission tactics). German air service pilots were allowed to assess the situation's balance of opportunities and risks in their attacks. This balance is inherent in Oswald Boelcke's tactical philosophy as expressed in Dictum No. 1: 'Try to secure advantages before attacking'. It is even more succinctly expressed in German Erich Hartmann's short Dictum Number 5 from World War II:

> '*Coffee Break*. If you can't attack safely or without the enemy taking drastic action to evade you, take a coffee break, i.e. disengage and look for an easier victim.'[11]

The German air service had a difficult time at the beginning of 1915. Many pilots were still flying the unarmed and obsolete LVGs and Taubes, and there was an influx of inexperienced pilots as the service expanded. With the stormy winter weather of 1914-1915, there was limited flying. There also was inefficiency and a great deal of frustration among both staff officers and operations personnel. The problem was the dispersion of authority and the lack of air-qualified staff officers. This was natural in a service that was growing so rapidly; most qualified pilots were needed at the front. Yet direction and orders came from the staffs of the armies. There was no central aviation authority, and the numerous army headquarters lacked qualified air staff. On 9 February 1915, the German high command recommended to the Prussian war ministry that they create a chief of field aviation (Feldflugchef).The action was approved on 26 April.[12] The army appointed Hermann von der Lieth-Thomsen as the new chief of fliers and made him a liaison with the front. His deputy was Major Wilhelm

Siegert who previously had been OHL's bomber chief and advisor on aviation. Lieth-Thomsen and Siegert were authorised a small staff of ten officers and twenty-eight enlisted men with a headquarters at Charleville. Lieth-Thomsen became, de facto, the head of the German air service.

Boelcke described the spring of 1915 as a time of peace. There were no ground offensives. The weather was bad, with rain, snow and low clouds, so there was little flying. This caused extensive boredom for the pilots and observers. Boelcke's only diversion was playing with his big sheepdog, "Wolf". When the weather would break, Oswald Boelcke still flew with his brother, Wilhelm, but their partnership aroused jealousy in other members of the section. The jealousy was not professional. It also caused some conflict with their commander. He wanted to separate the brothers. In response, the two Boelckes asked for a transfer to another unit, but it was denied. The dissention rose to a peak when the commander attempted to assign Wilhelm to another pilot and give Oswald a new observer. The brothers objected verbally, and when their objections were ignored, they went on strike. This may be the only time in his life when Boelcke's behaviour was not professional. The commander relented for the moment, but he was not happy. He would get revenge.

At this time in 1915, the press was beginning to publicise the new breed of air warriors. The influence of airpower on public opinion was much greater than that of seapower, largely due the fact that it engaged the third dimension and was publicised by the new media technology of film production.[13] The sight of aeroplanes and their heroic individual pilots on film and in news reports caught the public imagination, and the pilots were bombarded by reporters and questions – some intelligent, some inane. In a moment of pique while he was being treated for his asthma, Boelcke penned a leaflet, "Aircraft Defences Against Troublesome Questioners", which he reproduced on the hospital's duplicating machine. The leaflet was subsequently distributed widely to curious visitors.

Aircraft Defences against Troublesome Questioners:[14]
'PLEASE!!!
Do not ask me anything about flying.
You will find the usual questions answered below:

- Sometimes it is dangerous, sometimes it is not.
- Yes, the higher we fly, the colder it is.
- Yes, we notice the fact by freezing when it is colder.
- Flying height 2,000-2,500 metres (6,500-8,200 feet)
- Yes, we can see things at that height, although not so well as at 100 metres.
- We cannot see well through the telescope because it waggles.
- Yes, we have dropped bombs.
- Yes, an old woman was supposed to have been injured and we put the wind up some transport columns.
- The observer sits in the front and can see a bit.
- We cannot talk to each other because the engine makes too much noise.
- We have not got a telephone in the machine but we are provided with electric light.
- No, we do not live in caves.'

In April 1915, the commander finally transferred Wilhelm to the aviation reserve section in Posen, many miles away in eastern Germany. Oswald asked for a transfer also, but was threatened with being sent to the infantry if he persisted. Oswald was saddened by the separation from his brother – his mentor. Oswald was destined to participate alone in Germany's surge to air superiority. Wilhelm was to go on to command Kasta 7 (Kampfstaffel – fighting squadron) and later Kasta 10 in 1916. He would survive both world wars and die peacefully in Wiesbaden, Germany, in 1954.

Mercifully, the doctor diagnosed Boelcke with murmurs in his bronchial tubes, and he was sent to a field hospital at Château-Procien, France, for three weeks to convalesce. He was relieved to get away from Section 13 and its commander, if only for a short while. Within three days, Oswald was bored with the inactivity of the hospital. After two more weeks he was trying actively to leave by getting transferred to a new flying section. However, upon being referred to the chief doctor he was told frankly that General von Pritzelwitz had been upset that he had lost Wilhelm, and he had ordered the doctor to keep the younger Boelcke in the hospital. Upon learning this, Boelcke relented and asked to be returned to flying. Within a week Boelcke had both of his wishes granted: he was released from the hospital and transferred to Section 62 at Döberitz, which was famous in flying circles because it was the location of the first pilot training base in Germany.

Staff Surgeon-Major Arendt wrote a letter to Boelcke's parents after his death confirming the details of this period.

'I made his acquaintance when he was sent to my field hospital in the spring of 1915. He was in low spirits because he had been separated from his brother, but even so he might well have been proud of the fact that the chief of staff took the trouble to come to me and discuss his immediate future in the most appreciative terms. It was not easy to get on intimate terms with our "little Boelcke" as he called him, because evidently he had no great opinion of medicine men. But the ice soon thawed, and this silent serious-minded young man became in his own fashion the cheeriest who shared those beautiful spring days and jovial evenings. Good music always put him in a happy frame of mind, and what a master of dancing he showed himself when he partnered our chief dispenser. We gradually became more intimate with him. A photograph that each of us will cherish shows him with Captain Przyskowki on one of his last evenings. Soon afterwards he left us, completely reconciled to his lot – so thoroughly reconciled in fact, that he appeared over our little town in his machine that same afternoon and waved his greetings to us.'[15]

On Sunday, 25 April 1915, he announced to his parents that at last he was being transferred away from his irksome commanding officer. Professor Werner cites this period of Boelcke's professionally strained relations as evidence that his 'star did not rise smoothly to its zenith. He experienced bitter checks and disappointments ... which he had to overcome.'

In May, another change occurred that buoyed the German air arm. Albatros, LVG and other manufacturers delivered C-Series biplanes, which were standard 1914 models, but modified to move the observer from the front to the rear of the pilot's seat and to add a flexible-mounted 7.92 mm (0.312 in) Parabellum MG14 machine gun for his use. The first Albatros and LVG C-1s featured a 150-hp Mercedes, inline engine, which gave them a marked speed advantage over similar British and French machines.

Meeting Max Immelmann

Oswald Boelcke reported to his new outfit, Feldflieger Abteilung 62, at Döberitz, Germany, on 25 April 1915. On 13 May, the unit moved to Pontfaverger, France. Boelcke left Pontfaverger and reported on 19 May to KEK Douai (located at the previously French aerodrome, La Brayelle). Since he had been at the front since August 1914 and had over forty-two flights over enemy territory by January of 1915, Boelcke was the most experienced pilot of the section. There he met a Lance-Sergeant Max Immelmann, a reserve non-commissioned officer (NCO) who had joined the unit in March. Immelmann had been born in Dresden in 1890, the oldest of three, one year before Boelcke. His father managed a cardboard factory, but the

ancestors had been government officials. Immelmann was a vegetarian and extremely clever with anything technical. He grew up loving gymnastics and cycling and was known for his acrobatic skills. At age 14, he entered the Dresden cadet school, and in 1911, he began the war academy at Anklam. Thus, all three of our stars – Boelcke, von Richthofen and Immelmann – attended a military academy. However, Immelmann felt he was not suited for officership.[16] Accordingly, he resigned from his regiment in April 1912 and transferred to the reserve. When the war started, his unit was activated, and he applied for the air service, entering Aldershof aviation replacement section on 12 November 1914.[17]

Immelmann had some difficulty and spent a very long period of pilot training, not soloing until after the fifty-fourth flight on 31 January 1915. In February 1915, he crashed a two-seater. It was not until 31 March 1915 that he passed his third and final pilot test, earning his Prussian wings. Assigned to Section 10, he had two more accidents, with only a small fracture to himself. After only thirteen days at Section 10, he was transferred to FFA Section 62 at Döberitz, Germany, in

Max Immelmann (Reprinted by permission of Greenhill Books, from Franz Immelmann, *Immelmann: The Eagle of Lille*)

May 1915 where he met Oswald Boelcke.

Boelcke and Immelmann became friends; both were from Saxony, they derived their knowledge from experience, not books, and they shared the adventure of flying. Max's brother Franz wrote in his 1931 biography that their friendship 'soon exceeded the type of intimacy formed by the common bond of the war experiences that was to be theirs so soon'.[18] Others observed that they had a friendly rivalry.

But the young fliers had very different personalities. Max was reported to be self-centred, arrogant and a risk-taker. Unlike Boelcke, who had crossed the threshold and was committed to a military aviation career, Immelmann was more interested in the flying. Boelcke was more mature, naturally more cautious and introverted but forced himself to be more socially outgoing. Boelcke was quoted as believing, 'You can win the men's confidence if you associate with them naturally and do not try to play the high and mighty superior.' There is a postcard in the Andreas Thies collection that reveals something about their re-lationship. The picture contains a publicity studio-portrait of Max Immelmann, signed by him, with the inscription: 'Leutnant Immelmann der erfolgreiche Kampfflieger' ('Lieutent-ant Immelmann the successful battle-flier'). On the reverse in Boelcke's handwriting is the question, 'Findet Ihr das schön? Ich nicht!' ('Do you find this nice? I do not!')[19]

They also differed on their attitudes toward publicity. Immelmann's attitude was revealed in a letter to his mother,

'Now I shall no longer object to being written up in the papers, since I have seen how everyone at home follows my successes. It is amazing. I have received at least eighty congratulations.'[20]

Anthony Fokker and his Marvellous Machine Gun

In April of 1915, the Frenchman Adolphe Pégoud was still shooting down airplanes, and another Frenchman, Roland Garros, had run wild with his innovative metal wedges that al-lowed the machine gun to fire through the propeller blades. Those that hit the metal wedge would theoretically be thrown off safely. Garros shot down three German aircraft in the first two weeks. Unfortunately, while strafing trench lines on 18 April 1915, his engine quit and would not restart. He landed behind the German lines. The secret to his unexpected success was out! It was easy to see why the improvised metal wedges on the propeller would deflect French bullets. The German air service called in a young Dutch engineer, Anthony Fok-ker, to examine the aircraft and its marvellous machine gun. Fokker analysed the deflector planes but commented that he was working on a better idea – to add a synchronising gear to the engine so that the gun would not fire when the propeller was in the way.[21] A contrib-uting reason to reject the propeller-wedge idea was that German machine-gun bullets had steel jackets that would have penetrated the French wedges.

Anthony Fokker did not invent the synchronising device, but his engineers had been developing an ingenious gearing system that allowed the machine gun also to be mounted on the fuselage cowling, but fire *through* the open spaces in the propeller blades. Fokker ma-chined this device on a Parabellum, and it was first mounted on a Fokker M5K powered by an 80 hp Oberursel U.0 rotary engine. Fokker in his autobiography described his initiative to show off the new invention:

'In order to demonstrate it myself, because I felt so elated over conquering the prob-lem, I installed the synchronised gun in a little monoplane we had at Schwerin, lashed the tailskid of the monoplane to my 80-hp Peugeot touring car, and set out for Berlin, 220 miles (372 kilometres) away, arriving there Friday morning.'[22]

Fokker demonstrated the M5K to the Feldflugchef's staff at Döberitz, west of Berlin, in what he hoped would be a convincing display. He was wrong.

> 'In my confidence, I had not figured on the conservative military mind, which not only has to be shown, but then wishes to be shown all over again, after which it desires a little time to think the whole matter over once more.'[23]

Fokker demonstrated the operation of the machine gun on the ground and again in an aerial strafing attack. The staff were impressed, but argued that the only certain test of the gun would be to have it shoot down an aircraft. He was directed to General von Heeringen's headquarters, Seventh Army. Again he performed a test firing from the ground and in the air. In a repetition of the Berlin response, the observers liked the performance, but said the Crown Prince, commander of the Fifth Army, should see it. Fokker then went to Stenay, France, about eleven miles from Verdun.

The Crown Prince was gracious and asked him if his father had invented the gun. After a detailed show-and-tell of the operation of the gun and airplane, Fokker demonstrated its capability once again. The Crown Prince was very impressed, invited Fokker to lunch, and then sent him back to the airfield with instructions to demonstrate the gun by shooting down an enemy airplane at the front.

Lest he be captured and shot for a spy, the Dutchman, Fokker, donned a German air service uniform and took off, looking for an adversary. Finding none, he moved his operation to Douai, France, where the KEK from Section 62 was stationed. He immediately became friends with Lieutenants Boelcke, Immelmann, Wintgens and the other pilots. Discovering that Immelmann was an engineer, Fokker even offered him a job after the war.

After a week of unsuccessful flying, Fokker found a French Farman two-seater and positioned himself behind it. However, with the Frenchman in his sights, his imagination conjured up a picture of the aircraft and crew in a ball of flames; he could not pull the trigger. He dove back to Douai and informed the commander that he was finished with flying over the front. After a short argument, they agreed that a regular German pilot should complete the demonstration.

A Myth is Created

Leutnant Oswald Boelcke was reportedly selected for the mission of shooting down the first airplane with the synchronised machine gun. Fokker explained the controls to Boelcke and then saw him take off. Fokker then departed for Berlin. Upon arrival he was told that 'Boelcke, on his third flight, had brought down an Allied plane'.[24] Thus, a myth was born.

Several historians[25] repeated and perpetuated the story that Boelcke then took up the Eindecker and shot down an aircraft with the new gun. This may have happened, but if it did, it contradicts several other facts about Boelcke's life. First, the incident was not credited to Boelcke in his official record book. It may be that the enemy victim had fallen inside Allied lines and the victory unconfirmed. Secondly, Boelcke does not mention the action in his *Fieldbook*. Thirdly, Professor Werner did not mention the event in his biography. Boelcke's first official victory is listed as occurring more than a month later, on 4 July 1915, when he was flying a two-seat LVG.

John Cuneo, in his excellent history of the German air service, reports on this incident and says only that when Anthony Fokker gave up the idea of shooting down an Allied airplane and departed, 'he left behind for Leutnant Boelcke the monoplane which he had been demonstrating'.[26] Franz Immelmann, in his biography of Max, does nothing to refute the myth.

Historical records show that two of the new machines were at KEK Douai, France, in May 1915, and Fokker and Boelcke spent much time together. Boelcke's enterprising spirit immediately grasped the implications of the new invention. When Fokker departed he left behind production number E.3 for Boelcke and the other pilots to try out. Boelcke flew the new machine and began to imagine the tactics that could be used to employ the new weapon. The German air ministry authorities liked the device, ordered production and re-designated the aircraft, Eindecker E.I.[b]

The engine on the E.I was a seven-cylinder 80-hp Gnome rotary. It was, in Fokker's own words:

'Tricky, unreliable, difficult to operate, the Gnome consumed an enormous amount of gas and oil for the small power supplied. Much of its power exhausted itself in the mere rotation of its parts. If the ignition was shut off without throttling down, gas flooded the engine. Then, it wouldn't pick up quickly again, but might catch fire. Every motor was different, so that a pilot had to learn the crotchets of each one he flew with. Engine trouble accounted for many of the captures and disasters in the early months at the front.'[27]

Fokker E-I, in which Boelcke got his second victory on 19 August 1915. (SDASM Archives)

At this point we should note that the rotary engine had a peculiar characteristic: the engine had only two speeds: full speed or off. Pilots controlled the engine with a throttle lever and shut the engine off when they wanted to descend or slow down. This made landing rotary-engine aircraft somewhat tricky.

Anthony Fokker was not content with the low power of the E.I, and within weeks the type E.II had been developed by changing the 80 hp engine for one of 100 hp. Although the

---

[b] German aircraft were designated by the first letter of their type. Fighters were: E = Eindecker (monoplane); D = Doppeldecker (biplane); Dr = Dreidecker (Triplane). The E.I was the first model of the Fokker fighter series. Reconnaissance and multi-purpose aircraft were C = Aufklärer und Mehrzweck; Ground-attack and close air support were: CL-, CLS-, J-, DJ = Schlachtflugzeuge; Big and Giant Bombers were G & R = Groß & Riesen.

aircraft was fast and manoeuvrable, it had one feature that limited its rate of roll. The aircraft had no ailerons to control the roll of the aircraft to the left or the right. The lateral movement of the stick pulled wires and warped the trailing edge of the wing. This was not initially a problem with the Eindecker, against the slower and not-very-manoeuvrable French and British machines of the period, but as faster and more advanced models were introduced it would become so.

Meanwhile, the strategic situation on the Western Front had changed in favour of the French. They attacked Artois, France, in May and Champagne and Artois again in July and August 1915. The Germans were forced onto the defensive, but this was a familiar strategy, right out of Clausewitz, *On War*, who wrote that the defence was stronger than offence on land. In turn, the German high command sent orders to the armed two-seater units to fly only barrier patrols, on the German side of the trench lines. With their army background and doctrine, the German generals had not yet realised that the air power was inherently offensive. Fate was not to sustain this defensive, doctrinal view of aviation, and Boelcke immediately objected to this order.

In June 1915, Boelcke was given KEK Douai's first LVG C-1, a two-seater aircraft with a machine gun for the observer. Boelcke wrote to his parents:

'Since June 14th, I have a battleplane of my own: a biplane, with 150-hp motor. The pilot sits in front; the observer behind him, operating the machine gun, which can be fired to either side and to the rear. As the French are trying to hinder our aerial observation by means of battleplanes, we now have to protect our division while it flies. When the others are doing range-finding, I go up with them, fly about in their vicinity, observe with them and protect them from attack. If a Frenchman wants to attack them, then I make a hawk-like attack on him, while those who are observing go on unhindered in their flight. I chase the Frenchman away by flying toward him and firing at him with the machine gun. It is beautiful to see them run from me; they always do this as quickly as possible. In this way, I have chased away over a dozen.'[28]

The LVG represented a great leap forward because placing the gunner in the rear gave him a clear field of fire aft, the hemisphere from which most attacks came.

Germany's first air-to-air claim was in the Fokker E.I with one machine gun, flown by Leutnant Kurt Wintgens, FA-6b (Bavaria), on 1 July 1915. Had this victory been confirmed, it would have been the first in history for the German air service. It was not confirmed because it fell behind French lines, out of sight of German infantry. After that date, events for the German air service happened fast.

CHAPTER VI

THE ACE RACE

Oswald Boelcke was promoted to Oberleutnant (first lieutenant) in the summer of 1915 while with KEK Douai. On 4 July, he and his observer/gunner gained their first victory flying the LVG C-I.

Boelcke described the action:

LVG two-seater with gunner's position.

'We were just on our way to the front, when I saw a French monoplane, at a greater height, coming toward us .... Luckily, we were faster than he, so he could not flee from us by turning. We were higher and faster; he below us and slower, so that he could not escape. By all kinds of manoeuvres he tried to increase the distance between us; without success, for I was always close on him. It was glorious. I always stuck to him so that my observer could fire at close range. We could plainly see everything on our opponent's monoplane, almost every wire, in fact. The average distance between us was a hundred metres; often we were within thirty metres, for at such high speeds you cannot expect success unless you get very close together. The whole fight lasted about twenty or twenty-five minutes.'[1]

This event is considered by many to be the first confirmed victory for German aviation. While it may not be literally true, the earlier incidents were not documented nor verified.[2] The French aircraft was a Morane-Saulnier L Parasol two-seater monoplane, the same as Wintgen's first claim. Boelcke's opponent was from Escadrille MS15 with pilot Lieutenant Maurice Tetu and observer Lieutenant LeComte de la Rochefoucauld, the latter of whose body fell on the grounds of his own estate.[3]

Edward Sims in his excellent study, *Fighter Tactics and Strategy 1914-1970*, credits Oswald Boelcke with 'the first detailed description of combat tactics' in his account of his first victory, 4 July 1915, 'an engagement that he carefully planned beforehand.'[4] Others would follow.

The Fokker Scourge

Once arms were introduced into the reconnaissance mission, the pilots and observers began to value speed, altitude and manoeuvrability – the characteristics of the sport pilot. Public imagination became powerfully engaged as soon as one aircraft crew shot down an opponent. Indeed, success in aerial combat and the publicity heaped upon individual heroes became a driving factor in pilot motivation, politics and aircraft design. The high command – and doctrine – was receiving feedback that it was not entirely prepared for. As subsequent air offensive actions grew more numerous, and successful, German rules of engagement began to change, freeing the pilots from purely defensive patrols.

The deployment of this new scout or fighter by the German air service was piecemeal, one or two to each of the many sections to provide escort for the heavier and slower two-seaters. This initial concept of close escort was a mistake that many armies would later make with air forces. To avoid the new guns from falling into Allied hands, the pilots were forbidden to fly across the front. Boelcke ignored this direction and frequently went hunting over enemy lines. Boelcke's habit of seeking out quarry coincided with the German term, Jagdflieger, which one year later evolved into Jagdstaffel.

With Boelcke's experience and now an air-to-air victory, he started to become talked about. Boelcke's first combat flight in the Fokker monoplane was on 7 July 1915. Max Immelmann inherited and flew Boelcke's LVG. Within a few days, Boelcke gave Immelmann his first flying lesson in an Eindecker. Two days after his first ride, Immelmann soloed but had difficulty landing. He had never flown a monoplane in combat, and he had never before fired a machine gun. Immelmann learned quickly, and he was promoted to leutnant on 14 July 1915.

Boelcke was not much impressed with his name being published and lauded in the German press. In a letter of 16 July, Boelcke wrote: '... Father asks if it will be all right to publish my report in the newspapers. I don't care much for newspaper publicity, and I do not think that my report is written in a style suitable for newspapers. The people want such a thing written with more poetry and colour – gruesome, nerve-wrecking suspense, complete revenge, mountainous clouds, blue, breeze-swept sky – that is what they want. But if the publication of the report will bring you any joy, I will not be against it.'[5]

Leutnant Wintgens continued his pursuit of Frenchmen and shot down a Morane-Saulnier Parasol on 15 July 1915, which was confirmed for his first official victory. Then he shot down another the same week.[6]

Before August 1915, aviators on both sides could feel relatively safe when flying over the lines. The only serious threats were anti-aircraft fire and the unreliability of their own machines. All that changed in July as the Fokker Eindeckers were deployed and introduced a new and lethal threat. The Australian, Trevor Henshaw, in his milestone publication, *The Sky Their Battlefield*, comments on this change in July 1915:

'Until this time, however, if an RFC pilot saw an enemy machine, he nearly always attacked it as a matter of course, most times seeing it off, even if flying a B.E.2C. On some occasions the enemy would even be shot down. The Fokker totally changed this balance of engagement, removing the initiative from the British .... The Eindecker was a new and potent weapon, and it cried out to be experimented with tactically. It was the ability of a few early exponents of the Fokker to evolve the essentials of air fighting with such skill which made it the great weapon it became. These included aspects of manoeuvrability and superior positioning. The Fokker was to have its problems, but at its peak it was an extremely dangerous weapon because it combined several telling attributes which made it superior in combat to anything else in the sky. The Fokker Scourge was beginning.'[7]

The Ace Race

On 1 August 1915, Immelmann scored his first victory, flying an Eindecker E.I, shooting down a two-seat B.E.2C over his own aerodrome at Douai. The B.E.2C was the initial aircraft product of the Royal Aircraft Factory and derived its name from its layout, similar to the French Blériot. Therefore, it was designated the "Blériot Experimental" (BE). With this first loss and the many to come, the airplane soon was dubbed "Fokker Fodder". The ace race was on. Wingtens,1; Boelcke, 1; Immelmann, 1.

Boelcke's Second Victory

Boelcke won *his* first single-seat victory (his second overall) on 19 August 1915. He described the day's events in a letter to his parents:

'I fly mostly in the evening to chase the Frenchmen who are out range-finding, and that evening [19 August] there were a lot of them out. The first one I went for was an English Bristol biplane. He seemed to take me for a Frenchman; he came toward me quite leisurely, a thing our opponents generally don't do. But when he saw me firing at him, he quickly turned. I followed close on him, letting him have all I could give him. I must have hit him or his machine, for he suddenly shut off his engine and disappeared below me. As the fight took place over the enemy's positions, he was able to land behind his own lines. According to our artillery, he landed right near his own artillery. That is the second one I positively left my mark on; I know I forced him to land. He didn't do it because he was afraid, but because he was hit.'[8]

Fokker E.I on take-off for a combat mission. (San Diego Air & Space Museum)

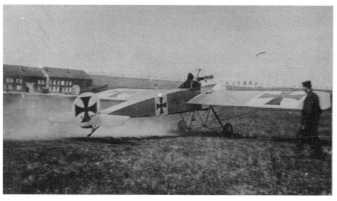

Historian Norman Franks asks, thoughtfully, what was the difference between Boelcke's claim and Wintgens' first one. While Boelcke seemed certain his machine-gun fire caused the opposing pilot to land, no one can be sure. In these early days of air combat, it was common for pilots to escape a dangerous situation by going down to land. They seemed confident that with high feelings of chivalry in place on both sides, it was safe to do so. However, 2 Squadron reported in British records that one of their Bristol biplanes was in combat with a German machine on this day. The German's machine guns severed the Bristol's fuel pipe, causing it to force land.[9]

A week later, the KEK Douai unit received Fokker E.IIs with upgraded 100-hp rotary engines by adding two more cylinders (to nine). The Fokker Eindeckers were beginning to plague the Allied pilots. The little Fokkers had three advantages over their competitors: 1) They could climb higher and attack their prey from a sloping dive, using stealth and gaining speed; 2) They were much more manoeuvrable in a fight than the stable, slower enemy machines; and 3) The volume of fire from their single machine gun was greater than their opponents because the gun was fed from long belts of bullets in the fuselage, while opposing aircraft with the over-the-wing Lewis gun were generally limited to the forty-seven rounds in the circular, pan magazine.

Despite the continuing deployment of new airplanes, there were three ongoing problems with the Eindecker. First, the aircraft used a wing-warping method, like the Wright Flyers and the Taube, which was inefficient and slowed its flight manoeuvres. Second, the Eindeckers were flawed with reliability issues. The new synchroniser mechanism sometimes malfunctioned, allowing the gun to shoot off the propeller. If the lower wing lift cables were slack, they were prone to getting tangled in the wheels, causing landing accidents. In addition, pilots who were used to the heavy, stable aircraft of the previous year did not adapt quickly to the light, nimble monoplane. In July and August 1915, three of the aircraft had fatal crashes at the Döberitz training station in Germany, resulting in the inspectorate grounding all the Fokker E.Is and disbanding the training unit at Döberitz.

Third, the E-Series production was slow. The Fokker Es never exceeded a production rate of thirty-two per month. With this rate and the inevitable losses due to accidents and enemy action, there were only fifty in service at the front at any one time. Those deployed were dispersed, two to a section – violating the principle of mass – and reducing their effectiveness.

A brief explanation of the wing warping may be due. The early Fokker aircraft were controlled by light-weight cables that ran from the stick and rudder to the wing and tail sections. When the pilot wanted to climb, he pulled back on the stick, and the attached cable pulled the elevator up, causing the nose to rise. The force on the stick for this movement was very slight because the elevator was large and the moment arm long. When the pilot wanted the airplane to turn left, he put the stick to the left and applied left rudder, causing it to bank in that direction. The rudder was very effective and easy to move, but the cables for the wing movement ran to the top of a post on the fuselage and then down to the trailing edge of the left wing, which caused the wing to warp upward. Conversely, the cables to the right wing were routed through a pole extending directly downward from the fuselage and then to the wing tip, pulling (warping) it downward. Because the wing had to be fairly rigid to withstand the forces of lift and drag, moving the stick to the left or right was very difficult, and the aircraft movement relatively slow.[10]

The French were not idle; Adolphe Pégoud became the first ace with five victories in the summer of 1915. This was the same Pégoud who had so amazed young Boelcke with his aerobatics in the Frankfurt air show in 1913. He was to be shot down and killed on 31 August. He had six total victories. Max Immelmann shot down his second aircraft on 26 August 1915, and the score was tied at two.

On 27 August, Oswald Boelcke became a hero on the ground. While strolling around the village of Douai near his aerodrome on a day off, he noticed a young French boy trying to balance on the edge of a concrete wall over a canal. When the boy fell in Boelcke dived into the canal fully clothed, and rescued the drowning lad, Albert DePlace. 'When we got to the land the mother of the boy came running up to me and thanked me most profusely. The rest of the population gave me a real ovation. I must have looked funny, because I had jumped in as I was and the water was streaming off me.'[11] Two weeks later, he visited the boy's parents, and they expressed their gratitude. They wanted Boelcke to be awarded the French *Légion d'honneur*. Oswald noted in his letter, 'that would be a good joke'. The German government would have none of that; instead, he received the Prussian lifesaving medal.[12]

Max Immelmann was an aggressive pilot. He flew the Eindecker to its limits and invented the "Immelmann Turn", a half-loop followed by a half-roll. The manoeuvre was performed by putting the aircraft into a shallow dive to gain speed, then pulling back on the stick to take the aircraft into the first half of a loop. When on his back at the top of the loop, the pilot relaxes back pressure and uses the ailerons and rudder to roll the aircraft right side up. The manoeuvre is useful to reverse direction and gain altitude, which could put the plane into a firing position behind an opponent. By the end of August, both Boelcke and Immelmann had victories in the Eindecker. They often flew together, just the two of them, in the evening 'to chase the Frenchmen there'. They were not content to fly barrier patrols and remain on the defensive.

With Pégoud, Garros, Wintgens, Boelcke and Immelmann shooting down airplanes, air combat became a prominent feature of military aviation. Their efforts led to the first successful attempt to establish a mission of what today we would call air superiority. What the French and British called it was the Fokker Scourge.

In September/October 1915, the unit received Fokker E.IIIs. This model had the same 100 hp engine, with the only change being a larger fuel tank that extended the aircraft's endurance to 2½ hours. With the Fokker E.I and the more powerful II and III and their synchronised guns and their experienced pilots, the Germans established and held air superiority from July 1915 through to the winter of 1916.

In reality, the psychological effect of the Fokkers' success was probably larger than their physical effect. The fear of meeting a Fokker was widespread, but the British losses to the early Fokkers tended to be exaggerated. There were actually only eight Fokkers operational on 1 October. Still, the spell of the scourge continued, amplified by the enormous publicity given to their success.

The public became caught up in the ace race but it was not so much a back-and-forth sequence of events as it was a "leader-follower". In the midst of clear skies and otherwise excellent flying weather, Boelcke got his third on 9 September, and Immelmann got his third twelve days later, 21 September 1915.

Boelcke's Fourth Victory

On 22 September 1915, Boelcke was transferred south to a secret unit at Metz. The unit was named BAM (*Brieftauben Abteilung Metz* – carrier pigeon unit, Metz), but this was actually a cover for a mobile combat unit, KEK Metz. Boelcke's own Fokker was sent from Douai but had not yet arrived, so the commander loaned him his aircraft. Boelcke took off early on 25 September and saw anti-aircraft artillery fire in the distance. He soon saw hostile airplanes. At first there were three, then seven. Undeterred by the numbers, Boelcke positioned himself behind and below one of them and closed to 100 metres before he opened fire. He hit the Frenchman who began to descend toward his own lines. Suddenly Boelcke realised that he was behind the French lines in an area he was unfamiliar with and without a map. He broke off the attack and luckily found his way back. Soon a report came in to the unit from front-line observers that they had seen an aircraft flutter down to German Hill 368, whereupon the pilot was dragged from the wreckage and into a trench. This provided the necessary confirmation of a victory. The same day German Sergeant Eduard Böhme downed a double.

Immelmann got his fourth on 10 October to once again tie the score. By this time, he and Boelcke were both flying the Fokker E.III. Although Boelcke's little unit at Sivry had at first only two Eindeckers, he initiated the tactic of flying them together. One would attack while the other remained at altitude, protecting the leader and watching for any approaching aircraft threats. As Trevor Henshaw notes, the RFC pilots were so shocked with the Eindeckers' firepower and new tactics that they were almost mesmerised.[13] Britain and France desperately needed a new fighter.

Oswald Boelcke in a Fokker E.III with one machine gun. (Johan Ryheul)

British Leadership Changes

Brigadier General Sir David Henderson was promoted to major general in the summer of 1915 and transferred back to London as the commander-in-chief of the RFC. Lieutenant Colonel Hugh Trenchard was promoted to brigadier general and replaced Henderson as the chief of the RFC in France. Shortly afterward, the British were heavily engaged in the Battle of Loos (September-October 1915). The initial phase of this battle was poorly handled by British Commander-in-Chief Field Marshal Sir John French, and he was replaced in December by General Sir Douglas Haig. Haig had known about Trenchard since the Salisbury Plain manoeuvres, and he had worked closely with him during the Loos affair.

Trenchard was brash, intolerant of failure and noted even by his friends as being a martinet. He was devoted to aggressive aircraft operations over enemy lines. As British historian Peter Hart described him: 'Trenchard has a remarkable gift for prophecy coupled with a peculiar ability to develop policy almost by instinct.'[14] As a result of his aggressive policy and

German proficiency, the RFC lost eighty-two aircraft shot down in the period July-October and lost another fifty pilots and observers between November 1915 and January 1916 during the Fokker Scourge.

Although these losses were miniscule compared to those on the ground, the publicity surrounding them was sufficiently controversial to provoke concern in the British House of Commons and the French Chamber of Deputies. Noel Pemberton-Billings attacked the Royal Flying Corps by labelling its aviators as nothing more than "Fokker Fodder" adding that 'our pilots are being murdered rather than killed!'[15]

Known informally as "Boom", Hugh Trenchard responded by dictating squadron tactics from headquarters. His January 1916 decree was:

'Until the Royal Flying Corps are in possession of a machine as good or better than the German Fokker it seems that a change in the tactics employed becomes necessary. It is hoped shortly to obtain a machine which will be able to successfully engage the Fokkers at present in use by the Germans. In the meantime, *it must be laid down as a hard and fast rule that a machine proceeding on reconnaissance must be escorted by at least three other fighting machines. These machines must fly in close formation and a reconnaissance should not be continued if any of the machines become detached* .... From recent experience it seems that the Germans are now employing their aeroplanes in groups of three or four, and these numbers are frequently encountered by our aeroplanes. *Flying in close formation must be practised by all pilots.*'[16] [Emphasis added.]

Flying close formation is mentally and physically difficult, and the ability to do it is often the major difference between those airmen in pilot training who choose fighters versus those who elect to fly larger airplanes or helicopters. Once the student gets into a fighter unit, he learns that there are many other types of formation that are used in tactical situations.

Although Hugh Trenchard was a genius in organisation and leadership of the RFC and later the Royal Air Force, this is an example of tactics being the "opinion" of the senior officer present. Close formation is without a doubt the *worst* formation to use in combat, exceeded only perhaps by trail formation. The concentration of the pilot (wingman) flying close formation (defined as flying with the wingtips overlapped or within a very few feet of one another) on a leader is so intense that they have virtually no chance of seeing an attacker in time to manoeuvre safely. The aircraft on the wing is so close to the leader that he is also part of the attacker's target.[17]

Trail formation may be worse because the trailing pilot's view is focused forward, with no possibility of seeing an attacker from the rear. In addition, all other pilots are looking forward, following the leader. No one in the flight can see an attacker closing in on the last aircraft. The Germans and Americans would much later develop a better formation for air-to-combat called "fighting wing" (in German, the "Rotte") where the wingman positions himself about 45 degrees back from the leader and well away (300-600 feet in the early days). This gives both the leader and wingman excellent visibility, and the wingman's position can be maintained even under hard manoeuvring. The Allied air forces of WWII forgot the lessons of WWI. The RAF entered WWII air combats with its flights often in trail formation, sometimes wondering what happened to "tail-end Charlie". The German Luftwaffe with the Condor Legion in Spain in the 1930s went one step further and developed a fighting formation of four aircraft called the "Schwarm" (flight). Three schwarms would constitute a squadron. In English, the schwarm is called the "Finger Four" because the fingers of either hand represent the position of the aircraft, although spread far apart for maximum pilot visibility.

The RFC's woes continued and morale declined as losses mounted to the swift and deadly Fokker monoplanes. British training and experience appeared to be inadequate to counter the threat. In October, Trenchard (then still a lieutenant colonel) requested the War Office in London to train pilots and observers in air combat tactics before they were sent to continental squadrons. This request must have struck Whitehall as peculiar as it was in direct conflict with Trenchard's overall demand that pilots be sent to France in ever greater numbers and faster.

At this time, the RFC was described as a "company of individualists". The organisation sought recruits primarily from public (private) school graduates and university men with experience in sports or officer training. Subaltern Sholto Douglas, from Oxford University, had transferred from the Royal Horse Artillery to the RFC as an observer in 1914. Upon arrival in his first squadron, Douglas was struck by the lack of formality:

'After the rigid discipline that I had known in the Royal Horse Artillery the free and easy way in which things were done in the RFC was very much to my liking. Although most of the pilots were regular army officers ... they were all men of a different breed from what I had become accustomed to since joining the artillery. I was now in the company of individualists, some of whom, I was soon to find, could even be regarded as at least eccentrics – if not downright crazy'.[18]

Another British pilot explained that 'in those days the Flying Corps was a highly individual service. Each officer had his own machine, housed in its own tent, with his own rigger and his own mechanic to attend to it. He regarded himself as a separate fighting unit. As a unit, he was willing to cooperate, but he certainly could not be bossed about as though he were an air taxi-driver'.[19] To counter this tendency for individualism, the RFC did not permit the recording or publishing of an individual pilot's combat accomplishments. That was soon to change.

Sholto Douglas flew combat missions as an observer and entered pilot training in May 1915. He returned to France in the summer of 1915 with 40 hours and 5 minutes of flying time. Concerned about the lack of experience of new pilots, he found that the average flying experience for newly assigned pilots was only 20 hours, and some had only 14. Douglas described this policy as 'sheer murder'.[20] In December 1915, he would narrowly survive an air engagement with Oswald Boelcke. In WWII, he became a squadron commander, commanded Fighter Command after the Battle of Britain in 1940, and retired as a marshal of the Royal Air Force.

Meeting von Richthofen

On 1 October 1915, Oswald Boelcke was on a train to Rethel, France, to fly barrier patrols over the lines. Manfred von Richthofen was also on that train, having been transferred as an observer flying two-seater bombers for Section Ostende on the 4th Army Front at Flanders. Richthofen's new unit was to be Section Metz at Rethel, flying the same airplane. Richthofen related the story of his first encounter with Boelcke:

'In the dining car, at the table next to me, was sitting a young and insignificant-looking oberleutnant. There was no reason to take any note of him except for the fact he was the only man who had succeeded in shooting down a hostile flying man not once but four times. His name had been mentioned in the dispatches. I thought a great deal of him because of his experience. Although I had taken the greatest trouble, I had not brought an enemy down up to that time. At least I had not been credited with a success.

'I would have liked so much to find out how Oberleutnant Boelcke managed his business. So I asked him: "Tell me, how you manage it?" He seemed very amused and laughed, although I had asked him quite seriously. Then he replied, "Well it is quite simple. I fly close to my man, aim well and then he of course falls down." I shook my head and told him that I did the same thing but my opponents unfortunately did not come down.'[21]

Von Richthofen's Background

Rittmeister Freiherr Manfred Albrecht von Richthofen was born on 2 May 1892, in Breslau, East Prussia. This made him one year younger than Oswald Boelcke and two years younger than Max Immelmann. Other comparisons and contrasts are inevitable. He was descended from a noble and aristocratic family. Manfred was enrolled in the Royal Prussian Cadet System at age 11. He proceeded to the Senior Cadet Academy and graduated in 1911. However, he did not at first pass his ensign's examination, so he joined the Uhlan Cavalry Regiment as a sergeant. He took the test a second time, passed and was made an ensign, but he was chastened by the experience and determined to never let that happen again. Months later he was detached from the Uhlans and posted to the Military Academy in Berlin. He graduated in 1912 with a commission as a leutnant. With the onset of WWI, von Richthofen, back with the Uhlans, led cavalry patrols into Russian Poland. By the middle of August 1914, the Uhlan Regiment was transferred to participate in the German advance through Luxembourg toward Belgium. He again led patrols and saw battle with French dragoons, winning the Iron Cross Second Class.

Manfred von Richthofen, the Red Baron.

Von Richthofen served in the northern section of the trenches for some weeks, but was soon transferred south to the Verdun Front and given the job of adjutant, a staff job behind the lines. Deeply frustrated, he wrote his commanding general a short letter in May 1915: 'Dear Excellency, I did not go to war to gather cheese and eggs, but for another purpose.[22] His request for transfer to the air service was denied. However, some staff officer changed his mind, and within a few days his transfer was approved.

When faced with a choice: pilot training (three months) or observer training (two weeks), he chose the latter because it was shorter. In his own words, 'I wanted to go to the front quickly, for I was afraid that I would be too late for the war.'[23]

Von Richthofen need not have worried. He flew dozens of missions as an observer and gained valuable experience. He then entered pilot training in late October and passed his final examination on Christmas Day 1915. He was assigned to Kasta 8 of Kagol No. 2 on the Eastern Front. He and Boelcke would meet again in the summer of 1916, and Boelcke would invite Richthofen to join his Jasta 2, where Richthofen would earn his first sixteen victories.

The Ace Race Creates Public Figures

As the ace race continued, both Boelcke and Immelmann became more famous. Boelcke's attitude toward publicity was revealed in a humorous incident. Apparently a firm in Berlin had asked his father for a photo of the young pilot. Boelcke replied to his parents in a letter of 10 October 1915:

'The Berlin Illustration Company will manage quite well without my photo – I beg you not to send them one. I don't like all this publicity – I find quite enough articles in the papers about myself to be sick of it. I am told an English paper lately announced that I bolted to America before the war because I could not pay my debts as a leutnant and worked as a liftman in a New York hotel.'[24]

Boelcke's Fifth

In the month of October 1915, the number of RFC squadrons rose to twenty-five, which with the increase in French planes, helped to offset the success of the Fokkers. The full impact of the Fokker Scourge was still to be felt because the numbers were small, and the aircraft was having engine problems. But Boelcke and Immelmann were discovering that with their modest advantage in speed and a greater advantage in altitude, they could stalk and position themselves to achieve a surprise attack. This was aided by the Allied observation crews who were sometimes overly intent on spotting and plotting artillery positions, which diverted them from looking out for attacking fighters. On 16 October, Boelcke found a French two-seat Voisin B-1 (No. V839) west of Metz and shot it down.

The fifth victory would normally have made him an ace, a pilot with at least five victories if that designation had been accepted at the time in the German air service, but it was not. The Germans had a term, "kanone", literally translated as "cannon" derived from "tube" for aviators who had downed four aircraft. While Boelcke's letter of 17 October 1915 records the victory over the French while he was flying a Fokker Eindecker, he makes no mention of the ace achievement. This is most probably due to the early nature and delayed evolution of this designation and it not being formally established.

Germany already had distinctions at the level of six victories, when it became customary to award the Royal Order of the House of Hohenzollern Knights Cross with Swords. Then the level of eight victories was designated for the award of the *Pour le Mérite*. When the Germans decided to adopt the terminology of ace the officials initially selected the level of ten victories as the threshold. With either of the two levels one chooses to use, it is the author's belief that Oswald Boelcke was the first German ace. Boelcke's fifth victory was on 16 October 1915, and Immelmann did not get his until seven days later, on 23 October. Similarly, Boelcke shot down his tenth aircraft on 12 March 1916, and Immelmann shot down his tenth the next day, 13 March.

By this time, the British were developing a healthy respect for the Fokker monoplane. As Lieutenant Bernard Rice, RFC, related to his father in a letter, 23 October 1915 in describing a specific engagement of one of his mates:

'The Fokker was the Eindecker or monoplane with a single forward-firing Spandau machine gun. The machine itself was much more than a match for the BE and I can only assume that the German pilot was a gentleman and a sportsman to break off the engagement as he did. To pilots of all nationalities the problem of staying in the air and then returning to earth safely were shared by all as a mutual respect was being built up. Fire was of course the paramount fear, no parachutes in those days and if your aeroplane burnt it cremated you and saved the grave diggers a job. Of course, you could always jump for it.'[25]

With the aerial success of the early Fokker monoplanes the opinion of the high command changed, and they demanded more aircraft. Finally, the inspectorate allowed Fokker training to resume – but only at the factory at Schwerin, Germany. More broadly, the inspectorate changed its policy that had separated pilots from factories in 1914; in the summer of 1915 pilots were allowed to express their views to aircraft designers at the factories. In return, many manufacturers feted famous pilots in Berlin suites at luxurious hotels.

By October 1915, the war had been raging for fourteen months. Yet the features and capabilities of aircraft were still not understood. The differing roles of fighter or scout, bomber or observation were not defined. If an aeroplane could fly it was expected to fulfil any of these functions at any time.

The Cult of the Fighter Pilot as Hero

In Germany, meanwhile, a new breed of hero had become the people's darling. He was the air fighter, a Wagnerian knight riding a winged charger and jousting with gay abandon in dramatic tournaments high above the clouds. Boelcke and Immelmann personified this dramatic image, which the pilots themselves would concede was somewhat distorted. Their personal courage was no less than advertised, but their tilts against Allied flyers were made easier with the synchronised gun.

Boelcke's Sixth and the Hohenzollern Medal

On 30 October, to support an offensive near Tahure, all seven Fokkers were assembled together in a temporary Staffel as a test to see if massing the fighter was more effective than their current deployment in ones and twos.

Boelcke was assigned to fly a defensive barrage patrol when he spotted three French aircraft 'mucking about behind their own lines for observation purposes. As it was urgent for us to stop those fellows, I decided to go across and make it hot for them.' Boelcke continues the story in a letter to his parents on 2 November 1915:

'The following incident was very funny. I had hardly opened fire before the head and upper body of the French observer appeared above the top wing. Then he vanished quickly and reappeared with an old blunderbuss in his hands. Owing to my great speed I was so close to him the next moment that he got a thorough fright and popped his head in again – perhaps I had hit him as I was blazing away the whole time.

'But the pilot was quite a tough fellow. His machine turned this way and that and refused to fall. Then I headed straight for my opponent until it looked as if the two machines must collide, when I was only three or five metres away, I pulled mine to one side and saw the Frenchman go down by the right wing at the same time. The whole business only lasted about a minute, during which I fired 500 rounds at the enemy.

'I have written you an exact description so that you need not imagine it is at all much in reality. As long as one keeps one's head and judgment, my fast, nimble Fokker makes a fight in the air hardly more dangerous than a motor trip. So don't worry about me. Promise me that.'[26]

When Boelcke got his sixth victory, it was the highest number of any German pilot up to that time.[27] In response to this, he received a telegram on 1 November 1915 from General von Falkenhayn, chief of the General Staff: 'I am pleased to inform you that HM [His Majesty] is pleased to invest you with the Knightly Cross of the House of Hohenzollern, with Swords, in recognition of your magnificent achievements against enemy airmen.'[28] The House of Hohenzollern medal soon became a virtual prerequisite for the award of the Blue Max. Immelmann duplicated the feat and got his sixth victory six days later. The score was again tied.

Royal Order of the House of Hohenzollern Knights Cross with Swords. (OMSA)

Meanwhile, Anthony Fokker had developed another model of the Eindecker. In his own words, 'Because of Immelmann's great success, I built a special monoplane, powered with a 160 Le Rhône and equipped with three machine guns shooting 1,800 bullets a minute, for him. A terrorising hail of lead spurting from its nose.'[29] The increased power of the engine was achieved by placing a second 80-hp rotary engine behind the front one and connecting the two engines together. The first problem that arose was that the synchronising mechanism for the three machine guns was very complicated and prone to jam. When this became apparent in testing, Fokker removed one gun and equipped succeeding models with only two. Then both Boelcke and Immelmann had problems with the reliability of the E.IV engine. Many fights had to be broken off when the engine malfunctioned.

On 9 November 1915, Boelcke was invited to dinner with the chief of the air service, Oberstleutnant Lieth-Thomsen, where he was loudly introduced as 'the famous Boelcke' and awarded two medals. His advice was solicited on how best to employ the new air weapon. The next day he was sent to the Fokker factory at Schwerin, then to Berlin. During these visits he was requested to write several reports on tactical, technical and organisational issues.

Still based with KEK Douai, Immelmann got his sixth victory on 7 November, for another tie. Then on 15 December he shot down an RFC Morane from 3 Squadron.[30] Immelmann now was leading with seven while Boelcke's count still stood at six. Other Fokker pilots were doing well too. The German air service had ten single-seat pilots listed with a total of twenty-eight victories.[31]

Another tradition was inaugurated at the end of 1915. On Christmas Eve, Section 62 held a celebration for the enlisted men in one of the hangars. Then in the evening, the officers retired to the casino to continue the festivities and exchange presents. Boelcke tells the story, 'For me there was a very beautiful silver cup, among other things. This cup was inscribed, "To the Victor in air combat" ["*Ehrenbecher für den Sieger im Luftkampfe*"] and was given to me by the commander-in-chief of the Aviation Corps. Immelmann received its mate.'[32] These two cups inaugurated the tradition of rewarding every pilot on the occasion of his first aerial victory. The original cups were authorised by the Kaiser and commissioned to a silversmith. Later, they were sponsored by German industrialists and awarded by the army. Sometime in late 1917, the criterion for award was raised to eight or nine (and the silver changed to iron) as the requirement for the award of the *Pour le Mérite* was increased. Boelcke and Immelmann, in 1915, were the first aviators to be so honoured.[33]

The Ehrenbecher was awarded to Oswald Boelcke on Christmas Eve, 1915, and was inscribed, "To the Victor in air combat". (Walter Waiss)

The Protagonists at the End of 1915

The employment of the German air service in 1915 concentrated on reconnaissance, artillery spotting, some tactical bombing and air combat with the monoplanes. The service had increased its single-seater force over the course of the year, but they were still outnumbered. There were 107 fighter aircraft spread among the two-seater units on the Western Front (eighty-six Fokkers and twenty-one Pfalz). However, the employment of the fighters was faulty. Ordered to remain on their side of the front and to implement an aerial blockade the force was much too small to be effective. 'Their futile attempts at an air blockade by constant patrols back and forth among the lines only dissipated their sparse numbers.'[34]

Meanwhile, the French were experimenting with air support for ground operations by the use of wireless communications. This was very effective, especially in those areas where ground observation was limited. However, they had no real opposition to the Eindeckers, and only the small numbers of the German fighters prevented a French disaster.

The British, who had pioneered wireless communications, developed a standardised system of air-ground cooperation. They also increased their tactical bombing force. Air historian John Cuneo continues his assessment:

'But the great advance of the RFC over the German air service should be clear. Where the latter was trying hard to re-establish itself with observation and the sole novelties were the small trickle of fighter monoplanes to the front and the system of defensive patrols, the RFC was experimenting with new tactics. The bombing raids were excellent attempts on paper to isolate the battlefield but insufficient airplanes nullified the theory. The conception of the aerial isolation of the battlefield which it and the French air service were then developing, is still one of the most profitable employments of aircraft developed in cooperation with ground forces. Crude and limited equipment, plus bad weather, prevented any outstanding results but aside from one annoyance the future seemed bright. That annoyance was the Fokker monoplane.'[35]

The Fokker Scourge continued. Though its numbers were statistically small, they were huge in relation to 1914 and dramatic beyond imagination. The RFC lost 137 aircraft due to enemy action in 1915, versus only twenty-two for 1914. Of the 137, seventy-one can be documented to air combat, with another thirty-two downed due to unknown causes.[36] There was worse to come.

How do we find Boelcke at the end of 1915? First, he continues to evolve his fighting techniques. He has developed as a leader, but retained his humility. He is quoted as saying, 'I do not try to play the high and mighty superior'. He is now serving in an even more dangerous part of his profession – aircraft combat. And his expertise is increasing rapidly. In fact, he is increasing in all of the four elements of combat expertise: total flying time; time in a particular machine; time in theatre; and number of combat missions. What happens next catapults him further into the public and professional spotlight.

CHAPTER VII

Boelcke and the Blue Max – 1916

Boelcke began 1916 with six victories, one behind Immelmann. The new year brought winter storms, gales and rain, and there was very little flying. It also brought a new model of the Eindecker with two machine guns, the Fokker E.IV.

Boelcke's Seventh

The weather cleared a little on 5 January 1916, and Boelcke took off eagerly in his new E.IV. He intercepted two Royal Flying Corps B.E.2Cs, the old, reliable, stable workhorse of the reconnaissance community. The aircraft had been designed by Geoffrey de Havilland and produced by the Royal Aircraft Factory. It was Boelcke's seventh victory. The full story of this action was told in the Prologue. This battle was so memorable that Bernard Rice, RFC, also wrote about it in a letter to his father, 26 January 1916:

> 'Splendid news of our lost people. Russell is untouched but was taken prisoner. Willie Somervill and Formilli are all right too, the former grazed his cheek and Formilli a bullet in the shoulder. One is in hospital, both in Germany. The Huns flew over and dropped a message bag containing notes from each of them for us. Jolly nice of them wasn't it? Poor old Russell, we are so relieved, I could not bear to think of the poor old chap being done in all alone out there. It appears a Fokker hit him in the engine just after he had dropped his eggs. Willy put on his note that it was Boelcke who shot him down.'[1]

This victory was widely reported in German newspapers. The *Anhaltischer Staats-Anzeiger* published a front-page article:

British B.E.2C aircraft. Boelcke shot down one of these on 5 January and a total of nine of this type.

> 'Headquarters 6th January. (Notice via wire) Western Front. Two English Aircraft Shot Down: The first one from our Oberleutnant Oswald Boelcke, who scored his seventh victory. [Elsewhere] at the front, there was heavy artillery action, and an enemy air attack against Douai was without success.'[2]

Boelcke and Immelmann's Eighth

Boelcke's description of the next momentous event shows his humour. He noted in his *Field-book* that on the evening of 11 January the section had a little party in which he stayed up late and had more than a little to drink. The next morning he 'did not feel like getting up', but the day dawned clear and bright, so he strolled out to the field at Douai. He took off in his Fokker about 9:00 am. Max Immelmann had gone off about 30 minutes earlier. Boelcke intercepted two R.E.7s near Ypres: one dived away and landed just on the British side of the trenches; the other remained airborne but headed for the lines. Inexplicably, he did not ma-noeuvre as Boelcke closed in, firing. The aircraft crashed behind the German lines with the pilot killed and the observer wounded.

Meanwhile, Immelmann intercepted a Vickers F.B.5 Gunbus and set it on fire. Immel-mann's encounter with his British counterpart is interesting and similar to Boelcke's with Lieutenant Formilli. Immelmann's victim was 2/Lieutenant Herbert Thomas Kemp who crashed the burning machine. Immelmann landed nearby, ran over to the crash site and engaged the pilot in conversation. Lieutenant Kemp asked if he was Immelmann, and upon learning he was correct, congratulated him on 'a fine sporting success'.[3] The two were tied again.

That same evening, Boelcke was called from dinner to receive a phone call. He was told that he and Max Immelmann were awarded the *Orden Pour le Mérite*. This order had been originally established by Friedrich Wilhelm I, the electoral prince, but the name was changed by Frederick the Great in 1740. The badge is a Maltese Cross in deep blue enamel with gold trim, hung on a black and white ribbon and worn around the neck.

Left: *Orden Pour le Mérite* – The Blue Max. (Walter Waiss)
Right: The Blue Max as worn around the neck. (Walter Waiss)

One story has it that the blue enamel reflected a blue cast against Immelmann's skin, and from this, observers named it the Blue Max (*der blaue Max*).[4] This historic order originally was reserved for those who had performed an extraordinary achievement (successful de-fence of a fortification or victory in battle). Previous awards had been made to: Gerard von Scharnhorst, 1807; Gebhard von Blücher, at Waterloo, 1815; Otto von Bismarck, 1884; and Paul von Hindenburg, 1914. Boelcke and Immelmann were the first aviators to receive this award, each having achieved the required eight aerial victories.[5]

Boelcke's Ninth

On 14 January 1916, two days after receiving the *Pour le Mérite*, Boelcke shot down his ninth aircraft, but only after a long turning battle, the hardest he had been in. Finally, the bullets from his twin Spandau machine guns hit the BE's engine, and the plane caught fire. The pilot dived for the British lines but crashed just short in the barbed wire.

On the way home, Boelcke's plane was down to emergency fuel, and he had to land at Flers, France. This was about 10:30 am, but because he had an invitation to dinner at 5:30 pm with the King and Prince of Bavaria in Lille, he spent a stressful day in a car back to Douai and then had to dress for dinner in his best uniform while driving off to Lille for the appointment.

Two days later, Max Immelmann is reported to have flown an E.IV, with three machine guns. However, the synchronising device on this model proved to be erratic, and most of the E.IVs went to a two-gun configuration.

The Effects of Fame

The award of the *Pour le Mérite* was noticed around the world. The event was especially the subject of newspapers in Great Britain, Germany and the United States. For example, the *Salt Lake Tribune* published an article with three subtitles: "GERMAN AVIA-TOR IS GIVEN GREAT HONOUR; Emperor Decorates Boelcke with Order *Pour le Mérite*; AIRMAN TALKS OF FOE; Says British Airmen are Most Daring and Courageous in Work; LIEUTEN-ANT BOELCKE, famous German aviator, who is smothered with correspondence."[6]

"Fokker attacks British Pusher" German *Flieg-erkarten* Series I. Card Nr. 2. Artist F. Schulz-Kühn. (Heinz-Michael Raby)

Over the next days, the two aces received telegrams from the King of Saxony, the Crown Princes of Prussia and Saxony, Prince Sigismund, the chief of war aviation, and many others. As invitations flooded in, the two realised a banquet circuit had begun in full swing. They were the rock stars or football heroes of their age. All Germany knew of their fame. The two new celebrities had to learn to balance social commitments with flying. The author can testify from personal experience that maintaining equilibrium and modesty in this new situation is not without stress. Sons of royalty and public school boys were probably better trained, practised and may have found it easier than lower-middle class youth, who usually have a steep learning curve to climb in social circles. Some do it better than others, and some distain what they consider this diversion from flying. What makes the balance more difficult is the complete difference of flying from other enterprises. Even the most articulate fliers find it difficult to describe their skill, exhilaration and fear of combat flying.

For insight into Boelcke's personal feelings about answering questions, see his leaflet, "Aircraft Defences Against Troublesome Questioners", in the previous chapter. Still, he was gracious and kind to his admirers. As seen in this never-before-published Fieldpostcard Boelcke wrote to a German citizen, Robert Lechner, who had congratulated him on the award of the Blue Max. Boelcke's message was, 'For the friendly congratulations my sincere thanks.'[7] On the front of the card it was stamped *Artillerie Flieger Abteilung 203*, which

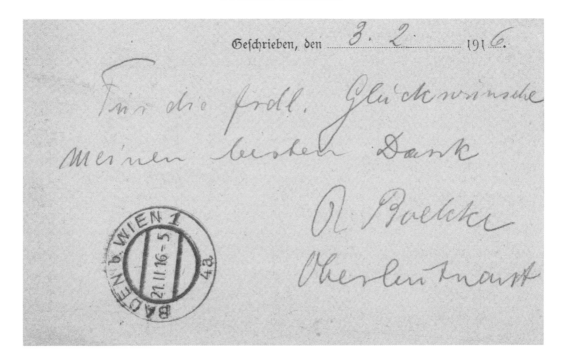

Oswald Boelcke's postcard, 3 February 1916, in response to an admirer. (courtesy of Heinz-Michael Raby)

was at Jametz, near Verdun. Boelcke had been reassigned from KEK Douai to the secret KEK Jametz in February 1916 in anticipation of the Verdun offensive. The card was sent to Lechner's address in Baden close to Vienna, but it seems that Mr. Lechner changed his address so the postal service corrected it and forwarded it on 21 November 1916, after Boelcke's death. The aviators continued to catch the imagination of the public.

Over the next months, invitations to social events continued to flow in. In April Boelcke was again invited to dinner with General Falkenhayn and the Grand Duke of Saxe-Weimar. Even personal dining changed, as Boelcke told his parents that he got butter, ham, sausages, cakes and 'even more of the otherwise rare eggs than I can eat .... That is all very well – if only I had not to answer such a terrible lot of letters. I really do not know what I am going to do about all these new honours.'[8] In the last days of April, he was invited to have lunch with the Emperor, who made him tell all about his tactics and latest victories. Finally, with a few days off, the 24-year-old Boelcke went to the opera in Wiesbaden. He related the experience in a letter to his parents, 29 April 1916:

'In those two days I learnt by experience how conspicuous a young officer with the *Pour le Mérite* appears at home – it is worse than having a warrant out against you. They stared at me all the time in the streets, both in Frankfurt and in Wiesbaden, where I was on Wednesday afternoon. Also the people in the opera crowded round me in each interval – it was terrible.

'But the worst was yet to come. When the opera singer Schramm sang the well-known aria "Father, mother, sisters, brothers," he was loudly applauded and encored.

At last he reappeared to start his encore. But just imagine –I could hardly believe my ears – the fellow did not sing the proper words but a verse in my honour which they had hastily strung together behind the scenes – it sounds like it. The singer himself sent me a copy round:

> "Listen, friends, our airman glorious,
> Leutnant Boelcke's here to-night,
> Many times he proved victorious,
> Made the foeman feel his might.
> May this hero go on winning,
> Send another hundred spinning,
> And how lovely if we may,
> Greet him here another day.'"[9]

World War I Aircraft

One of the reasons these two aviators were so successful was that the Fokker Eindeckers I, II and III were almost 20 per cent faster than their adversaries, and the 160-hp IV was 30 per cent faster. Even though their force was small in number, the Fokker Eindeckers dominated the air wherever they flew for over six months, from July 1915 to the winter of 1916.

Brief Comparison of Early WWI Aircraft (Author with data from: *Nieuport 11/16 Bébé vs Fokker Eindecker* by Jon Guttman, © Osprey Publishing Ltd, and James Miller, *DH- 2 vs Albatros D I/II*)

Aircraft Type	Nationality Crew	Machine Guns	Top Speed (mph)	Speed Increase (over B.E.2C)
1915 Combatants				
B.E.2C Pusher	British/Two	One Lewis	69	–
F.B.5 Pusher	British/Two	One Lewis	70	1.4%
Fokker E.I, E.II E.III	German/One	One (thru prop)	82	18.8%
Fokker E.IV	German/One	Two/three Maxim	90	30%
1916 Combatants				
F.E.2B	British	One Lewis	72	4%
D.H.2 Pusher	British/One	One Lewis	93	35%
Nieuport 11	French/One	One Lewis	97	41%
Albatros D.I & D.II	German/One	Two Maxim	109	58%

By early 1916, the advantage began to shift to the French. They had superior numbers and introduced the fast and nimble Nieuport 11 C1 "Bébé". They were also assisted by the Morane-

French Nieuport 11 "Bébé".

Saulnier Type N and the French reorganisation into squadrons and groups.[10] The British contributed to the effort with the deployment of the F.E.2B, a Farman experimental pusher. Their first F.E.2B squadron was operational in January 1916. But this aircraft lacked manoeuvrability and was only marginally faster (72 mph) than the B.E.2C.

The British also introduced the de Havilland D.H.2 in March 1916. This was a single-seater, still a pusher, but much faster at 85-93 mph, a stable gun platform and more rugged. However, it was slower than the Fokker E-Series in rate of climb. It became operational with 24 Squadron in February 1916 under the command of Major Lanoe Hawker. Hawker had been awarded the Victoria Cross in 1915, and by all reports he was an outstanding squadron commander. He would later be killed in an epic dogfight with Manfred von Richthofen in November 1916.

It should be noted that these pioneer pilots faced serious dangers, not just in combat, but in routine flying. Most of the machines were made of wood covered by fabric, but rigged and virtually held together by cables and wire. Without these wires holding the wings and landing gear in position, the parts would collapse. It was an apt description to call them "kites". Moreover, the training of new pilots was rushed and conducted without any systematic application of instructional techniques. Driving a motor car or riding a horse required some forceful arm and leg motions, but nothing in their civilian lives prepared a novice pilot for the minute adjustments and smooth application of an aircraft's controls. Many pilots were rough and jerky on the controls. They lacked coordination of stick and rudder that was necessary for good flying.

A three-point landing in an aircraft with a tailwheel is accurately described as a complete wing stall one inch off the ground. (A stall is a condition where the air over the wings becomes turbulent and loses lift.) A stall from 20 feet would result in a bounce, and a stall from 50 feet would wipe out the landing gear and propeller. Undercarriages frequently gave way or got caught in the mud, flipping the plane over on its back. Narrow landing gear and low wings were especially difficult to land in a crosswind. Many pilots "ground-looped" to their

embarrassment (a situation where the aircraft turns abruptly, usually 180 degrees, collapsing a wheel or damaging a wingtip). Engines were prone to quit exactly when needed most, and few pilots were trained to fly the ensuing heavy glider. Spin recovery was not taught at all, yet this was a common result of aerial combat, either as

British de Havilland D.H.2 single-seat pusher fighter.

the result of being hit in some vital part or the pilot losing control. Aircraft of this era were not very stable and tended to spin and fall rapidly.

Once the novice got a little experience he often tended to become overconfident. Leslie Horridge of the RFC's 7 Squadron recorded:

'I am beginning to think that you cannot be killed in an ordinary aeroplane smash. I have seen so many, and no-one has been killed, that it seems to be very bad luck if you are ever hurt. If the pilot knows how to fly, flying is as safe as motoring, probably more so, as you never have to worry about being run into. Nearly every smash is caused through carelessness, either in getting off or landing.'[11]

This quotation is an excellent example of overconfidence from too narrow a viewpoint. Overall, many more pilots were killed in training than in combat. Of the official number of 14,166 British pilots who died in the war years, less than one half (44 per cent) died in combat.[12] The German response to the British and French introduction of newer and faster aircraft was to accelerate the development of the new D-type machines and deployment of the C-type machine (including an Albatros). The Albatros C.1 was a two-seater with the pilot in front and a gunner/observer in the rear cockpit with a ring-mounted Parabellum MG14 machine gun. At the same time, the 6th Armee's staff officer in charge of aviation formed specialised units of two to four Fokkers or Pfalz Eindeckers. The units were described earlier as single-seater fighter detachments (KEKs). Despite the fact that these unit organisations were only on a temporary basis, they formed the immediate predecessor of the Staffeln.[13]

The RFC was also experimenting with different organisational models. On 30 January 1916, the RFC formed two air brigades, each one containing two wings paired together. Each brigade then had a corps wing that directly supported the ground forces in artillery spotting, reconnaissance, photography and some local bombing and reported to the corps headquarters. The other wing was called an army wing with the mission of air combat and longer-range reconnaissance and deep bombing raids.

One could say that the fight for some sort of air superiority was well underway. The first three battles for air superiority were: the Fokker Scourge; Verdun; and the Somme. I have already discussed the contribution of the Fokker Eindecker with Boelcke and Immelmann to the scourge in 1915 and the first quarter of 1916.

The Battle of Verdun

On 21 February 1916, the German army launched a battle of attrition at Verdun, hoping to capture this historic citadel and bleed France to the point where she would give up the war. It was a desperate objective, which required the massing of hundreds of thousands of men, artillery and aircraft. The offensive was aided by the concentration of a large number of captive balloons and bombing raids on rail junctions with bombs of ever-larger weights (220 lbs with later ones 660 and 2,200 lbs).[14] The German air service massed 168 aircraft, including twenty-one single-seat fighters available for Verdun. The fighters were split into three KEKs: Avillers, Jametz and Cunel.[15]

The French had more aircraft, but their strategic doctrine was dominated by the ground generals. The flying units were given orders to concentrate their aircraft on the front lines to provide ground support. The ground generals wanted to see planes overhead. The French air commander, Commandant Paul du Peuty, initially demurred and went along with his superiors' insistence on the aircraft attacking ground targets and merely escorting reconnaissance aircraft. But the aggressive KEKs, led by Immelmann and Boelcke, were having great success picking off the orbiting French aeroplanes. Du Peuty reversed his policy (that he had opposed all along) and ordered his single-seat units to attack the German aircraft directly. This freed them from their "sheepdog role" of protecting the ground forces on the front line. It also allowed offensive bombing and strafing German airfields behind the lines. These tactics and the simultaneous fielding of the forward-firing Nieuport enabled the French to challenge the Fokker's dominance and gain air superiority over the Verdun battlefield. One of the most famous French squadrons that participated in this battle was that of the "Storks" (Escadron de Chasse 01-002 "Cigognes"). The French air order of 29 February 1916 is instructive in its clarity:

'The mission of the escadrilles is to seek the enemy in order to engage and destroy him ... They will fly by escadrilles [six] or half-escadrille [three]. They will take an echeloned formation in three dimensions.'[16]

This is one of the first records of formation flying in combat, but the policy's effectiveness was seriously diluted by two factors: 1) French pilots were not trained in formation flying, and 2) Most French pilots were fierce individualists and frequently abandoned the formation at the first opportunity. John Cuneo records:

'The French lack of skill in formation flying, the heavier losses resulting from the fact that the fighting was over the German lines and the inspiration of Lieutenant Boelcke began to give the Germans the edge in the air.'[17]

On an operational scale, the policy of "attack and destroy" was so successful that the Frenchman, du Peuty, shared the details of his thinking with General Hugh Trenchard, and the two became good friends.

This unlikely friendship reinforced Trenchard's inclination to use his air force offensively, and so the policy became combined doctrine. At the same time, Trenchard split his forces into specialised units of army cooperation and fighter operations.

The French leadership also was concerned about the effectiveness of the German fighters. Knowing the French had numerical superiority, General Pétain called his chief of air operations and gave him an order, 'I am blind! Sweep the skies for me!'[18] The French generals also centralised their air units into a single aviation command for the Verdun sector and assembled fifteen pursuit units there.

The French air offensive reinforced the German policy of fighting defensively, and the French began to dominate the skies. While the German KEKs flying the Fokker monoplanes seized the initiative and gained local air superiority where they flew, their small numbers and limited range/loiter time hampered their effectiveness. French reconnaissance aircraft became successful, and the French army began to regain lost ground. However, French aircrews paid the price of the "sweep the skies" policy. From 21 February to 1 July 1916, France lost 100 pilots and observers in a force that by 1 June had grown to 1,120 aircraft. Despite the massive resources in men and material that were thrown into the Verdun battle on both sides, it gradually devolved into a stalemate, with huge losses and little movement in the front lines.

Lieth-Thomsen's Reorganisation Memo

Oberstleutnant Lieth-Thomsen, the chief of the German air service units in the field, assessed the French air resurgence and applied the lessons of Verdun in an iconic memo on organisation. On 10 March 1916, he wrote to the high command that it was becoming increasingly apparent that to develop the full power of air forces it was necessary to provide 'unity of command'. There needed to be 'the unified command of our entire aerial equipment, the systematic development, training, preparation, deployment and employment of all air forces and anti-aircraft defences, and the organic union of the entire air arms of the army and navy'.[19] The chief's memo was the opening shot in what would become a radical reorganisation of the German air service.

Boelcke Flies at Verdun

Boelcke's health problems never left him, and at the end of February 1916, he was hospitalised with intestinal disease. By the end of the first week in March, he was feeling better and asked to be discharged. He was refused. So he decided to 'make a bolt for it'. He disappeared from the hospital early the next day and caught a ride back to his section with a passing lorry.

Boelcke had been at KEK Jametz on the Verdun Front since February. He was early to recognise that air power was inherently offensive. He became concerned that Jametz was too far from the front to be effective, and he tried continually to get moved closer. Finally, the staff officer in charge of the aircraft on the Verdun Front agreed, and he was given permission to establish and lead one of three "groups" or sections of scouts deployed forward. These "groups" were really "flights" (USAF designation) or "divisions" (USN designation) of four to six aircraft. He chose a beautiful meadow on the banks of the Meuse River, close

Two of Boelcke's Eindeckers at Sivry-sur-Meuse. (*Voler Nemsch*; Johan Ryeul)

to the town of Sivry, only 12 kilometres behind the line. This deployment of an independent "group" of scouts was significant because it was another step on the road to organising fighter squadrons. The unit became known as KEK Sivry (-sur-Meuse) [Sivry-on-the-

Meuse].[20]Boelcke arrived on 11 March as the commander. He was accompanied initially by Leutnant Werner Notzke and several enlisted men, with two airplanes. The day after Boelcke's arrival he shot down a Farman pusher – his tenth victory, and on 13 March, a Voisin, his eleventh. Later, the number of his aircraft increased to six and the number of pilots and support personnel accordingly.

Boelcke (on right), Ltn Notzke (seated) and four visiting officers lounging at Sivry-sur-Meuse. (*Voler Nemsch*; Johan Ryheul)

Boelcke continued flying a Fokker E.IV, with the double-row rotary engine and two machine guns. The increased power of the new engine allowed the fighters to climb to higher altitude, which aggravated Boelcke's shortness of breath, but it did not deter his determination. On 19 March, he downed another two-seat Farman for victory number twelve.

A humorous incident followed. On 20 March, Max Immelmann called on the telephone from Douai and congratulated Boelcke on his latest accomplishment, but chided him that he had violated their "agreement". Immelmann said Boelcke should have waited for him to catch up. Boelcke promised solemnly to wait a week before his next kill, but he was unable to keep his promise. He got number thirteen the next day.

Sivry-sur-Meuse was close to Stenay, which was the headquarters of Crown Prince Wilhelm. When Boelcke was invited there, which was frequently, the Crown Prince would send his own car and driver. The Crown Prince also visited Sivry several times, and he and Boelcke developed a friendship. The relationship was so close that when the prince had not heard from Boelcke for a few days, he would telephone to inquire. Despite this contact with royalty, Boelcke remained modest and only mentioned it to his parents on one occasion. On 21 March 1916, he was surprised to receive a handwritten letter from the Kaiser:

'It has been reported to me that once again you have emerged victorious from a fight with enemy aircraft. I have already shown you, not long ago by the bestowal of my highest war order, the *Pour le Mérite*, what importance I attach to the results of your daring courage. But I cannot let the occasion of your twelfth victory, whereby you have now put out of action the strength of two enemy flying sections, pass without expressing to you again my fullest appreciation of your excellent achievements in aerial warfare.'[21]

In this period of aerial success, Boelcke had his worst ordeal of combat. While flying opposite the French at Verdun, a Nieuport got behind his Fokker and stayed for countless minutes, firing frequently. Boelcke felt fear as he banked, yanked, climbed and dove, but the Nieuport remained behind in this life-or-death battle. The Frenchman's bullets whizzed by his head and chewed up the fabric on his fuselage and right wing. Finally, in a last-ditch effort he pulled up into a stall and kicked the rudder, forcing the airplane into a tight spin. Fortunately, the Frenchman did not follow, and Boelcke escaped, unharmed. He breathed a sigh of relief and swore to himself never to be caught unaware again. When he landed he and his ground crew counted more than ninety bullet holes in his plane. Boelcke immediately knew the days of the Fokker Eindecker domination were over. There would have to be a new fighter for the German air service.

Fokker E.IV with two machine guns.

The Fokker E.IV did not meet the bill. In March, Immelmann had his propeller cut off by machine-gun bullets when one synchroniser broke. It happened again in May. Motivated to communicate his conclusions to the high command, Boelcke sat down and wrote two memoranda. The first was on the 'wretched' use of German airpower. In it he said, 'The only proper kind of war to engage in the war is an offensive war. We have remained on the defensive too long.'[22] Boelcke's second memo responded to a headquarters' request for technical evaluations. This document, "Report on the 160 HPE. Machine", 23 March 1916, is the only one that survives today. It was objective, but critical of the Fokker E.IV and stated the operational requirement for a new aircraft, a 'modern biplane fighter machine.'

The "misuse" allegation was to be corrected by a reorganisation of the German air service to include *Kampfeinsitzerkommando* ("fighter single-seat commands"). In the technical report, Boelcke detailed his pilot assessment that 'the speed is sufficient, climbing capacity falls off considerably at great heights. The manoeuvring power of the 160-hp machine is considerably inferior to that of the 100-hp and 80-hp types, because of the difficulty in counteracting the active force [torque] of the heavy engine.' Also, 'the mounting of the guns at an elevation of fifteen degrees is unsatisfactory.'[23] To restore good climbing performance, he recommended 'a light biplane', a requirement that was to be met by the Albatros firm four months later. His report was also very critical of the 160-hp rotary engine, which he considered to be too finely balanced and unreliable for combat.

Anthony Fokker was quite incensed by what he considered to be criticism of his aircraft, and his attitude toward Boelcke became cool. It never recovered. From that point forward he favoured Max Immelmann in his dealings and writings. However, he began to consider the advantages of the in-line, liquid-cooled engine. Although he would soon produce the Dr.I triplane with another rotary engine, he switched to the in-line Mercedes 160-hp engine for the Fokker D.VII. Thus, Boelcke was among the first to recognise the limitations of the rotary engine in general, which began to decline in favour.

Boelcke's concerns over the E.IV were borne out by Max Immelmann. Fokker commented on Immelmann's misfortunes and admitted later in his autobiography:

'It was an unlucky machine, though he [Immelmann] gained two victories in it. He nearly lost his life when a rocker arm of the Gnome rotary motor broke in flight. Flailing through the air like a revolving knife, it cut through the steel supports attaching the engine to the nose of the fuselage. The loosened motor rocked and shook itself entirely loose from its bed, but was stopped before it tore completely away. With his motor hanging only by a single twisted tube Immelmann skilfully brought the plane to safety. His time had not yet come.'[24]

As a direct result of Boelcke's technical analysis and Immelmann's frightening experience, both he and Max Immelmann reverted to flying the Fokker E.III model with its 100-hp engine; less power but more reliable. At the end of March 1916, both aces had thirteen victories. In April each added one more, and they were still tied.

By the winter of 1916, virtually all German air service fighters were flying in pairs with a section leader and his wingman flying as a team. Boelcke determined that his wingman fly slightly *above*, back and to the side to guard the leader's tail. [Author's note: Modern USAF formation doctrine is for the wingman to fly slightly lower than the leader. If the leader banks and turns abruptly the wing can more easily slide under and retain sight at all times.]

Leutnant Boelcke's letter of 17 April to his parents outlines a little of the celebrity status that his success had brought him:

'I went to Charleville several days ago to discuss service matters with the chief of the air forces. On this occasion Falkenhayn [General Erich von Falkenhayn, chief of the general staff] asked me to dinner. It was very interesting to get a close view of this man who is moving the scenery in the theatre of the world. We all sat at little tables; I sat with Falkenhayn, General Tappen and the quartermaster general. I have already told you that the Grand Duke of Saxe-Weimar visited my aerodrome lately and that I dined with him that evening.'[25]

On 18 May, Boelcke had a non-combat experience that was so memorable he recorded it in his *Fieldbook*. It showed his humanity. 'Toward evening I went up and found our biplanes everywhere around Verdun. I felt superfluous there, so went off for a little trip. I wanted to have a look at the Champagne district once more, and flew to A. and back. Everywhere there was peace; on earth as well as in the air. I only saw one airplane, in the distance at A.'[26] During the rest of May 1916, Immelmann got one victory, but Boelcke got four. Their numbers were fifteen-eighteen, with the last two being a double kill on 21 May. The Emperor promptly decreed Oberleutnant Boelcke be promoted to Hauptmann (captain). This made Boelcke the youngest captain in the Prussian army and marked the first time that a man of only 25 years and 16 days would achieve that rank. There was a Prussian army regulation that required an officer to be at least 30 years old to be a captain. This was all the more exceptional because of his middle-class birth.[27]

The two famous pilots continued to be lauded in the German press and around the world. Immelmann became known as "The Eagle of Lille" his hometown. The unnamed editors of *The Red Fighter Pilot*, noted in their 2007 Introduction, 'Although Immelmann had gotten most of the attention from the German press, it was Boelcke who made the most lasting contribution of aerial combat.'[28] In June, Boelcke was to have an auspicious day, although he did not recognise it at the time.

One of the squadrons France deployed to defend Verdun was the famous "American Escadrille". This legendary outfit was composed of Americans who had entered the *Aviation Militaire* to fight for France. The unit was commanded by a French captain and designated N124. On 13 May 1916 France declared *l'Escadrille des Americains* operational and the squadron arrived opposite Verdun on 20 May. They flew their first combat sortie over Verdun on 22 May, and Bert Hall shot down a German Aviatik.[29] When the German ambassador in Washington, DC, complained soon afterward that this national name violated the neutrality of the United States, the name of the squadron was changed in December 1916 to the Lafayette Escadrille.

Oswald Boelcke met the Americans that June in the air over Verdun. Boelcke described the episode in vivid terms in his *Fieldbook*. A German pilot had just landed, and he ran up to Boelcke, all out of breath: 'The devil is loose on the front. Six Americans are up. I could plainly see the American flag on the fuselage. They were quite bold; came all the way across the front.' Boelcke continued:

> 'I didn't imagine things were quite so bad, and decided to go up and give the Americans a welcome. They were probably expecting it; politeness demanded it. I really met them above the Meuse. They were flying back and forth quite gaily, close together. I flew toward them, and greeted the first one with my machine gun. He seemed to be quite a beginner; at any rate, I had no trouble in getting to within 100 metres of him, and had him well under fire. As he was up in the clouds and flew in a straight course, I was justified in expecting to bring him to earth soon. But luck was not with me. I had just gotten my machine back from the factory, and after firing a few shots my gun jammed. In vain I tried to remedy the trouble. While still bothering with my gun the other "five Americans" were on me. As I could not fire, I preferred to retreat and when the whole mob came chasing after me, I hastened my homeward flight.'[30]

Boelcke humorously recorded in a footnote to a letter to his family, 'The direct result of this encounter was that the English wireless news service reported, "Yesterday Adjacent Ribiere succeeded in bringing down the famous Captain Boelcke in an air battle at Verdun." In the meantime I have relieved him of this misapprehension.'[31]

In early June, Boelcke was informed that he was to form his own Staffel with six Fokker E.IIIs. (This was a smaller, informal, group than would later outfit squadrons with eight to ten aircraft.) In a letter to his parents Boelcke wrote:

'I made no efforts to get this; they pushed it on me almost against my will. But now that I have taken the job on, I find it great fun and I shall take care to make it into a very special Staffel.

'The only snap is that my Fokker Staffel is not on the regular establishment and so can be disbanded again accordingly.'[32]

Immelmann's Death

However, before this change from KEKs to Staffels could be implemented the ace race came to an abrupt end. On 18 June 1916, Max Immelmann got two victories, for a total of fifteen, but was killed when his E.III Eindecker crashed. One account was that the synchronising mechanism malfunctioned, bullets shot off one propeller blade, and the unbalanced engine tore itself apart. A second version opined that he had been shot down by an Englishman. A third was that he had been shot down by anti-aircraft fire. Fokker's official investigation was that at least one of the control wires had been shot through. Boelcke's explanation was that a piece of his propeller flew off. The resulting vibration broke the restraining wires, and the fuselage broke into pieces. Immelmann was 25 years old.

Boelcke is Grounded

Boelcke attended Immelmann's funeral and was devastated by the death of his friend. No one knows the full extent of his sorrow as it was not recorded, but it certainly came as a shock. Within days he received a telegram that provided another shock, 'Hauptmann Boelcke is to report at once to the commander-in-chief of the Aerial Division. He is to be at the disposal of the commander-in-chief of the army'. Boelcke was elated because he expected to be transferred from Verdun, north to the Somme, where the English were massing for an offensive. Much to his dismay, when he reported as ordered to the chief on 24 June, he learned he was to be grounded with an effective date of 27 June and was to be sent on leave for his "nerves". The Emperor and the Crown Prince did not want to risk losing their two most famous aces of the war. Boelcke was outraged. He protested vigorously, although the chief was not moved. In a rare fit of anger, Boelcke stormed out.

'When I got outside I cursed the adjutant and other pen-pushers in a most offensive fashion, which only, however, provoked mirth from all concerned. One of the fellows gave me a wise lecture to the effect that I was no longer a private individual who could play with his life at will but the property of the German nation, which still expected much from me.'[33]

One of the staff officers suggested that rather than take mandatory leave, Captain Boelcke could make a visit to Turkey and tour other fronts. Boelcke immediately recognised this would be better than sitting idly by on the ground, and he agreed. His attitude gradually accepted his fate, and he wrote to his parents:

'Even though this was nothing that replaced my work [flying], it was at least a balm for my wounded feelings. I immediately went to Sivry to pack my things and use the remaining two days to fly as much as possible. I flew twice that night, because I had to utilise the time.'[34]

And use the time he did. Boelcke returned to Sivry-sur-Meuse and flew twice that evening, 27 June, over Verdun. On the second sortie he met five French fighters and shot down one of them, his nineteenth victory.[35]

Sometime in this short period between 18 June and 10 July, Boelcke was reportedly interviewed by a reporter from Berlin. One of the newspaper articles that was based on this interview appeared in the *Salt Lake Tribune* on 3 August 1916:

'BERLIN. A correspondent of the *Berliner Tageblatt* on the Western Front describes a meeting with Captain Boelcke, the German aviator who has shot down twenty enemy aeroplanes and been decorated with the order "*Pour le Mérite*" by the Emperor.

"'In the afternoon, after a vain search to Boelcke of several hours we came upon a half demolished farmhouse," the correspondent writes, "A broken propeller of an aeroplane was fastened to one of the walls of the little building and here I found the young airman who with his recently killed comrade, Leutnant Immelmann, has become an idol of the German nation.

"'When I asked him for the secret of his success as an aviator he said: "There is no secret to it. My excellent eye does it. When I am thousands of feet above the earth I can observe the movements of the enemy machines for which I am lying without a spyglass, and my aim is always good. Of course, sometimes it takes a little nerve to attack, but that every German has. Courage is no special distinction."'[36]

Observations About the Ace Race

The German public created the ace race in their imagination, and the newspapers named and exploited it. One can decry this adulation of the civilian citizens of the various countries, but we would be well advised to keep in mind Abraham Lincoln's opinion, 'In this and like communities, public sentiment is everything. With public sentiment, nothing can fail; without it, nothing can succeed.'[37] The race was 50 weeks long, from 4 July 1915 to 18 June 1916. In the end, it was not so much a race as a leader-follower sequence. Boelcke led ten times, and Immelmann led five. Of the 50 weeks of the "race" Boelcke led 30; Immelmann 4; with 16 weeks of ties.

The ace race was an important part of the initial air combat in WWI. It characterised the growth and development of air fighting in the eyes of the public; it gave birth to the phenomenon of the Fokker Scourge to the military profession; it highlighted the importance of speed and manoeuvrability as performance factors that changed the aircraft industry; it was witness to the development of air superiority as a military concept of dominance that remains in language today; it resulted in the escalation of air casualties; and it ushered in an era of formation flying that changed the nature of air warfare from lone eagles to teams of talented aviators.

The Boelcke Dicta are Born

Chief of air service Colonel Lieth-Thomsen recorded many years later in his book that Boelcke had spent several days in this period with his air staff officers in considering and writing down the basic principles of air warfare and the organisation and tactics that would further the development of this new aviation arm. Some of these ideas were codified and became the famous Boelcke Dicta.

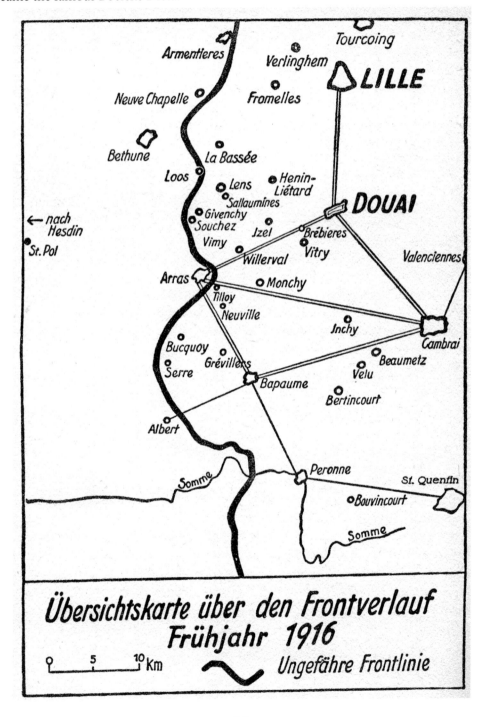

Übersichtskarte über den Frontverlauf Frühjahr 1916

0 5 10 Km Ungefähre Frontlinie

CHAPTER VIII

Boelcke's Dicta

Tactics

In the beginning, there were no fighter tactics because there were no fighter missions. Tactical thinking was limited by the technology available and the doctrine of the time. Many believed that aircraft should not be armed, and others felt that rifles, pistols and bricks might be effective if you could get close enough to your enemy to hit them. The mission of air superiority had not even been invented, so there was no military requirement for fighter aircraft or the tactics to employ them. Fighter pilot and author, Edward Sims, noted that tactics were 'primitive and experimental'.[1] However, the early military pilots knew instinctively that something was missing – something to codify their random thoughts about air warfare.

The idea of developing fighter tactics had been with Oswald Boelcke since he began combat flying, but he did not write them down until June 1916. He described his actions in letters to his family. He discussed his ideas with Max Immelmann and other pilots, but Immelmann did not share his views. Immelmann wrote to his mother in 1911, 'The study of military tactics, which are the basis of an officer's career, leave me completely cold.'[2] Boelcke wrote what were to become his famous dicta in conjunction with the air staff while he was grounded following Immelmann's death. The term "dicta" was chosen because it means "authoritative pronouncements" a "formal state of principles". Derived from the Latin, dicta is the plural of dictum.

Dicta Boelcke[3]

- Always try to secure an advantageous position before attacking. Climb before and during the approach in order to surprise the enemy from above, and dive on him swiftly from the rear when the moment to attack is at hand.
- Try to place yourself between the sun and the enemy. This puts the glare of the sun in the enemy's eyes and makes it difficult to see you and impossible for him to shoot with any accuracy.
- Do not fire the machine guns until the enemy is within range and you have him squarely within your sights.
- Attack when the enemy least expects it or when he is pre-occupied with other duties such as observation, photography or bombing.
- Never turn your back and try to run away from an enemy fighter. If you are surprised by an attack on your tail, turn and face the enemy with your guns.

- Keep your eye on the enemy and do not let him deceive you with tricks. If your opponent appears damaged follow him down until he crashes to be sure he is not faking.
- Foolish acts of bravery only bring death. The Jasta must fight as a unit with close teamwork between all pilots. The signals of its leaders must be obeyed.
- For the Staffel: Attack in principle in groups of four or six. When the fight breaks up into a series of single combats, take care that several do not go for one opponent.

These ideas may seem like common sense to those who have seen countless movies of documentary and fictional air battles, but before they were common sense, they were unique, unproven and often controversial, like hypotheses in a scientific journal. That they are flexible, capable of adaptation to local circumstances and emerging technology is a tribute to their enduring value.

What made these dicta so valuable was that they had been developed from actual experience, primarily from flying the Fokker Eindecker against French and British foes in trial and error. Boelcke would take off, climb to altitude and search for an enemy aircraft. Often the sight of German anti-aircraft fire would be an indication of a hostile aircraft crossing the lines. He would get into a favourable position, between the victim and the sun if possible, then descend in a long, slanting dive, gaining speed, hoping to remain undetected until very close behind the opponent, in what became known as the "six o'clock" position. Then he would open fire, in short bursts, closing to within a few yards. Thus, he used concealment, high speed, attack from the rear blind spot, and close-in firing, all tactics that aces have used over the decades since. Edward Sims wrote, 'Using these tactics, Boelcke pioneered in air combat'.[4]

The German air service printed Boelcke's rules in pamphlet form and distributed them to all prospective scout pilots. Although several Allied pilots had discussed and even written notes on their own tactics, no such list was published or distributed with either the Royal Flying Corps or the *Aviation Militaire* until 1918.[5] Their knowledge was passed by word of mouth and usually kept within squadrons. Pilots continued to be trained with only the barest knowledge of flying skills and virtually no systematic education in combat tactics. That is why the new pilots had such a high attrition rate; many of them surviving less than two weeks.

Over the century since they were written, the dicta have been printed and reprinted in numerous volumes. For example, they are reproduced in total in Robert Shaw's book, *Fighter Combat: Tactics and Manoeuvring*,[6] but he says nothing about Boelcke himself. On the opposite end, Edward Sims discusses Boelcke's tactics and their evolution in great detail, but does not actually reprint the dicta.

Principles one, two and four of Boelcke's Dicta can be summarised as "gain surprise". This is a principle of war shared by airmen, sailors, infantrymen and tank crews over the decades. Edward Sims wrote that: 'Boelcke was probably the single most important figure in the development of air fighting during the first part of the First World War.'[7]

The Value of Firing First

Boelcke's first dictum was always try to secure an advantageous position before attacking. This principle of tactical flying is vital to allow the attacker to fire first, and firing first is the most certain way to win the engagement. The major benefit is that the attacker gets to fire at a non-manoeuvring target. In fact, in many of Boelcke's victories, the defender never fired at all because he never saw Boelcke coming. The current emphasis on designing stealth into the airframe is a follow-on corollary to Boelcke's dictum. If the opponent cannot see you, he cannot attack. In addition, the instinct of the defender is to flee rather than fight, which gives the attacker another advantage.

All pilots, even the early ones in WWI, knew this instinctively. The data to support this tactic was not compiled or analysed until much later – in the Second World War from after-action reports. The analysis appears in an unpublished US army staff study based on 300 WWII platoon-to-company-size armour engagements in France. These data revealed and its analysis confirmed the importance of firing first.[8] If the attacker gains surprise and fires first, his historical probability of successful attack is between 80 and 99 per cent. (See the figure below.) If the attacker has a near equal force ratio (e.g. one attacker and one defender) his probability of success is at the lower end. If the attacker has a numerical advantage (say two to one or four to one) his historical probability of success increases toward the upper end. Conversely, if the defender gets off the first shot, the attacker's probability of success is only 10-15 per cent, and even increasing the force ratio to 6:1 only improves it to 60 per cent. The results of the analysis and the principle itself are confirmed by the professional knowledge of fighter pilots, submariners, snipers, tankers. The infantry corollary is the ambush, with claymore mines and automatic weapons. It embodies one of the ancient principles of war – surprise attack.

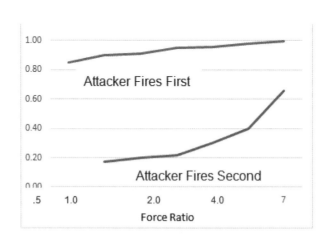

The attacker who fires first has an enormous advantage. (Reprinted with permission of Johns Hopkins University Press.)

Fighter Formations

Some authors give credit to Boelcke's Dicta for the initiative to use two aircraft together to double the look-out capability of the attackers and reduce the inherent vulnerability of a single aircraft armed solely with a forward-firing gun. Edward Sims is more assertive, 'He [Boelcke] decided scouts should fly in pairs. Each pilot could cover the blind spots the other could not cover visually and detect an aircraft approaching the other from the rear.'[9] From the author's research it appears that the French were the first to recognise the power of formation flying. The French order of 29 February 1916, during the Battle of Verdun, probably documents the first tactic of flying in formation.

Initially, two pilots would fly a loose formation, but gradually the following aircraft would be moved forward, so that the two ships would essentially be in a line abreast formation. In 1916, this was defined as 60 yards between aircraft, which was the turning radius of the Albatros D.I and II fighters. The purpose of this spread formation was to maximise lookout and provide mutual protection, both of which are impossible for the wingmen (now wings) in close formation or close trail formation; in those two formations, only the leader can look around freely. The author can attest that flying in line abreast is difficult and tiring. It is easy to get too far ahead or behind. Fortunately, the German pilots, who on the average were more experienced than the Allies, learned the technique quickly. The lack of flying experience, and the limited opportunities for training in formation flying among Allied air services, exacerbated this problem.

We do know from reading Boelcke's journal and contemporary accounts that he used the tactic of grouping multiple aircraft together in the hunt for opposing planes. Once the Albatroses arrived in his squadron, he routinely scheduled them in groups of four or five. This technique of massing fighters was developed to its logical extreme by Manfred von Richthofen, whose Flying Circus is legendary.

Boelcke also pioneered another aspect of combat flying. He wrote a second brochure, on enemy capabilities entitled, "Experiences of Air Fighting". It included a brief summary of the performance and vulnerabilities of three types of enemy aircraft. (Note: The Germans used the term Vickers to refer to virtually all types of British pusher-engine aircraft.)

> '*Vickers Single-Seater*: Very agile, somewhat slower than the Albatros, generally loses height in steep turns. Defenceless in the rear.
> '*Vickers Double-Seater*: Not so agile or fast. Two pivotable machine guns for observer sitting in front, one of which can incline upwards. Can shoot well forward, upward or sideways, but rear fire limited by necessity of shooting clear of propeller.
> '*Nieuport Single-Seater*: Very fast and agile. Armament and shooting possibilities very similar to our own. Generally loses height in prolonged turning action. Attack from behind if possible and at close range.'[10]

Boelcke was not alone in developing tactics for the new arena of warfare. A Royal Flying Corps observer penned his "Notes on Combat in Air":

> 'Attack on the same level if possible. In B.E.2C use side mounting [for the machine

gun]. Don't open fire over 500 yards. You don't carry enough cartridges to waste. Fire in bursts of not over ten. Switch your gun quickly to back mounting as he passes and fire remainder of drum: i) If Hun dives replace gun on side bracket. ii) Attack as before. iii) Put gun on front mounting and dive for position under tail. Never follow a machine directly behind as he will take you through and through. Never let a machine get under your tail. Never let a machine swoop down on you unawares from behind. At first sound of a shot from behind, turn to the right and left with nose down before looking round even. It is with his first burst of fire that the Fokker Scout gets his machine down. If an EA [enemy aircraft] Scout pressed his attack home and persists, follow into a slow spiral losing as little height as possible.

Lieutenant Bernard Rice, 2 Squadron, RFC'[11]

However, these notes are located in a manuscript in the RAF Museum in London, and there is no indication or evidence that they had any official sanction or were ever widely distributed among the RFC.

Boelcke's Dicta inspired other pilots to write down their thoughts about fighter tactics. Several examples, including those of Manfred von Richthofen are reproduced in the Appendices. These writings fostered numerous tactics manuals and some evolved into tactical doctrine. This led eventually in all military forces to the development of what are called, "tactics, techniques and procedures". These are formalised rules that guide and standardise the consensus of ways to operate in military services. The USAF publishes manuals on Tactics, Techniques and Procedures (AFTTP). The US Navy has Naval Air Training and Operating Procedures (NATOPS).[12] The US Joint Chiefs of Staff publish Joint Tactics, Techniques and Procedures (Joint Publication 3-Series). All of these publications are military doctrine, which are 'fundamental principles that guide the employment of military forces'.[13]

In the United States, the central unit for the development of air force tactics is the Fighter Weapons School of Air Combat Command at Nellis Air Force Base, Nevada. Ironically, neither the United Kingdom nor Germany currently have a specific organisation tasked with this mission.

Meanwhile, Boelcke was withdrawn from flying to save him from loss as a hero to the country, and ordered on an inspection tour of the east.

The Tour

Although a couch-bound observer could opine that the tour was a reward for Boelcke's success, no fighter pilot would have looked upon it that way. He was still grounded, and he would be missing some good flying. The tour of the east began in Vienna on 10 July 1916, when Boelcke was hosted by the head of the Austrian air service. He then visited an Austrian aerodrome and took a flight over the city. He found it much more relaxed and "residential" compared to the bustling Berlin. At each of the locations, he was beset with autograph hunters and reporters. Departing on a steamboat down the River Danube to Budapest, he caught the Balkan train.

The destination of the journey was Constantinople, the capital of the Ottoman Empire.

He was met with officers from the local German contingent and the war office. He then paid a courtesy call on Enver Pasha, the war minister and commander-in-chief of the Turkish armed forces. He was only 10 years older than Boelcke and was one of the three leaders of the "Young Turks" movement that came to power in 1908. He had spent 1909-1911 as military attaché in Berlin. After the coup in 1913, which brought his faction of the Young Turks to power, he led Turkey into the war on the side of the Central Powers. After a boat trip through the Bosphorus, Boelcke visited a German submarine which he had been anxious to see. On 17 July, he toured an air station, talked to the men and got a look at the aeroplanes that had been fighting the Russians.

Boelcke was then hosted on board the battle cruiser *Goeben*, which with the cruiser *Breslau*, had escaped the British and French Mediterranean fleets in 1914, and entered the Dardanelles. There the admiral turned the two warships over to the Turkish government, thus ensuring their entry into WWI.

After an elegant train ride to Smyrna (now Izmir) on the Aegean seacoast, Boelcke had dinner with his old instructor from 1914 at Darmstadt. On visiting the aerodrome, he was impressed with Turkish enlisted men, but the officers, pilots, and observers, he thought, 'not so good'. He toured the ancient ruin of Troy by air and flew over the British positions at Gallipoli that had been evacuated just six months before. At the end of July, while touring the Dardanelles, he received news of the Battle of the Somme and the British air superiority there. Oberstleutnant Lieth-Thomsen sent Boelcke a cable asking him to return soon. As a result, Boelcke wrote in his travel diary, 'I am all impatience to be back at the front.'[14]

Boelcke left Constantinople on 1 August and travelled to Bulgaria by train. There he continued the rounds of formal dinners, visited a cadet school, some grammar schools and flying units, some of which had very little action on the Eastern Front. Again, he was hosted by numerous officials of the Bulgarian war ministry where he was awarded a "For Valour" medal. From there he accelerated his journey and caught a train to Kovel, in the Ukraine, on the Eastern Front. There he met once again with his brother, Wilhelm, who was commander of Kagohl 2. Upon arrival, Boelcke received a more urgent message from the air force chief to, 'Return to Western Front as quickly as possible to organise and lead Jagdstaffel 2 on the Somme Front.'[15]

On his return trip he called on General Ludendorff who introduced him to Field Marshal Hindenburg, with whom he had lunch. In the final days of his journey he flew to Warsaw, then took a train to Berlin where he conducted business with air force officials in the inspectorate of flying troops and at the Johannistal airfield, where the Albatros factory was building D.I and D.II biplanes.

As the tour of the east concluded in mid-1916, the evolution of Boelcke's character was not complete, but he had matured. He learned to balance notoriety. He had become an international public figure. He didn't necessarily like it, but he accepted his role with equanimity. He did not embarrass anyone with outbursts or drunkenness. He accepted foreign medals and praise and honoured his hosts. His expertise had broadened beyond what a Saxon boy could have dreamed of. He was a man of the moment, and he wore the honour lightly. Still, he was called back to flying. As soon as his business in Berlin was finished, Boelcke travelled to Dessau, saw his family and set off immediately for the Somme.

CHAPTER IX

THE BATTLE OF THE SOMME – JULY 1916

The Strategic Situation

British and French planning for a combined offensive astride the Somme River began in December 1915. General Sir Douglas Haig had just been appointed commander of the British Expeditionary Force, and his instructions from the War Cabinet were to offer the 'closest cooperation' to the French.[1] The original plan had been for the French to attack with sixty divisions south of the river, with the British conducting a lesser attack to the north. The German attack on Verdun in February 1916 changed the entire situation. The French poured hundreds of thousands of men and guns into that killing ground. By the late spring, it was apparent that the British would have to shoulder the greater burden of any new offensive. The numbers shifted so that final planning was for fourteen British divisions to attack north of the river and five French divisions to the south. Thus, nineteen combined divisions were pitted against seven German dug in divisions, nearly the 3:1 offence/defence ratio touted in war colleges as needed for success.

Yet other factors were not equal. The Allies did not have "unity of command", the Germans did. The British infantry was composed overwhelmingly of fresh recruits with little training, led by inexperienced officers. The Germans had more experience. The British had been in the Somme location less than a year; the Germans had been there for two years, had taken the high ground sloping westward and had used the time to build a formidable network of well-constructed trenches and bunkers. And, most important, the Germans had machine guns.

General Haig had been trained at Sandhurst, the British Military Academy, and was a cavalry officer for nine years, chiefly in India. He had participated in the Omdurman campaign in the Sudan (1898) and the Second Boer War (1899-1902). In 1916, he was 55 years old. Most of the fighting in the Great War was new to him, and he was openly sceptical of three new weapons: the tank, the airplane and the machine gun, which he said specifically was 'overrated'.

Originally planned for August 1916, the combined Somme offensive was moved up and changed dramatically. From being a diversionary and secondary attack, the objective became to break the stalemate of trench warfare and force a decisive breakthrough of the German lines that would end the war.

Active preparations for the offensive began in April with greatly expanded air reconnaissance of the German defences in the front three lines. This expanded mission was facilitated by the increased production of Britain's aircraft factories, and in the period of

October 1915 to June 1916, fifteen new squadrons deployed to France, bringing General Trenchard's forces to twenty-seven squadrons. The British gained overwhelming numerical superiority. Seven of these squadrons were equipped with the new and faster D.H.2s and F.E.2Bs. French Nieuport 11s and 16s were also increasing in number. The combination led to Allied qualitative superiority.

The British infantry assault was preceded by an intense artillery barrage from 1,537 guns that began on 24 June 1916, lasted for six days and expended three million rounds of ammunition. The objective of the artillery barrage was to clear away the German barbed wire emplacements, smash the lines of fortifications and destroy their artillery. Just before the infantry advance, the artillery would concentrate on the German front lines and obliterate any defence. Peter Hart wrote:

> 'As there was not going to be any opposition there was, therefore, no need for any haste. According to the tactical instructions issued by the Fourth Army the advance across no man's land would be made at a steady walking pace in long lines of men just 2 or 3 yards apart. This would ensure that the relatively untrained troops did not lose their alignment and would thereby arrive upon the German line at exactly the same time.'[2]

However, the fire plan was faulty. When the time for the infantry attack arrived, the artillery was lifted from the German front lines and moved further back. The deep, concrete fortifications in the German front line had, for the most part, protected their soldiers. As soon as the artillery barrage ended, the German infantry came up out of their bunkers, manned their machine guns and waited for the inevitable infantry assault.

The British infantry went over the top at 7:30 am on 1 July 1916. With the bulk of their air service still deployed opposite Verdun, the Germans almost immediately lost air superiority, and thus began the 'blackest days in the history of German war aviation'.[3]

British Air Superiority

The British and French held quantitative and qualitative superiority in the air. The RFC fielded 185 aircraft for the Somme, with seventy-six of them scouts. The French had 201 aircraft. The German flying service could only muster 129, with only nineteen scouts. The Fokker Eindeckers were outclassed by both D.H.2s and Nieuports.[4] The Allied advantage in the air was also about three-to-one.

When the Allied offensive began, the German air service was still heavily engaged opposite Verdun. Immelmann had been killed, Boelcke was on tour, and the remaining KEKs were overwhelmed. The British also linked a bombing campaign with their air offensive that attacked the German aircraft on the ground as well as in the air. The combined effort led to a dominating air superiority for the Allies. This superiority had a devastating effect on the German air service, the ground troops and the high command.

General von Below, Headquarters 1st German Army, accurately assessed the situation:

> 'The beginning and the first weeks of the Somme battle were marked by a complete

inferiority of our own air forces. The enemy's aeroplanes enjoyed complete freedom in carrying out distant reconnaissances. With aid of aeroplane observation, the hostile artillery neutralised our guns and was able to range with the most extreme accuracy on the trenches occupied by our infantry; the required data for this was provided by undisturbed trench-reconnaissance and photography. By means of bombing and machine-gun attacks from a low height against infantry, battery positions and marching columns, the enemy's aircraft inspired our troops with a feeling of defencelessness against the enemy's mastery of the air.'[5]

As Professor Johannes Werner described it in Boelcke's biography, 'The great lesson taught by the first battle of the Somme is that all fighting on the ground is dependent on the fighting above and the supremacy in the air.'[6] Aerial reconnaissance and ground attack were increasingly recognised as vital missions.

The initial infantry attacks did not go well for the Allies. When the opposing German infantry came up out of their reinforced bunkers, their machine gunners had a field day. The result of the first day's offensive was 57,000 British casualties in an attacking force of 120,000 soldiers, with over 20,000 dead. All this for a few hundred yards advance. However, the performance of the RFC had been effective in keeping German fighters and reconnaissance aeroplanes out of the skies over the Somme Front.

Two Types of Fighters Emerge

By this time in the summer of 1916, there were two types of motors powering aircraft in the war: rotary engines and in-line engines. The rotary engines were the Le Rhônes, Fokkers, Oberursels, Gnomes, Siemens, and Clergets. Rotary engines were air cooled, lighter but had less horsepower. Their aircraft tended to be somewhat slower in level flight, but had amazingly tight turning capabilities. The high turn rate was especially apparent in a right-hand turn because that was the direction the engine torque was operating.

In-line engines included the Daimlers, Hispano-Suiza, Rolls-Royces, Sunbeams and BMWs. They were water cooled, heavier and generally produced higher horsepower. Their aircraft tended to be faster because of the more powerful engine, but their turning capability was less. These inherent capabilities tended to favour the rotary-engine aircraft in twisting, turning and vertical battles. The in-line-engine aircraft were superior in diving, slashing attacks because the rotaries could not catch them and could not get away themselves.

The performance of the German air service in the first two months of the Battle of the Somme was so bad that the German army lost whatever faith it had in aviation, and parliamentary deputies in the Reichstag accused the air officers of not supporting the army. These arguments were partially true, but overstated. Ground commanders are trained to employ and direct "combined arms" (artillery, infantry and cavalry [armour]). They wanted to have aviation placed under their direct command, but aviation is not a battalion, or regiment, or brigade asset. It is not even a creature of the higher level unit, the division. It is at minimum a corps-level or army-level resource, also with an independent mission at the tactical and strategic levels. On the tactical level, the mission of air superiority is vital to combat on the ground, but these air operations are usually out of sight of front-line troops, and therefore not appreciated by the ground forces. Air-to-air battles were occasionally visible to friendly forces, but this became less so as the speed and altitude capabilities of fighters increased. On the strategic level, airpower is capable of massing, dispersing and attacking on a theatre-wide scale, or even deeper as a strategic weapon.

As the Verdun Front wound down, more German aircraft were transferred to the Somme, and by August 1916, the German air force had some sixty single-seat fighters there, composed mostly of outdated Fokker E.III and IV monoplanes with some Fokker and Halberstadt biplanes.[7]

German section strength opposite the Somme increased steadily from nine flying units on 1 July 1916 to thirty-four units by September and forty-six units in October. By mid-October the Germans had 540 aircraft engaged on the Somme, virtually two-thirds of their 885 aircraft force. Army leadership also changed. On 29 August 1916, von Hindenburg replaced General Falkenhayn with General Erich Ludendorff, a long-time supporter of aviation. Von Hindenburg officially terminated the Verdun offensive and accelerated the transfer of assets to the Somme.

Trenchard's Offensive Spirit

The RFC's success had come at a high price. As the British aircraft ranged ever deeper into German airspace the losses from anti-aircraft fire and German fighters mounted. Still Brigadier General Trenchard's offensive spirit, by now the RFC's mantra, was maintained. At times the offensive became blind aggression. Trenchard believed that the high losses of pilots and observers – as visually represented by empty chairs in the mess – were demoralising to his crews. RFC policy was to stage newly arrived aircrew from England at the Northern Pilots' Pool, St. Omer base. Then they would be assigned to various squadrons as the need arose. The problem in Trenchard's mind was that they were not being delivered promptly. Therefore, he issued his historic order that casualties must be replaced on the very day they occurred. As mentioned previously, Trenchard's order read that there must be, 'a full breakfast table, with no empty chairs'.

> 'If as an ordinary pilot you see no vacant places around you, the tendency is to brood less on the fate of your friends who have gone forever. Instead your mind is taken up with buying drinks for the newcomers and making them feel at home.'[8]

That was the theory. Observed behaviour of combat soldiers and airmen from World Wars I and II is that there is a tendency for veterans to avoid befriending newcomers for fear of attachment should the inexperienced man be soon killed.

The policy of no empty chairs reverberated through the nearly forty squadrons, the wings, headquarters and back to the War Office and the training bases in England. Trenchard's firm belief was that the official establishment was indifferent to his need for more pilots and squadrons. All this was to maintain the broader policy of aggressive "offensive spirit".

General Trenchard enforced his policy ruthlessly. One of the officers who dissented from Trenchard's policy was one of his wing commanders, Lieutenant Colonel Hugh Dowding. This indomitable leader was one of the public school fellows who had joined the army early and served with distinction in India and the Orient. Back in England, he had learned to fly at his own expense and joined the RFC in his mid-thirties. He had many of the same qualities as Hugh Trenchard – highly competent but uncompromising. The difference was that he had a passionate concern for his aircrews and the high rate at which they were being killed. While not opposing the offensive spirit in principle, he believed and advocated to Trenchard and others that the crews be given realistic and adequate training before being sent into combat. Instinctively, he knew the truth of the high loss rate curve that ruthlessly eliminated inexperienced pilots in their first few combat missions. Dowding's wing contained four squadrons, one of which had suffered 50 per cent casualties by early August 1916. After one of his squadron commanders and two flight commanders had been shot down, Dowding went to Trenchard and requested the squadron be withdrawn from the line for a few weeks' rest. Trenchard was upset with this request, and although he approved it, he privately thought Dowding's compassion outweighed his duty. In official correspondence, he referred to Dowding as a 'dismal Jimmy'. Trenchard removed him from command and sent him back to England. Never being allowed back to the front in WWI, Dowding nevertheless rose to become the commander of Fighter Command in the Battle of Britain. Trenchard never forgot this episode. When the Battle of Britain ended in late 1940, Trenchard was one of the voices that persuaded Winston Churchill to retire Dowding.[9]

The Rise and Fall of Albert Ball

The "offensive spirit" did not claim high-ranking commanders only. Albert Ball enlisted in the British army in 1914, joining the "Robin Hood" battalion (officially the Sherwood Foresters) in his hometown of Nottingham. He was promoted to sergeant and in October 1914, received a commission as a second lieutenant. While still in England in 1915, Ball paid for and earned his pilot's license. Transferring to the RFC, he joined his first squadron in France in February 1916, flying B.E.2Cs. On 7 May 1916, he was transferred to fighters with 11 Squadron. He shot down his first airplane on 16 May flying a Bristol Scout. Transferring to a Nieuport, he shot down five more aircraft and a balloon in six weeks. He was an ace at age 19. But the strain of combat flying became evident. In a letter to his family on 16 July, he confessed he was feeling 'very rotten'. His nerves, he said, were 'poo-poo. Naturally I cannot keep on forever, so I went to see the CO [commanding officer] and asked him if I could have a short rest and not fly for a few days.'[10] His squadron commander was sympathetic, but the brigade commander was affronted. Ball was not only refused, but he was immediately transferred to a squadron that was flying reconnaissance and bombing, again in old B.E.2Cs.[11]

After his banishment period was over, Albert Ball was returned in August 1916 to 60 Squadron, then commanded by Major Smith-Barry. He quickly learned that Ball was more effective flying alone, and he was given free rein. He was also given his own Nieuport. Later, he was assigned a personal S.E.5. Within hours he had taken off and destroyed a Roland reconnaissance aircraft. Six days later he shot down three more Rolands in 45 minutes, bringing his total to eleven. One of Ball's secrets was that he trained himself and practised regularly firing the Lewis gun on the squadron's firing range.[12] In September 1916, Ball performed a triple victory, shooting down three German aircraft on three different days. By then his total was thirty-one. Again he requested leave; because of his nerves he was taking unnecessary chances. This time, it was granted, and he returned to England a hero.

Generals in the British War Office were overwhelmingly conservative and officially opposed publicising the names of famous fliers for two reasons: they wanted to stress teamwork, and they considered praise of fighter pilots would be detrimental to equally brave bomber and reconnaissance crews. The result was that the British did not publish official statistics on the victories of individuals. However, when Albert Ball attended a solemn civic ceremony in Nottingham and was honoured, the event was featured in the *Daily Mirror*, and the *Daily Mail* published his picture next to that of Oswald Boelcke. Following that exposure, he was invited to Buckingham Palace where the King presented him with a clutch of three Distinguished Service Orders and one Military Cross.[c]

Albert Ball would go on to achieve forty-four victories before he was shot down during his second combat tour. His loss on 7 May 1917 is the subject of some mystery and dispute. Ball and von Richthofen's Jasta 11 were involved in a huge air battle on that day with aircraft diving in and out of cloud cover. Ball's aircraft was last seen entering a cloud layer in pursuit of a German opponent. He was not seen exiting the cloud, but he crashed behind German lines. Lothar Richthofen, Manfred's younger brother, claimed and was awarded the victory, but he described Ball's aircraft as a triplane, which was an error. Whether he was shot down by Lothar, hit by anti-aircraft or lost control in the cloud is one of the mysteries of the war. Ball was awarded the Victoria Cross posthumously.

The Germans were also improving the quality of their aircraft, and over the next several months four new types of fighters were deployed: The Fokker D.II/III; Halberstadt D.II; the Roland D.I and finally, the Albatros D.I/D.II. Of these, the Albatros was destined to be the clear star.

In September and October 1916, the Battle of the Somme continued. Before the battle was over, Boelcke would make significant contributions to the outcome by the formation of his new squadron Jagdstaffel 2 (Jasta 2).

---

[c] The Distinguished Service Cross (DSO) is second only to the Victoria Cross in British military medals. It was initiated in 1886 and its award to such a junior officer as Albert Ball, then a captain, was extremely unusual. Being awarded three is unprecedented. The Military Cross ranked below the DSO and was originated in 1914 specifically to reward junior officers.

CHAPTER X

THE FORMATION OF JASTA 2

The British and French clearly had air superiority over the Somme from the first day of the offensive. With the Fokker Eindeckers being outclassed, Immelmann's death and Boelcke's absence, the German air service was on its heels. The air service recognised that the situation demanded a man who would be able to lead and to inspire. The only person available was Captain Oswald Boelcke. The chief of the air service informed Boelcke on 8 August that he was to organise and command Jasta 2.

At the same time, the high command decided on a radical reorganisation and implemented it on 10 August 1916. The German air service Chief of Staff, Oberstleutnant Hermann von der Lieth-Thomsen, ordered the two-seater sections to consolidate into permanent bomber units designated Kastas and the single-seat scouts into Jagstaffeln or Jastas. This reorganisation implemented a concentration of force – one of the classic principles of war.

This order established seven Jastas. Royal Prussian Jasta 1 was formed out of KEK Nord at Bertincourt, France, under the leadership of Hauptmann Martin Zander on 22 August 1916. The unit moved to Bertigny two days later. Their aircraft were Fokker D.I and D.II biplanes and a small initial deployment of Albatros D.Is. The superior performance of the Albatros fighter was soon demonstrated. In the last week of August, Jasta 1 claimed six victories, more than their parent KEK unit had scored in three months.[1] Eight more Jastas were formed in September; none in October; nine in November; and another nine in December. By the end of 1916, there would be thirty-three Jastas.[2]

Jasta 2 was officially established on military orders on 10 August 1916. Lieth-Thomsen recalled Boelcke from his tour of the Eastern Front on 11 August. He was assigned to command this second Jasta, also at Bertincourt, opposite the British main thrust on the Somme. Jasta 1 and most of the other Jastas had been formed from existing KEK units, but Jasta 2 was an orphan. It had been officially listed to receive fourteen aircraft, but it had no parent unit, no pilots and no airplanes. Boelcke, however, was given authority to select his own fighter pilots. This should surprise US readers because the ability to select pilots or any other skilled personnel, is severely limited, virtually non-existent at the level of squadron commander, as this privilege is limited to very senior officers in the US.

As soon as Boelcke reported back from his tour on 27 August, he learned that the squadron's base had been moved to Vela, actually a short walk up the road to the north end of Bertincourt.

Recruiting Böhme and Richthofen

When Oswald Boelcke visited Kovel, Ukraine, on the Eastern Front in mid-August to see his brother, he was looking for fighter pilots. There he recruited several pilots for his squadron. The first was Erwin Böhme, a 37-year-old civil engineer who had worked in Germany, Switzerland and East Africa. After pilot training, he was an instructor for a year and then served with Wilhelm Boelcke on the Eastern Front. Wilhelm had recommended Böhme, and Boelcke was glad to accept his advice. Böhme also had become known for his daring as a reconnaissance pilot in the Battle of Verdun.

The second pilot was a young former cavalry officer (Uhlan), Manfred von Richthofen, whom Boelcke had met in early 1916 on a train. Von Richthofen related the occasion of his recruitment at Kovel:

'While we were chatting among ourselves one of my comrades said: "Today the great Boelcke arrives on a visit to us, or rather to his brother." In the evening the great man came to land. He was vastly admired by all and he told us many interesting things about his journey to Turkey. He was just returning from Turkey and was on the way to headquarters. He imagined that he would go to the Somme to continue his work. He was to organise a fighting squadron. He was empowered to select from the flying corps those men who seemed to him particularly qualified for his purpose.

'I did not dare to ask him to be taken on. I did not feel bored by the fighting in Russia. On the contrary, we made extensive and interesting flights. We bombed the Russians at their stations. Still, the idea of fighting again on the Western Front attracted me. There is nothing finer for a young cavalry officer than the thrill of the chase in the air. The next morning Boelcke was to leave us. Quite early somebody knocked at my door and before me stood the great man with the *Pour le Mérite*. I know him, as I previously mentioned, but still I had never imagined that he would come to look me up in order to ask me to become his pupil. I almost fell upon his neck when he inquired whether I cared to go with him to the Somme.'[3]

This transfer of von Richthofen from flying two-seaters on reconnaissance and artillery-spotting missions to the single-seat fighter squadron of Jasta 2 was the most important event in Manfred's life. Without Boelcke's sponsorship and recruitment, von Richthofen would be an unknown name in aviation history. With Boelcke's mentorship and instruction, he became WWI's "ace of aces".

Boelcke also selected three other pilots there who were unidentified. However, historian Norman Franks deduced they were probably Leutnants Hans Imelmann (no relation to Max Immelmann), Christian von Scheele and Herwarth Philipps.[4] Apparently these three had some other assignments or time en route because they do not appear on the Jasta 2 roster until much later. When Boelcke got back to the aerodrome at Vela, France, he found an empty airfield with only four permanent hangars and a few aircraftsmen mechanics. Jasta 2 was a hollow shell.

On 1 September, Leutnant der Reserve Hans Reimann and Leutnant Manfred von Richthofen arrived along with Offiziersstellvertreter Max Müller and Feldwebel Leopold Rudolf Reimann (no relation to Hans Reimann). Müller was 29, from Bavaria and was one of the outstanding non-commissioned pilots of the war. At this point, he had flown more than 160 front-line missions and had received both classes of the Iron Cross, the Bavarian Military Merit Cross 3rd Class with Crown and Swords and the Bavarian Bravery Medal in silver. Erwin Böhme and Oberleutnant Günther Viehweger arrived next. At age 37, Böhme was the father-figure of the squadron, and he and Boelcke became good friends.

Jasta 2 also got its first three aircraft on 1 September 1916. Leutnant Hans Reimann flew

his new Albatros D.I over from Jasta 1. Reimann was 22 years old and had previously flown with Kasta 8. Boelcke, upon hearing that he could have two Fokker biplanes from the aircraft park, took NCO Reimann, and together they ferried the two Fokker D.IIIs from Armee Flug Park 1 to Jagdstaffel 2 at Bertincourt. One of these was number 352/16, which Boelcke took for his own.

Boelcke's Fokker D.III, No. 352/16, September 1916. He flew this aircraft from 2 to 19 September and scored eight victories with it. (via the League of WWI Aviation Historians)

The D.III featured the Oberursel U.III 14-cylinder, two-row rotary engine, the same engine as the Eindecker E.IV. The aircraft mounted two Maxim machine guns that gave it excellent firepower. But it retained the wing-warping method of the Eindeckers, which made it heavy on the stick and slow in roll. Boelcke flew this aircraft until the Albatros Ds arrived, shooting down eight aircraft during September 1916. Its performance was better than previous models of the same design, but Boelcke found it to be too slow. On Boelcke's recommendation, the D.III was withdrawn from heavily contested sectors of the Western Front, but it continued to serve in quieter sectors. Boelcke's personal D.III, serial 352/16, survived the war and was on display at the Zeughaus museum in Berlin until the aircraft was destroyed by Allied bombing in 1943.

Boelcke's Fokker Logbook

The author was fortunate to obtain a copy of the only known logbook detailing Oswald Boelcke's flights in this aircraft. It is curious that his pilot logbooks are not available but we do have records kept of the airplane. What we have is the book for the airplane, Fokker D.III 352 produced in 1916 (*Bordbuch fuer das Flugzeug: Fok. D.III 352/16*), the document being prepared under the direction of the chief of field aviation in the west from 5 April 1916.[5] The entries of interest are those beginning 1 September 1916, the day that Boelcke and NCO Reimann went to the aircraft park at Cambrai and ferried two new D.IIIs to their base.

The aircraft log entries document twenty-three flights: twenty combat; two ferry flights; and one test flight. Flight number two was a local test flight where Boelcke tried out the airplane for 30 minutes over Bertincourt on 1 September, to see if it was ready for combat. All the flights were with Oswald Boelcke as the pilot, except the second ferry flight, on 22 September, when Warrant Officer Reimann flew the aircraft in a nine-minute trip from Bertincourt to Lagnicourt, when Jasta 2 was transferred to get out from under the guns of British artillery. From 2 September to 16 September, this was the only aircraft Boelcke flew – eighteen combat (hunting) flights in 15 days.[6] In this period he shot down seven aircraft (victories twenty to twenty-six), for an average of 3½ victories per week. Since the squadron had only a few aircraft, and the pilots had not yet been trained in the "Boelcke system" most of his flights were alone: one at dawn; nine in the morning; four in the afternoon; and four at dusk. Boelcke later wrote that he believed solo flights were too dangerous for his untrained squadron, and he preferred to fly alone. However, once the Albatros D.IIs arrived on 17 September, he led the squadron in flights of four or five aircraft. After that date, he only flew the Fokker twice, on 19 and 23 September, gaining his twenty-eighth victory over a Morane-Saulnier Bullet on the 19th.

The flights were usually short, varying from 30 to 55 minutes. Only one was nearly two hours – and unproductive. The average was 43 minutes. During this month of September, he was also still recruiting pilots, organising the squadron, constructing facilities, training the pilots and writing reports.

Jasta 2's pilots

The original squadron at the beginning of September 1916 had only six pilots: Boelcke (nineteen victories) and five leutnants: Hans Reimann, Wolfgang Günther, Otto Walter Höhne, Ernst Dierner and Winand Graffe. Only Graffe had victories (two). In the month of September, the squadron added Leutnants Erwin Böhme (two), von Richthofen, Herwarth Philipps and Wolfgang Günther, plus officer for special duties (OzbV) Ltn Hellmuth von Zastrow and Oblt Günther Viehweger (one). Offz Max Müller and Offz Leopold Reimann (two) also reported. Sometime in September Leopold Reimann was promoted to warrant officer. Thus, for the month of September 1916, they had on average ten to eleven pilots.

The new pilots did not fly immediately. Boelcke planned and executed a rigorous training programme of firing machine guns on the ground range, assembling and disassembling the weapons to fix stoppages that often occurred in flight. Then there were long sessions with the newly-arrived Halberstadt aircraft, followed by classroom lectures using a blackboard. Boelcke reportedly had models made of the principal Allied planes and trained his men in the strong and weak points of each.[7] Aircraft recognition, tactical-formation flying and tactics rounded out the training regime.

Boelcke battles Captain Wilson

On 2 September 1916, Boelcke took off in his new Fokker on Jasta 2's first operational sortie and scored his twentieth victory in a 50-minute flight against a British D.H.2.[8] The British pilot, Captain R.E. Wilson, 32 Squadron, RFC, later described the air battle and its aftermath in a letter home, written from the German prison camp at Osnabrück:

'It is some consolation to me that I was brought down by Captain Boelcke, the greatest German airman, and that my life was preserved in a fashion that is almost miraculous.

'As you know, I fly a fast Vickers Fighter. While on a reconnaissance flight I saw a German scout about to shoot down one of our slow B.E. machines. I came along just in time to save it, and after I had fired several bursts at the German he turned and flew home. I followed him and noticed that he was luring me further and further into his territory, and after I had followed him for 15 miles he turned round and attacked and with unbelievable speed climbed above me. He was flying a type of aircraft I had never seen before and I had no idea of its speed and rate of climb. My machine gun had jammed after I had fired a few rounds, and under those circumstances the only thing I could do was to flee. I tried every trick to get away, but he was able to skilfully [sic] follow my every move, and stayed right behind me. He shot through all my control cables except two – and these were jammed. The machine was riddled – the petrol control knob was shot from my hand – and then the petrol tank (was hit). My coat was also holed in two places, and soaked in petrol.

'Naturally, I had lost all control over my machine whose nose dipped down, while I sat there and waited, anticipating the crash that was imminent – not a very nice feeling. When at about fifty feet above the ground I pulled the controls back and forth, and somehow, at the last moment obtained enough control to prevent a crash, and was able to make some sort of landing – during which the machine and my coat burst into flames. I found it was possible to jump out, and throw my coat off – and was not burnt. The German came down low, and after seeing that I was out of the fight – he flew away.

'Next day Boelcke [visited the POW collecting station and] invited me to his aerodrome and entertained me in his mess. We were also photographed together. I got a very fine impression of him both as a pilot and a man, and this fight will remain the greatest memory of my life, even though it turned out badly for me.'[9]

Wilson also is reported to have said that he asked the identify of his captor. Upon hearing the name, Wilson smiled, shook Boelcke's hand and replied, 'If I had to be shot down, I'm pleased that it should have been by so good a man.'[10] This first victory of

Captain Robert Wilson with Oswald Boelcke. (Taken from *Knight of Germany*, Professor Johannes Werner, Casemate Publishers, 2009.)

Jasta 2 was also memorable to Boelcke, who wrote to his parents on 4 September:

'*Bertincourt, 4.9.16.* You will be astonished to read of my "twentieth" because you will have imagined me still organising my Staffel but not yet flying.

'A few days ago Fokker sent two machines for me, and I made my first flight in one of them the day before yesterday. There was a fair amount of enemy aerial activity at the front. These fellows have grown very imprudent. One of them tried to have a go at me when I was flying peacefully behind our lines, but I refused to let myself be drawn – he was flying much higher than I. Somewhat later in the day I saw shell bursts west of Bapaume. There I found a B.E., followed by three Vickers single-seaters, i.e. an artillery plane with its escorts. I went for the B.E. but the other three interrupted me in the middle of my work, so I beat a hasty retreat. One of those fellows thought he could catch me and gave chase. When I had lured him somewhat away from the others, I gave battle and soon got to grips with him. I did not let him go again; he did not get another shot at me.

'When he went down his machine was wobbling badly, but that, as he told me afterwards, was not his fault, because I had shot his elevating gear to pieces. The machine landed north-east of Thiepval; it was burning as the pilot jumped out and beat his arms and legs about because his [flying coat] was on fire too. I then flew home and took off again with fresh supplies of ammunition because other Englishmen had appeared. But I did not score any further successes.'[11]

Boelcke's descriptions of his air-to-air combats frequently used the term, a "battle of curves", which in German was "Kurvenkampf", a true depiction of the twisting, turning fights with opposing planes. The English term "dogfight" is somewhat of an equivalent, although some RFC pilots reserve this term for much larger, multi-aircraft battles.

Most of his other pilots were not yet flying because of a lack of airplanes, but another one of them recorded a wonderful anecdote during this period.

'Whenever Boelcke returned from a flight, we asked him while he still sat laughing in his machine: "Well, got another, Hauptmann?" whereupon he replied with another question: "Have I got a black chin?" (i.e., from the smoke [cordite] of the machine gun[s]). "Well, that's all right, then." In which case he had brought down another victim [or two].'[12]

Boelcke's stated objective with Jasta 2 was 'not merely to assemble pilots together, but to train them to cooperate and work together'. His leadership ability was emerging. Boelcke's early success – and that of most of the adventurous fighter pilots of the Great War, had been obtained by individual effort – solo sorties over the front with victories won in one-on-one combat. Boelcke believed this tactic was the best for himself and other outstanding pilots, but for those with more limited abilities there was a better way. He observed that when a pilot is chasing another aeroplane, he tends to concentrate on the opponent, often to the exclusion of his own safety. A second pilot, flying in loose formation with the leader, is in a better position to look around and spot a dangerous situation developing with a new enemy entering the fray. This new tactic of flying with wingmen had originated in the spring of 1916, but by the autumn it was better supported by the increasing numbers of aircraft in the sky. The days of the lone hunter were coming to an end. Teamwork was becoming more important than individual heroism.

Boelcke's Personality

Boelcke's personality in this period was later described by his biographer, Professor Johannes Werner:

'We may also state from these personal recollections that Boelcke was extremely moderate in his mode of life. He was never a smoker; the most he ever did was to light a cigarette in company when courtesy required it of him, but he always laid it down after a few whiffs. He was a very moderate drinker and lived almost abstemiously, but he was too natural a personality to ever make a principle of this abstinence or refuse to take a glass of wine on suitable occasions in the company of friends. His chief recreation seemed to consist of going to bed as early as possible. When the weather was good for flying, nothing existed for him except the service.'[13]

Werner's view is verified by the first-person account of Erwin Böhme who wrote to his girlfriend, Annamarie, 'This unpretentious young man, far from allowing fame to turn his head, exhibits a maturity and detached presence that is straight away incredible ....'[14]

Fame also extracted a price on Boelcke's time. By August 1916, he was receiving 800-1,000 letters a day. Reading them became a drain on his time and energy.[15]

As new pilots reported in, he began training them in tactics, teamwork and formation flying. The textbook was primarily verbal, based on his published dicta.

With his new Fokker D.III, Boelcke flew frequently alone in early September 1916. On the 8th, he downed an F.E.2B from 22 Squadron as his twenty-first victory; a D.H.2 from 24 Squadron on the 9th was the twenty-second; and he got doubles on the 14th and 15th. Number twenty-three was a Sopwith 1½ Strutter two-seater from 70 Squadron on a reconnaissance mission. The enemy aircraft fell in a spinning nosedive, and one of the wings came off. Victory number twenty-four was a D.H.2, again from 24 Squadron on the same day.

On 25 September, the British launched the third phase of the Somme offensive in the Battle of Flers-Courcelette, which produced the largest air battle thus far. Before the day was over three squadrons would lose two aircraft each, and 70 Squadron would lose four. On a dusk patrol, Boelcke shot down number twenty-five, another Sopwith 1½ Strutter, from 70 Squadron, which went down in flames. Number twenty-six, his second victory 30 minutes later on 15 September, was another Sopwith 1½ Strutter, from the same squadron. The pilot of the first Sopwith was Captain G.L. Cruickshank, DSO, MC, who was an experienced flight commander. He was 26 years old and had been flying since 1913. Alan Bott, the author of *An Airman's Outings*, recalled Guy Cruickshank:

'Cruickshank was one of the greatest pilots produced by the war. He was utterly fearless, and had more time over the German lines to his credit than anyone else in the Flying Corps. It was part of his fatalistic creed that Archie (AA fire) should never be dodged, and he would go calmly ahead when the AA guns were at their best. Somehow the bursts never found him. He had won both the DSO and MC for deeds in the air.

'Only the evening before, when asked lightly if he was out for a VC [Victoria Cross], he said he would rather get Boelcke; in the end, Boelcke probably got him, for he fell over the famous German's aerodrome, and that day the German wireless announced that Boelcke had shot down two more machines. Peace to the ashes of a fine pilot and a very brave man!'[16]

This was 70 Squadron's third loss in two days.

The British Estimate of the Situation
The official British order that sent out this flight of aircraft on 14 September 1916 is instructive in its estimate that the situation was favourable to continue the Somme offensive and that a cavalry charge would be successful:

Operation Order 488
By Major-General H.M. Trenchard CB DSO ADC
Commanding Royal Flying Corps In the Field

Tuesday, 14 September 1916

- The 4th and Reserve Armies are taking the offensive of zero [hour] pm on the 15th with a view of gaining in the first instance, the line Morval-Les Boeufs-Gueudecourt-Flers, and thence south of Martinpuich to our present front-line R.54.b. The French are attacking on the right of the 4th Army. When the infantry are established on the above line, the cavalry corps will push through to the high ground between Rocquigny and Bapaume.
- The C-in-C considers that the situation is so favourable as to justify and demand very bold and vigorous action on the part of all arms, including the RFC.
- The 9th Wing will cooperate as shown in table 'A' attached.
- The Sopwith patrol (3) will be carried out whether (1) or (2) start or not.

Attachment A:

Item (3). Eight Sopwiths. Escort to (1) and (2). As soon after B.E.12s as possible. Remain out – three hours. During bombing will patrol E. of Bourlon and Havrincourt and will subsequently patrol in the area Havrincourt-Epéhy-Roisel-Bapaume.[17]

It does not take too much imagination to see that this order, two-and-a-half-months after the initiation of the Battle of the Somme, still reflects the optimism of the planners – that the ground offensive would be "a piece of cake". The high command was so confident that the artillery had obliterated the front-line trenches and their occupants that they ordered the infantry to walk at a slow pace, keeping their lines straight. This was almost as if the artillery had prepared the battlefield to be a "walk in the park".

Personnel continued to report to Jasta 2. On 10 September, two more officers arrived. The first was Leutnant Hellmuth von Zastrow, age 25, of Berlin. He had served in the Prussian infantry before entering flying training. Boelcke had met him earlier when they were both serving at KEK Jametz, opposite Verdun. Zastrow had been flying with Artillery Flying Section 203 until he was wounded. No longer on flying duty, Zastrow became Jasta 2's adjutant. The second officer was Leutnant Herwath Philipps, born in Kiel, Germany, transferred from KEK Vaux.

The squadron's aircraft inventory still contained only five aircraft: one Albatros D.I; one refurbished Halberstadt and three Fokker biplanes, one each of the early Fokker D-Series (D.I, D.II and a D.III). This diversity of aircraft types in one unit was common in the German and other air services at this time. This created obvious difficulties with multiple types of spare parts, but it did not seem to affect the in-commission rate of the aircraft. Most likely, the simplicity of construction made them easy to repair. There did not seem to be many occasions when a large number of aircraft were out of commission for maintenance. The pilots were frustrated with the lack of regular flying. Boelcke continued to fly Fokker 352/16 daily, and the other pilots flew when they could.

Meanwhile, the RFC's policy of aggressively patrolling deep inside German airspace, the ever-present anti-aircraft fire and the increasing German fighter presence were claiming large numbers of English victims. Into this dismal situation for the Allies, the Germans introduced a weapon that would change the nature of the campaign. On Saturday, 16 September, Jasta 2 was notified that the factory and the procurement system had delivered six new Albatroses to the aircraft park at Cambrai, France. Six pilots hurriedly drove there and ferried the aircraft to Bertincourt. The long-awaited Albatros fighters had arrived.

CHAPTER XI

Introduction of the Albatros Fighter

'Superior weapons favour victory!'
– I.B. Holley, Jr., American historian, Ideas and Weapons

There have been countless times in history when the people have been ready, the technology has come. This was certainly the case with the German air service in September 1916.

The Albatros Flugzeugwerke GmbH (flying machine works) had been established by Walter Huth and Otto Wiener on 20 December 1909. By 1914, Albatros was the leader of the German aircraft companies, which included ten other firms. In order of their productivity, they were: Albatros, Aviatik, Luftverkehrsgesellschaft (LVG), Rumpler; Deutsche Flugzeugwerke (DFW), Euler, Gotha, Jeannin, SEG, Fokker and Luft-Fahrzeug-Gesellschaft (LFG).[1] The Albatros factory was based in Johannisthal Airfield, Berlin, which was the centre of German aviation. By the end of the war, they would be the largest aircraft manufacturer in Germany with a total of 10,350 aircraft produced.

One of the technical engineers was Ernst Heinkel who designed the Albatros B-Series reconnaissance biplane in 1913. The Albatros B.I was a two-bay[d] reconnaissance-biplane with the pilot in the rear seat and the observer in the front. The wing and the forward seating severely restricted the observer's field of vision and later, his field of fire when machine guns were introduced. The C-Series appeared in 1915 and reversed the crew cockpits so that the pilot sat in front and the observer in the rear with a 7.62 mm Parabellum machine gun on a ring mount. This configuration was defensively superior to previous German reconnaissance aircraft and to the Allies' pusher designs with the gunner in the front nacelle.

Albatros technical director Robert Thelen, a rated pilot, designed the D.I in response to the Allies fielding the single-seat Nieuport 11 Bébé and the D.H.2. The D.I was the first of the D-Series, which were single-seat, one-bay biplanes. The D.I was developed to incorporate the 1916 Mercedes D.IIIa engine that was being produced by the firm of Daimler Motoren Gesellschaft, Stuttgart-Untertürkheim.

---

[d] The term "two bay" refers to the number of closed sections between the fuselage and the wing tips. "Two bay" means that there were two sets of struts between the wings, which created two "bays" between the fuselage and the outboard strut.

Albatros D Prototypes

In June 1916, the Idflieg, the bureau of the German Empire that oversaw German military aviation prior to and during WWI, had ordered twelve pre-production (prototype) aircraft of the new D-Series. Albatros developed eleven of them as D.Is and one as a D.II. The D.I design was sleek and aerodynamic with streamlined struts. The fuselage surface was constructed of shaped plywood, with no internal bracing (technically known as semi-cantilever). This made it both lighter and stronger than truss and fabric designs that were in common use. The 160 hp Mercedes engine could drive the Albatros 20 per cent faster than contemporary aircraft. The only detraction from streamlining was the set of Windoff "ear" radiators that stuck out on each side of the fuselage with a water tank mounted on the top of the engine. The cabane struts that connect the wing to the fuselage were in an inverted "V" configuration, with the top wing set high above the fuselage. The armament was two Maxim 7.92 mm machine guns manufactured at the Spandau arsenal in Berlin. Ammunition was 1,000 rounds, 500 for each gun.

Albatros D.I, probably flown by Leutnant Walter von Bülow, *Pour le Mérite*. (James Miller)

The Albatros D.I reaffirmed the old pilot's aphorism, 'don't fly the A-model of anything'. "A" models, the first off the production line, have been notoriously in need of numerous modifications that only become apparent in a rigorous test and evaluation phase or operational squadron use. In the case of the D.I, this meant that the pilots did not like the inverted "V" configuration of the cabane struts, the high placement of the upper wing and the "ear" Windoff radiators on the fuselage. The struts were directly in line with the pilot's vision forward, and the high upper wing limited his view upwards. The fuselage-mounted radiators were lower than the engine, which let the coolant drain out with any leak or combat damage.

Albatros D.II Differences

The D.II was designed and constructed simultaneously with the D.I in the summer of 1916. It was not the result of operational feedback or a change in government requirements. Nevertheless, the D.II contained several improvements, and these continued with subsequent models. They included the inversion of the cabane struts in an "N" configuration and splayed them outward from the side of the fuselage to the upper wing. The builders also lowered the upper wing by 250 mm (9.8 inches), which greatly improved the pilot's visibility. On the prototype D.II, and all of the later production models, the Windoff radiators were replaced with a Teeves & Braun design that fit smoothly into the upper wing, providing a streamlined surface.

Boelcke's prototype Albatros D.II 386/16, 1916. (James Miller)

The Cockpit

The pilot sat in an open, egg-shaped (ovoid) cockpit with edges covered by a padded leather coaming. It had more room than contemporary French and British designs, and the lack of a firewall provided some heat. The pilot's seat was an upholstered bucket, which adjusted fore and aft. He was fastened in with a four-point seat belt and shoulder harness. The stick was a metal control column with two wooden hand grips that straddled the two machine-gun triggers, operated by the pilot's thumbs. The engine throttle was also on the stick, with an alternate on the left quarter panel.

There were very few instruments. There was no instrument panel as such. The only gauge directly in front of the pilot was a tachometer. Altimeter and airspeed indicators were not included in the factory machines, but some were retrofitted in the field. There was no clock, but many of the early aviators wore a pocket watch, modified to be worn on the wrist. The only navigation instrument was an alcohol magnetic compass mounted in a pedestal on the floorboard, similar to that on a boat. The engine and fuel controls were located to the pilot's right. The left cockpit wall held the engine magneto switch, which was used to start the engine.

Albatros Production and Factory Expansion

By July 1916, the central acceptance commission recommended the Albatros D.I for production, and Idflieg contracted for 100 aircraft (fifty D.Is and fifty D.IIs). Excluding the twelve prototypes, Albatros produced and delivered a total of fifty D.Is and 291 D.IIs. Based on the general inspectorate of military transportation's large production contracts for D.IIs, Albatros was able to expand its workforce considerably. The firm averaged 1,500 workers January through July 1916 and expanded to 2,000 in August. This work force boosted aircraft production from ninety in July-August to 120 in September and 135 in October. By January 1917, there were 274 Albatros D.II airplanes flying in twenty-two Jastas. Over the next few months most of the D.Is were converted to D.IIs.[2]

The Albatros D.II cockpit with its two machine guns. (James Miller)

Albatros impact on the Battle of the Somme

During the first phase of the Battle of the Somme in July 1916, the English gained undoubted air superiority. However, by the end of August the tide began to change as the German air service introduced its new aircraft, new tactics, and renewed willpower into the battle. The first sighting of an Albatros D.I was on 31 August, as Captain J.O. Andrews and 2/Lt A.E. Glew, of 24 Squadron RFC flying D.H.2s, encountered:

The author's model of Oswald Boelcke's Albatros D.II 386/16 now on permanent display in the San Diego Air & Space Museum.

'... a new type, extremely fast and climbing quickly. Biplane with streamlined propeller boss, apparently single-seater .... The tailplane was very large and rounded, not a fish tail. The HA [hostile aircraft] kept above the de H's diving, firing and climbing again. The encounter lasted 30 minutes, during which time Capt Andrews and 2/Lt Glew were only able to fire a few shots, owing to their inferior position underneath, and their inability to outclimb the hostile machines. At 12:40 pm the hostile aircraft turned away east.'[3]

On 16 September 1916, Jasta 2 received five D.Is and one D.II prototype (No. 386/16), which Boelcke took for his own. These initial Albatros designs were superior to the Fokker monoplanes and biplanes and virtually all French and British aircraft in several respects. They were faster, more powerful, had a higher ceiling, faster rate of climb and two machine guns. Lt Raymond Money, 12 Squadron, RFC, was even more specific in his evaluation of the Albatros D.I/II: 'On 17 September, we were to learn what a powerful and dangerous enemy the Germans still could be.'[4] Peter Hart continues his narrative and pinpoints the turning point of air superiority on the Somme Front:

'The impetus for change was the delivery on 16 September of the Albatross [sic] D.I [and II] earmarked for Boelcke's Jasta 2. Although new German scouts, such as the Fokker D.II and the Halberstadt D.II, had been arriving on the front throughout the summer of 1916, they all had only one fixed forward-firing machine gun. The Albatross [sic] D.I [and II] was [were] the first scout[s] to be armed with twin Spandau machine guns firing forward through the propeller without a corresponding loss in aerial performance, due to its careful streamlining and the awesome power of its 160 hp Mercedes engine which took it up to speeds of nearly 110 mph. The new aircraft was clearly superior to any Allied scout then flying on the Western Front and its sleek appearance and deadly bite soon earned it the nickname of "shark". Boelcke was delighted with his new machines.'[5]

The Mercedes D.III engine was a marvel of its time. First produced in 1914, the engine was a six-cylinder, in-line, water-cooled internal combustion engine with 150 hp. The engine was powerful, and it was not until 1916 that an airplane could be designed to handle that much power. By then, the horsepower had been increased to 160 and would increase to 217 by the end of WWI.

Even at full power these early Mercedes ran at very low rpm. The 160 hp was measured at 1,450 rpm, with the maximum rpm being slightly higher. Current aircraft reciprocating engines perform between 2,000-2,700 rpm. The stroke was short with a correspondingly low compression ratio (4.73:1). For comparison, the compression ratio in a current automobile is 9.0-9.5:1, featuring small pistons and long strokes.

The engine was limited by the fuel available. Most of the WWI fuels were benzene, an elementary petrochemical and a relatively light extract from crude oil. All were of low octane, which limited the compression ratio and thus the power. The octane rating of 1916 aviation gasoline varied by country and grade of petrol. The Allies used four types with their respective octanes: Old Export Grade (62.0 octane), New Export Grade (65.9), Fighter Grade (68.0), RAF or French Fighter Grade (71.0). Germany had three grades: Heavy Benzene (67.5), Medium Benzene (70.5) and Light Benzene (71.2).[6] The German petrol was slightly higher octane, which could then support engines with somewhat higher compression ratios, and correspondingly, a little more power. However, the result for all the engines in WWI was that they could only achieve low revolutions per minute.

Boelcke's reward: Jasta 2 victories

The arrival of the Albatros fighters was the reward Boelcke had been looking for. As soon as he landed from the ferry flight on 16 September 1916, Leutnant Otto Höhne had his Albatros D.I armed and refuelled. He then took off on a solo combat mission. Around 6:00 pm Höhne's machine-gun fire crippled a pusher F.E.2B of 11 Squadron RFC. The pilot, Second Lieutenant A. L. Pinkerton, landed his smoking airplane and was immediately made a prisoner of war. After his release in 1918, he claimed his plane had been hit by anti-aircraft fire, damaging the propeller, but was then "riddled" by the attacking fighters.[7] Whatever was the major cause, Höhne got credit for the kill, and the Staffel was overjoyed. One of the regular pilots, other than the Staffel commander, had downed an enemy aircraft. If Höhne could do it, so could they, especially in the new Albatros. They could hardly wait for the next morning. The score was: Boelcke twenty-six; other pilots, one.

Sunday, 17 September, is the real birthday of Jagdstaffel 2. In a letter to his father Boelcke described the joy of being Jasta commander, and his anticipation of leading his squadron in combat:

> 'Yesterday at least six [Albatros aircraft] arrived, so that I shall be able to take off with my Staffel for the first time today. Hitherto, I have generally flown Fokker biplanes, but today I shall take up one of the Albatroses. My pilots are all passionately keen and very competent, but I must first train them to steady teamwork – they are at present rather like young puppies in their zeal to achieve something.'[8]

Manfred von Richthofen was one of them. He had been raised as a hunter for sport in East Prussia, and he was keen to get into the fight. He vividly recalled his feelings before his first flight in the Albatros fighter with Jasta 2:

'We were all beginners. None of us had previously been credited with a success. What-ever Boelcke told us was taken as gospel. We knew that in the last few days he had shot down at least one Englishman a day, and many times two in a single morning. The morning of the seventeenth of September was a wonderful day. We could rely on brisk English flying activity. Before we took off Boelcke gave us precise instructions and then, for the first time, we flew as a squadron under the leadership of the famous man whom we followed blindly.'[9]

Erwin Böhme, the other pilot who had been recruited with von Richthofen, downed his first victory at 7:45 am on the dawn patrol, 17 September. The aircraft was a 1½ Strutter from 70 Squadron.[10]

The rest of Boelcke's flight landed from the first mission without further action. Rearmed and refuelled, they took off in late morning in search of a British squadron that was reported crossing the front. They found their quarry. The British flight was on a bombing mission of a railway station with eight B.E.2Ds of 12 Squadron with six pusher F.E.2Bs from 11 Squadron as escort. (The B.E.2D was identical to the B.E.2C, with the exception that it had dual flight controls, one in each cockpit.) Each B.E. had been given a maximum load, even leaving off the observer. Boelcke's flight of fledglings tore into the escorts. Seven other German fighters joined the fight. Boelcke, Hans Reimann and von Richthofen each got one, and Leutnant Wilhelm Frankl from Jasta 4 got another. Boelcke's adversary was Lieutenant L.B. Helder, the pilot, and Captain D.B. Gray, observer and a flight commander, flying an F.E.2B, with colourful streamers on his wings. The streamers were used by most of the air forces to identify flight and squadron commanders in the air. Some photos show streamers of red, white and black on Boelcke's aircraft. Boelcke described this fight in a letter to his parents:

'*17.9.16. Afternoon.* Meanwhile the status quo has altered once more. This morning I ran into an enemy squadron with two of my pilots (Ltns. Reimann and Richthofen). We cleaned them up thoroughly; each of us got one. I engaged the leader's machine, which I recognised by its streamers, and forced it down. My opponent landed at Equancourts and promptly set fire to his machine. The inmates were taken prisoner; one of them was slightly wounded. The pilot had to land because I shot his engine to pieces. So that was number twenty-seven. The Staffel is making itself! We have got five English machines since yesterday evening.'[11]

Von Richthofen's First Victory
Manfred Von Richthofen flying Albatros D.II 491/16 shot down Lieutenant Lionel Morris, pilot, and Captain Tom Rees, observer, in another F.E.2B, which crashed behind German lines. Richthofen landed nearby and inspected his first victim. His description of his engagement with the two-seater is graphic:

'Apparently he was no beginner, for he knew exactly that his last hour had arrived at the moment I got at the back of him. I was curious to see if he would fall. At that time, I had not yet the conviction, "He must fall!" which I have now on such occasions, but on the contrary, I was curious to see whether he would fall. There is a great difference between the two feelings. When one has shot down one's first, second or third opponent, then one begins to find out how the trick is done.

'My Englishman twisted and turned, going criss-cross [flying in zigzags, which only allowed the attacker to close the distance]. I did not think for a moment that the hostile squadron contained other Englishmen who might conceivably come to the aid of their comrade. I was animated by a single thought, "The man in front of me must come down, whatever happens". At last a favourable moment arrived. My opponent had apparently lost sight of me. Instead of twisting and turning he flew straight along. In a fraction of a second I was at his back with my excellent machine. I give a short series of shots with my machine gun[s]. I had gone so close that I was afraid I might crash into the Englishman. Suddenly I nearly yelled with joy for the propeller of the enemy machine had stopped turning. I had shot his engine to pieces; the enemy was compelled to land for it was impossible for him to reach his own lines. The English machine was curiously swinging to and fro. Probably something had happened to the pilot. The observer was no longer visible. His machine gun was apparently deserted. Obviously I had hit the observer and he had fallen from his seat.'[12]

Von Richthofen was on his way to becoming Boelcke's star pupil. When he got back to the squadron he found the other pilots having breakfast, and he proudly reported, 'One Englishman shot down. Everyone rejoiced for I was not the only victor. Every one of the beginners had gained his first aerial victory.'[13] The score was Boelcke: twenty-seven; others: four. Boelcke hosted a party that evening for all his pilots and mechanics to celebrate their triumph. He personally rewarded Erwin Böhme by pinning the Iron Cross to his tunic. Then Boelcke presented Böhme and each of the other victorious pilots with a commemorative first-victory silver cup, the Ehrenbecher.[14] This tradition continued throughout the war and into the Second World War. On that same night von Richthofen ordered his first (of sixty) plain silver cups from a Berlin jeweller inscribed, "1. Vickers 2. 17.9.16" for his personal collection.[15] The cups were about two inches high, much smaller than the Ehrenbecher he and other victorious pilots were given. Each of these sixty victories by von Richthofen were won while flying the Albatros; the remaining twenty were in the Fokker Dr.I., and for these there were no silver cups as the supply of silver in the country was exhausted.

The view from the other side of the trenches was expressed in the British official history of the air war. It is lavish in its praise of Jasta 2 and the Albatros:

'Their success against seasoned opponents, achieved on aeroplanes which had only arrived the previous evening, constituted a remarkable performance. It gave Boelcke's new fighting squadron immediate prestige.'[16]

Erwin Böhme went on to get five confirmed victories by the end of October 1916. He had the utmost confidence in his Albatros D.I and wrote a handsome endorsement:

'Our new aircraft border likewise on marvellous. Compared to the single-seater which we flew before Verdun [the Fokker Eindecker], they are improved. Their rate of climb and turning radius are amazing. It is as if they are living, feeling creatures that understand what the pilot wishes. With them one may risk everything and succeed.

'[Dogfighting] would be unthinkable in the heavy two-seaters. However, with our light single-seaters, the pilot is in a completely different situation. It is, if I may say, a personal unity with the machine. One no longer has the feeling that he is sitting in and flying an airplane, but it is as if there was a spiritual interaction. It is similar to a good horseman who is not only letting the horse carry him and is attempting through various commands to communicate with the horse his intentions, but who has grown so completely together with his horse, it immediately feels what the rider wants. Both have total understanding of and trust in one another, and they are motivated with one will. I can only compare the true joy of a horseman with the bliss I feel in being completely one with my Albatros.'[17]

So effective was the teamwork of Boelcke's Jasta that von Richthofen asserted, 'I would mention that since that time no English squadron ventured as far as Cambrai as long as Boelcke's squadron was there.'[18]

The British Notice the Arrival of the Albatros

The German army counter-attacked on 20 September 1916, and met considerable success under the local air superiority that Jasta 2 provided. One of the results was that the airborne barrage defensive system was abandoned, and the German aircraft ranged offensively over the Somme battlefield in patrols of three or more aircraft. In this time period the average life expectancy of the Royal Flying Corps pilot at the front was only eleven days. For those flying opposite Jasta 2, it may have been less.

Major General Hugh Trenchard wrote to Brigadier General Brancker on 21 September, announcing the effects of the Albatroses and asking for more pilots:

'My Dear Brancker,

'We are fighting a very big battle and fighting in the air is becoming intense, and will increase I regret to say and not decrease. It is only a question of our keeping it going longer than the Huns. If we cannot do that then we are beaten; if we do it then we win. I must warn you now that in the next ten days if we get fine weather I anticipate a very heavy casualty list. There are many more German machines, fast and much better fighters which have suddenly appeared on our front opposite us than there have been before.'[19]

RFC pilots most often saw the Albatros fighters in multiples, so they labelled them in the plural – the "Albatri". New Zealand historian Ian Mackersey provides his own assessment of the Albatros aircraft:

'No other aircraft then in existence could compete with this superb aerial gun plat-form. Its big Mercedes engine gave it a top speed of 109 mph and the ability to whistle up to over 3,000 feet in five minutes. In one dramatic stride the German air service had brought to the Western Front an aeroplane which no Flying Corps machine ex-cept perhaps the Nieuport, in expert hands, could compete. The D.H.2 and the Fees (FEs) were doomed. They could no longer protect the trundling old B.E.2s, the obser-vation workhorses upon which the army had become so hugely dependent to range its big guns and locate the enemy.

'To add to the menace of the "Albatri" the Germans flew them with a new breed of unusually gifted fighter pilots hand-picked and highly trained in the techniques of aerial combat.'[20]

Opposing pilots were quick to recognise the outstanding performance of the Albatros D.I and II, but many of them did not distinguish between the two models. James McCudden, a famous British ace who compiled fifty-seven victories before he was killed in an aircraft accident in April 1918, wrote:

'Outclassed. We continue doing our offensive patrols, but we never did much good as at that time the German Albatros D.I was very superior to the de Havilland Scout, and we rarely had a look in. The Huns simply climbed above us, and there they re-mained until they wanted to go home. These shows I liked, so long as I came out of them, but it was no fun fighting an enemy who was 15 miles faster and had almost twice the climb.'[21]

Mackersey also provides observations on Boelcke's fighter tactics:

'For his skill as a combat pilot they regarded Boelcke with reverence. The wolf cubs were eager to learn his fighting techniques and the master spelled these out for them in an historic document. The Dicta Boelcke laid down the basic principles and tac-tics of aerial combat that were to endure through the Battle of Britain in the Second World War and into the era of jet aerial combat, where homing missiles succeeded the guns of old. It aimed to replace solitary hunters with highly disciplined groups of aircraft flying in close formation, protecting one another and sticking doggedly to their leader.'[22]

Once again, we have a reference to "close formation" where the wingtips are almost (and sometimes) overlapped like the USAF Flight demonstration team the Thunderbirds, the US Navy's Blue Angels, RAF's Red Arrows or the former Luftwaffe team, the Vikings. In reality, Boelcke and subsequent flight leaders had their wingmen fly a loose, more manoeuvrable fighting wing or spread formation. Von Richthofen instructed his fliers of Jasta 11 in 1917 to leave enough room so the leader could perform a complete u-turn.

On 19 September 1916, Boelcke got another victory, number twenty-eight. He was flying the Fokker on another dusk patrol (6:30 pm), and his victim was a British Morane-Saulnier Scout of 60 Squadron. Jasta 2's first loss occurred on that same day. Leutnant Grafe was shot down by a pilot from 19 Squadron flying a B.E.12. Grafe had been flying one of the Staffel's Fokker D.IIIs.

On 22 September, four of Grafe's compatriots got their revenge in another meeting with 19 Squadron RFC. Jasta 2 pilots, Leutnant Otto Höhne, Leutnant Hans Reimann and Offz Leopold Rudolf Reimann, each shot down an RFC B.E.12.

Training the Jasta Pilots: End of September 1916

On 22 September, Boelcke was stricken with another bout of asthma due to the wet autumn weather in north-east France. He refused to go to a hospital, but took himself off the flying list and transferred command of his squadron to Oberleutnant Günther Viehweger. On that day off from flying, Boelcke wrote another letter to his father in which he described his training regime, some frustration and a most important view of squadron teamwork:

'I have not yet been able to put up sheds for our machines, which must be accommo-dated in tents at present as we haven't the men to do the work. My first aim is to get huts built for my officers so they can be housed on the aerodrome instead of living in the village and be always ready for take-off. What a lot of work.

'Besides that *I have to give my pilots some training* [emphasis added]. This isn't easy because they are all inspired with such fiery zeal that it is difficult to put the brakes on them. They have certainly all learnt that the main thing is to get the enemy in your power and beat him down at once instead of arguing with him. But until I get it into their heads that everything depends on sticking together through thick and thin when the Staffel goes into battle and that it doesn't matter who actually scores the victory as long as the Staffel wins it – well, I can talk myself silly and sometimes I really have to get tough with them. I always give them some instruction before we take off, and deal out severe criticism after every flight and especially after every fight. But they take it all very willingly.'[23]

This is an extremely significant letter as in it, he articulated his vision of squadron unity of purpose and dictated the procedures he developed to implement his training regime. Boelcke was well ahead of his time when he insisted on pilots briefing their flights before taking off, supporting each other in the air in formation and upon landing, reviewing what had happened. His training was a combination of democracy and dictatorship. The de-mocracy element is exemplified when he gave everyone a chance to review the flight, ask questions and articulate what they had learned from it. This was democracy in action. Since 1916, there have been various technological aids to reconstruct flight manoeuvres and out-comes, but Boelcke identified the essence of the experience and the learning of each flight. It is ironic that this practice of discussion before and after every flight was a mandatory element of Boelcke's training in highly structured Germany, while there is no evidence that such a democratic practice was conducted in the Royal Flying Corps.

Professor Werner contrasts Boelcke's style respecting individual action with his application of "iron discipline". Everyone had to do their part to support the Jasta. Finally, Werner notes the 'enormous expenditure of energy' it took to organise the flying schedule, fly multiple times a day, enforce formation discipline in the air, train the pilots and maintenance personnel and look after his men. Other units in 1916 were flying in formation, but when the fighting began, devolved into individual combats. The power of mutual support was not well understood.

For several days in September, the British artillery had been shelling the village and airfield at Bertincourt, France. In the afternoon and evening of 22 September, Jasta 2 personnel moved all their aircraft and material back to Lagnicourt. That night, British infantry captured the aerodrome. Boelcke resumed command of the squadron on 23 September 1916.

Von Richthofen's Second and Third

Manfred von Richthofen flew the same Albatros D.II with a flight of five aircraft on 23 September and intercepted an RFC flight of six Martinsydes from 27 Squadron. Leutnants von Richthofen, Erwin Böhme and Hans Reimann each downed one. A few minutes later, British Lieutenant L.F. Forbes deliberately rammed Leutnant Reimann's Albatros, causing it to spin and crash.[24] It was the first casualty of Jasta 2 in the Albatroses. Forbes managed to get his damaged Martinsyde back across the lines to his airfield at Bertangles, but hit a tree on landing, injuring himself and smashing the aircraft. He received the Military Cross and later became an air marshal. Erwin Böhme claimed an aircraft shot down, but it was not confirmed. However, the records of RFC's 27 Squadron show it lost three Martinsydes that day.

On 27 September, Boelcke led a flight of five aircraft south-east of Bapaume, engaged two and shot down one of them. Then he engaged the second plane and saw it fall. The first kill was a G-100 from 27 Squadron RFC that was mortally hit on the first pass. The second was a British aircraft, serial number 7495, which he fought in a long engagement in a series of tight turns. On close inspection the pilot appeared to be slumped over in the cockpit, apparently dead. However, when Boelcke landed he learned that Leopold Reimann had also claimed a British aircraft with serial 7495. Boelcke suggested, and the administrative officer agreed that the victory should be credited to the squadron, but not to any individual pilot.[25]

On 30 September, Jasta 2 lost its third pilot when Leutnant Ernst Diener was killed in an engagement over Bapaume with a French Nieuport Scout. That same day von Richthofen got victory number three when he shot down an F.E.2B from 11 Squadron, RFC, that was directly overhead Jasta 2's base at Lagnicourt. Total scores: Boelcke twenty-nine; others eleven.

As squadron commander (Staffelführer), Boelcke wrote an official report on activities for the month of September:[26]

Combat Sorties	186	An average of >twelve per day for the last fourteen flying days
Air-to-Air Fights	69	37% of the total sorties
Victories	25	13% of the total sorties (Boelcke's portion was ten)
Losses	(4) 3ᵉ	2% of total sorties

Jasta 2 ratio of victories/losses = 8:1.

The overall score for September 1916 was: Germany 123; Allies twenty-seven. General Trenchard admitted in a letter to General Haig that the RFC had lost the edge. He wrote:

'Within the last few days the enemy has brought into action on the Somme Front a considerable number of fighting aeroplanes which are faster, handier, and capable of attaining a greater height than any at my disposal with the exception of one squadron of single-seater Nieuports, one of "FE Rolls-Royce" and one of "Sopwiths" .... All other fighting machines at my disposal are decidedly inferior. The result of the advent of the enemy's improved machines has been a marked increase in the casualties suffered by the Royal Flying Corps.'[27] This is the month it can be said that Germany won back air superiority over the Somme.

---

[e] Boelcke is counting in the number (4), Leutnant Hans-Joachim von Arnim, who reported to Jasta 2 on 27 August from FA(A)207. Since Jasta 2 had no aircraft he went back to fly with his old two-seater squadron on 28 August and had the unlucky fortune to meet Albert Ball, who shot him down.

CHAPTER XII

Jasta 2 in Ascendance – October 1916

Oswald Boelcke close up, 1916. (Walter Waiss)

At the beginning of October 1916, Jasta 2 was still at Lagnicourt. The squadron counted ten pilots on duty. Six of them had air-to-air victories: Boelcke, twenty-nine; von Richthofen, three; Böhme, three; Höhne, two; Reimann, two and Oblt Viehweger, one. Boelcke had done an amazing job of training his men. On 1 October, Boelcke engaged and shot down another British D.H.2 of 32 Squadron.[1] The day was marred, however, by the loss of Leutnant Herwarth Philipps, who was shot down by anti-aircraft fire near Bapaume.

The weather on 2 October turned foul, with nearly continuous rain for days on end. Boelcke's thirty-first victory was over a French Nieuport (probably a XII) two-seater on 7 October. Boelcke was elated, 'Everything goes well with me; healthy, good food, good quarters, good companions, and plenty to do.'² Von Richthofen shot down his fourth victim, also on 7 October, a B.E.12 from 21 Squadron RFC. The B.E.12 was the scout version of the slow B.E.2C, but the modifications did nothing to make the plane more manoeuvrable, and it was still slow. It was no match for von Richthofen's Albatros D.II, and von Richthofen was learning fast.

Von Richthofen was overjoyed at being a member of Boelcke's cadre. He admired and followed the master's instructions with zeal. Another flight from Jasta 2 intercepted a 25 Squadron bombing mission on 10 October near Arras. Von Richthofen attacked an F.E.2B and severely damaged it. However, he had to break off the attack when he was bounced by the F.E.'s wingman. Subsequently, his victim was attacked by a two-seater from FA22, and Fritz Kosmahl got credit for the victory. The German air service at this time had no procedure to share a score.

Formation of the German Air Force

In October 1916, General Ludendorff, the high command and the Kaiser decided the German air service needed more senior command with a general officer in authority over all the army's air combat and anti-aircraft units, both in the field and at home. The Kaiser's order was transmitted by the high command on 8 October 1916:

> 'The increasing importance of the air war requires that all air-fighting and defence forces of the army, in the field and in the hinterland, be united in one agency. To this end I command:
>
> 'The centralised improvement, preparation, and employment of this means of warfare will be assigned to a "Commanding General of the Air Forces" who will be directly subordinate to the Chief of the General Staff. The "Chief of Field Aviation," with the dissolution of that post, becomes "Chief of Staff to the Commanding General of the Air Forces".'³

General Ludendorff chose Lieutenant General von Hoeppner, commander of the 75th Infantry Division, as the new air commander. He was given the title of commanding general of the air force (Kommandierender General der Luftstreitkräfte) holding the rank of lieutenant general. Oberstleutnant von der Lieth-Thomsen was appointed his chief of staff. At the same time, the German air service was renamed, from Fliegertruppe to Luftstreitkräfte.

One of Lieutenant General von Hoeppner's first orders was to collect, reproduce and distribute experiences of 1916 combat, including Boelcke's Dicta, to his airmen. Simultaneously with the formation of the German air force, the war ministry initiated the Hindenburg programme, which decreed total mobilisation for the nation. German air force (GAF) units on the Somme Front were bolstered in this period by more transfers of squadrons from Verdun and increased aircraft production from home. By 15 October, the GAF on the Somme mounted thirty-eight units, numbering some 333 aircraft. In opposition, the RFC had 328 aircraft.⁴

Oberleutnant Stefan Kirmaier joined Jasta 2, also on 9 October. He was 27 years old and had served in the infantry since 1914, where he had served valiantly and earned four awards for bravery. After transferring to the air service, he flew two-seaters and then scored three victories flying Fokker Eindeckers with KEK Jametz.

On 10 October, the rain ended, and the day dawned bright and beautiful. The British sent out numerous offensive patrols including one of Sopwith 1½ Strutters from 70 Squadron over Velu aerodrome, one of the German's own airfields. Boelcke led six Jasta 2 Albatroses from Lagnicourt. The Sopwiths were supported by D.H.2s and F.E.2Bs. Jasta 2 intercepted the enemy at 10,000 ft, and a huge fight ensued. Böhme shot down an F.E.2B and Müller got a D.H.2, whilst Leutnant Imelmann downed a Sopwith. Boeckle shot the controls away on a D.H.2 of 32 Squadron. The pilot barely made it back over British lines, crashing in a shell hole, uninjured. Of Jasta 2's thirty-one sorties for the day, eighteen resulted in air combat engagements, and the Jasta pilots claimed five. Boelcke, Böhme, Müller, Imelmann and von Richthofen all scored.

Von Richthofen fired 300 shots at an F.E.2B of 25 Squadron, causing it to smoke and glide out of the battle. However, he had to break off the fight and was not able to follow it all the way down. The F.E. was then engaged by a two-seater crew from FA22. Both von Richthofen and the two-seater crew claimed the victory, but it was awarded to the two-seaters. Von Richthofen's claim remained unconfirmed.

The next big day was the 16th, when the squadron knocked down at least four more aircraft. Boelcke scored a double (a B.E.2D and a D.H.2); Offz Reimann and Leutnant von Richthofen each got one. Von Richthofen's was his fifth victory, making him an ace. Leutnant Sandel claimed one, but the claim was never confirmed. That evening Boelcke wrote a long letter to his parents describing the second of his engagements on that day:

'On our next flight that same afternoon we ran into a squadron of six Vickers single-seaters south of Bapaume at 5:45 pm. We went into some fine turns. The English leader – with streamers on his machine – just came right for me. I settled him with my first attack; apparently the pilot was killed, for the machine spun down. I watched it down until it crashed about a kilometre east of Beaulencourt and then looked around for a new customer.

'This was also a very good day for my Staffel. In addition to Müller, Leutnant von Richthofen (his fifth) and Leutnant Sandal each got one, so that the Staffel scored five [sic; the actual score was six] victories altogether. The total since September is thirty-seven victories, although we have had a lot of bad weather lately. They are really splendid, clever gentlemen – my Staffel.

'The development of my aerodrome has profited much of late by the bad weather we have experienced. I have allotted all my officers small rooms in the new huts I have built in addition to their quarters in the village. So now we are all warmly and comfortably housed on the aerodrome, close to our machines. Also Oberleutnant Kirmaier, my technical officer – a splendid Bavarian and a very fine pilot who joined the Staffel two or three weeks ago – has put up some fine large workshops, etc. My flights have been quite remunerative.

'By the way, mother need not paint such a ghastly picture of the circumstances and dangers in which I live. She only need think of the extra experience and routine with which I go into action, quite apart from all our technical advantages in flying and shooting gear.'[5]

This was to be Boelcke's last letter. From this point on, we have only the terse accounts he filed in combat reports to air force headquarters.

Boelcke was on a hot streak in the air. He shot down an F.E.2B on the 17th for his thirty-fifth victory, and three days later, he shot down his thirty-sixth. The weather cooperated again on 22 October, and the squadron launched thirty-three sorties, resulting in seventeen fights and six victories. Boelcke got another set of doubles (thirty-seven and thirty-eight) on that day by downing a B.E.12 and a British Sopwith 1½ Strutter. This was the *fifth* set of doubles that he had scored since May 1916.

Jasta 2's strutter victims on this day were all from 45 Squadron, which had been rushed into the battle with inadequate training. Their four losses were a harsh lesson dealt by the finest squadron on the Western Front.

The English pilots were quick to perceive that the battle for air superiority had changed against them. As the noted American historian, John Morrow, Jr. wrote, '... the appearance of the Albatros signalled the French [and British] loss of technological superiority in fighter aviation.'[6] One British ace recorded on 23 October that the new German aircraft had a higher combat ceiling and routinely used this feature to engage with advantage:

'I know I felt very uncomfortable with two HA well above me, and in spite of the fact that I climbed to about 13,500 [feet] they were still above, which is very demoralising. We shall have to bring out some very fine machines next year if we are to keep up with them. Their scouts are very much better than ours now on average ... the good old days of July and August, when two or three D.H.2s used to push half a dozen Huns onto the chimney tops of Bapaume, are no more. In the Roland they possessed the finest two-seater machine in the world, and now they have introduced a few of their single-seater ideas, and very good they are too, one specimen especially deserves mention [the Albatros D.I and II]. They are manned by bold good pilots, probably the best, and the juggling they can do when they are scrapping is quite remarkable. They can fly round and round a D.H.2 and made one look quite silly.

Second Lieutenant Gwilym Lewis,
32 Squadron, RFC[7]

On 25 October, Boelcke scored his thirty-ninth kill, a B.E.2D crew performing artillery spotting over Miraumont, France. Von Richthofen got his sixth that day, and Leutnant Höhne got his third. The next day, 26 October 1916, Boelcke shot down his fortieth. His victim was a B.E.2D two-seater from 5 Squadron RFC, which fell with a long plume of smoke. This was an incredible number for 1916, and it made Boelcke the leading ace of all the aviators, on both sides of the front. This record would not be exceeded until 13 April 1917, when Manfred von Richthofen scored a triple. On the same day, Stefan Kirmaier shot down two.

In all, there were some eighty air-to-air engagements over the Somme on both 20 and 26 October 1916.

Staffel pilots absorbed Boelcke's training, listening to him on the ground, following him in the air, and performing brilliantly when on their own. In the month of October alone, the Staffel scored thirty victories with the loss of only three pilots, a 10:1 kill ratio.[8]

In this month-and-a-half from 17 September to 28 October, Boelcke's rate of victories exceeded two per week. With Kirmaier's victories on the 26th, Jasta 2 had scored fifty with the loss of only six pilots. Von Richthofen wrote of his excitement in being with Jasta 2 and the way that Boelcke watched over and protected his wingmen:

'During my whole life I have not found a happier hunting ground than in the course of the Somme battle. In the morning, as soon as I had got up, the first Englishmen arrived, and the last did not disappear until long after sunset. Boelcke once said that this was the El Dorado of the flying men. It was a wonderful time for our squadron. We roamed the skies, happily diminishing our enemies.

'We had a delightful time with our chasing [hunting] squadron. The spirit of our leader animated all his pupils. We trusted him blindly. There was no possibility that one of us would be left behind. Such a thought was incomprehensible to us. Animated by that spirit we gaily diminished the number of our enemies.'[9]

Boelcke was not only a great squadron leader, but with his quiet, enthusiastic and friendly manner, his men felt that they could talk to him. Von Richthofen noted that everyone who got to know him felt they were his best friend. 'He had about forty of them.'[10]

By all accounts, Oswald Boelcke was modest in his personal life. He never smoked and only drank in moderation. He had a good sense of humour, and his chief recreation seemed to be to go to bed early. Nothing existed for him but flying, the squadron and his family.

The most in-depth description of Oswald Boelcke's leadership, his personality and his effect on his pilots was provided by Leutnant Erwin Böhme, his closest friend. Böhme's letter of 18 October 1916 is revealing. He wrote to a friend only ten days before Boelcke's death:

'You admire our Boelcke. Who would not? But you admire in him only the successful hero; you can know nothing of his remarkable personality. That is known to only the few who are privileged to share his life. This is most remarkable in view of the fact that he underwent no particular experiences in the course of his brief pre-war life. I assure you that not only do I admire Boelcke as my master, but – astounding as it may seem considering that he is only 25 years old – I honour him as a man and am proud that a friendly relationship has grown up between us. He may have been influenced towards this friendship because he sees in me an older and more mature man and is delighted to find me serving the cause he has at heart with an ardour that is quite youthful....

'No wonder the Staffel flourished. Victories are mounting up. And yet in spite of many fights and many daring deeds we have suffered no loss in the last two weeks.'[11]

During this short two-month period of Jasta 2, Boelcke's character blossomed into maturity. His flying skills were well-polished, and for the first time he had a unit large enough to challenge his leadership skills. What comes across in the testimonies of his men is his strength of character, which in the heat of death and battle, took them into a higher level of performance and loyalty. The opinions and performance of his men are more than enough testament to his character and leadership.

Under his inspired leadership, the Staffel achieved outstanding success with the new Albatros fighters. Between mid-September and mid-October, the German air service shot down 211 Allied aircraft with a loss of only thirty-nine of their own. Lieutenant General von Hoeppner, commanding general of the German air force, later wrote in his memoirs: 'If the enemy's superiority in the air that was so oppressive at the beginning of the Battle of the Somme was broken at its end, the merit is due in no slight measure to Boelcke and the Jagdstaffel he led.'[12]

Despite the losses being inflicted on the RFC, Trenchard did not back off from his aggressive, offensive doctrine. As an example, RFC Headquarters in September issued a memorandum, "Future Policy in the Air", which broadcast a hardening of Trenchard's position of pursuing the offensive, and maintained that the policy during the Battle of the Somme would be 'relentless and incessant offensive'.[13] But the intensified air war caused a change in RFC priorities. In August and October 1916, RFC Headquarters noted that the primary mission of the offensive wings was to win the air battle. It relegated reconnaissance to a secondary role and did not even mention close air support.[14]

Thus, in less than a month the German resurgence had not only challenged the British superiority in the air, but it had influenced the opponent to change his priorities away from the ground battle. Boelcke and Jasta 2 were part of this alteration of the operational situation.

On a personal level, some of the spirit and the enduring epic myth of the times is contained in a British report filed by Albert Ball, the British ace who fought against Jasta 2 in this period:

'We kept on firing [against a German two-seater] until we had used up all our ammunition. There was nothing more to be done after that, so we both burst out laughing. We couldn't help it – it was so ridiculous. We flew side-by-side laughing at each other for a few seconds, and then we waved adieu to each other and went off. He was a real sport that Hun.'[15]

Captain Albert Ball, 60 Squadron, RFC

Boelcke and his pilots continued to fly multiple times each day. While one or two sorties a day might have been considered average in a normal time, they were flying four or five in the intense air battle over the Somme. The record of Boelcke's eleven victories in October 1916 is:

30th, 1 October, D.H.2, 32 Squadron RFC, NW Flers.
31st, 7 October, French Nieuport two-seater, probably a XII

32nd, 10 October, D.H.2, 32 Squadron

33rd,16 October, B.E.2C, 15 Squadron

34th, 16 October, D.H.2, 24 Squadron, the second of a double

35th, 17 October, F.E.2B, 11 Squadron

36th, 20 October, F.E.2B, 11 Squadron

37th, 22 October, B.E.12, 21 Squadron

38th, 22 October, Sopwith 1½ Strutter, 45 Squadron, another double

39th, 25 October, B.E.2D, 7 Squadron

40th, 26 October, B.E.2D, 5 Squadron.[16]

Jasta 2's performance led the German air force to inflict a grim pattern of losses on the RFC. The British casualties were even more devastating because 86 per cent of them had been due to enemy fighters.[17]

The squadron roster grew in October 1916 and consisted of: Boelcke (forty victories); Oblt Stefan Kirmaier (seven); Ltns von Richthofen (six), Erwin Böhme (five), Otto Höhne (three), and Hans Imelmann (three); OffStv Max Müller (two) and Oblt Günther Viehweger (one). That left Ltns Karl Büttner, Erich König, Bodo Freiherr von Lyncker and Jürgen Sandel with Vfw Paul Ostrop, who had yet to score.[18] October was an especially productive month as the fifteen pilots produced thirty-two victories. With Oswald Boelcke leading Jasta 2 from the front, the squadron's score of thirty-two in October 1916 would remain the highest score for two years, until Black September 1918, when the Jasta Boelcke scored forty-six victories.

Of the twenty-one pilots who served and learned under Oswald Boelcke, nine would become aces. Together they scored 214 victories, 101 of which were done while a member of Jasta 2. Oswald Boelcke commanded Jasta 2 for two months of its twenty-seven-month existence in WWI. Yet in this short time he personally trained pilots that scored 30 per cent of the total tally of Jasta Boelcke in the war.

One of the reasons for the squadron's outstanding performance was the leadership and training Boelcke had developed and put in practice. Boelcke conducted fourteen of his victories in the Albatros D.II prototype, serial 386/16. He referred to those British and French he flew against with a variety of euphemisms; "patients", "inmates", "customers", "fellows", "poor fellows", "tough fellows", "beginners", "opponents", "dangerous opponents", "cheeky", "valiant men", "brethren" and "Haeschen" (rabbits).

The contribution of Oswald Boelcke's leadership, Jasta 2's skilled pilots and the powerful Albatros aircraft turned the tide of air superiority in September/October 1916. Peter Hart noted:

'It was clear that even the best available RFC scout, the Nieuport 17, was demonstrably slower and could also be out-climbed by the Albatross [sic] D.I and D.II scouts. This was a serious situation [for the British]. The German aircraft were also hampered by the weather, but their newfound sense of purpose was symbolised by the formal creation of the German air force on 8 October. The German aviators were once again taking heart, cheered by the arrival of the new scouts and the inspirational successes of Boelcke and his Jasta 2.'[19]

One of the factors that led to this German period of air superiority was the distribution of Boelcke's Dicta. He wrote his analysis of the air war for the headquarters staff, asking for approval and requesting to establish an information system to all flying units. Headquarters supported the ideas and distributed them to the other fighter squadrons then being formed. He developed the tactical rules; others mostly used them and, when noticing the effects, came up with more advanced tactics.[20]

In summary of his performance in the year of 1916, Boelcke had received the Blue Max, survived the Battle of Verdun and the death of his friend, Max Immelmann, wrote his dicta, travelled to the Orient, organised Jasta 2 and led a cadre of pilots to new heights of air combat. The German air force had recaptured air superiority over the Somme. At the same time, the British Somme offensive, which had never achieved much success on the ground, continued to be bogged down. The Germans were able to rebuild trench fortifications faster than the British could advance and capture them.

Boelcke's letters to his parents show the intensity and stress of his work during these two months of the Jasta. They are much less frequent, skipping from 4 to 17 September to 5 October and then the 19th. Then they drop dramatically to a few lines until his last flight.

Boelcke's character was now fully mature. He had earlier mastered the techniques of individual combat as evidenced by his forty victories. In the eight weeks with Jasta 2, he had expanded his leadership from the small two-airplane section at Jametz to a full squadron of pilots, mechanics and armourers. He was well-liked and respected by kings, princes, and peers and adored by people he had never met. He was at the top of his game.

Boelcke and his pilots of Jasta 2 had scored numerous victories and lost only a few comrades. But those periods of grief were nothing as compared to the tragedy that lay ahead.

CHAPTER XIII

BOELCKE'S LAST FLIGHT

Oswald Boelcke just before his fatal accident. (Johan Rhyeul)

On his last evening Boelcke left the mess and went back to his room. The scene was recalled by Ludwig Fischer, his loyal batman:

'My captain kept on growing thinner and more serious. The superhuman burden of seven take-offs and the worries about his Staffel weighed him down. General von Below, the commander-in-chief of our army, wanted to send him on leave because he was overworked, but he would not go. "I'm needed here," Boelcke said.

'He was always cheerful when he came back from a victory with the Staffel, but otherwise he was often in a very depressed mood in the last few days. When he came home from a flight a couple of days before his death, he said to me: "Fischer, I found an opponent who was a match for me today. There'll be hard fighting in the next few days."

'The last evening he soon left the mess and came back to his room. "There's too much noise for me," Boelcke said. He sat down by the hearth and stared into the fire. Then he said to me, "Fischer, put on the gramophone record, 'Father, Mother, Sisters, Brothers, have I in the World no more.'" [This was the same song sung as an encore during his excursion to the opera.]

'Then Leutnant Böhme came in and asked: "Can I keep you company for a bit, captain? There's such a row in the mess." Then they sat talking a long time by the fireside, until at last I said: "It's time we went to bed now, sir." "Who's on duty tomorrow?" Boelcke asked, and then he said, "Good night," and that was all.'[1]

28 October 1916 dawned a dark and dismal day. The clouds and mist hung gloomily over the Staffel at Lagnicourt. Boelcke scrambled the squadron at 7:00 am to engage British aircraft overhead. He came back an hour later, having had a firing engagement, and flew another three times that morning. The Staffel was heavily engaged with the British in the Battle of the Somme.

The Last Interview?

The New York Times published an article on 28 January 1917, that a Hauptmann Walter Bloem had coordinated an interview with Boelcke on the day of his death. While the author cannot confirm the authenticity of this article, it contains some interesting comments:

'The little group made their way toward the shed where Boelcke kept his aeroplane ... They found Boelcke quartered with seven other airmen, their machines all ready for a flight at an instant's notice. He was at the telephone, so that we had leisure to look him over before he could greet them. Captain Bloem was struck by the boyishness of his face. When the telephone conversation ended and Boelcke was introduced to his visitor, the latter was struck also by the "eagle eye" of the young airman. "No use; I must use that old expression," Bloem writes, "It is the only way of describing Boelcke's glance."

'A high wind was blowing. "Are you going up in this storm?" asked one of the visitors. "Yes, if an opponent shows up," answered the aviator. "In that case no storm counts." Then he turned to his aeroplane and the eagle glance softened somewhat. Somebody pointed to the many patches on the machine. "Bullet holes," remarked Boelcke. "Such things happen, you know."'[2]

The article continues to quote Boelcke in describing the role of the "war aviator" being to protect the other aircraft performing the missions of reconnaissance, artillery spotting and ground support. These missions were less glamorous, but no less important. They, unfortunately, have little chance of being mentioned in dispatches as often as the fighter pilots.

Just then, the article reports, a young lieutenant dashed in 'with eyes shining in triumph' as he described his first victory. Boelcke was quoted as saying he would 'report [the victory] at once so that he [the British pilot] may be buried.'

If this newspaper reporter is correct, on one of the busiest flying days of his life, Oswald Boelcke was concerned about the proper burial of a fallen adversary. The lieutenant's encounter certainly did not happen on 28 October, as Jasta 2 did not record any victories that day. The most recent "first claims" were on 10 October, two weeks before. The reporter may have made up the story or taken some poetic license and merged two events. In either case, the story does highlight the humanity of Boelcke in caring about the squadron's victims and his encouragement of young fliers.

The Accident

Later in the day, the pilots were resting from a hectic day of flying. Leutnant Erwin Böhme described the situation:

'On Saturday afternoon we were standing by in our little house on the aerodrome. I had just begun a game of chess with Boelcke – then, about 4:30 pm, we were called to the front because there was an infantry attack going on. [Boelcke led a flight of six, including Manfred von Richthofen and Erwin Böhme.] We soon attacked some English machines we found flying over Flers; they were fast single seaters that defended themselves well. In the ensuing wild battle of turns, that only let us get a few shots in for brief intervals, we tried to force the English down, by one after another of us barring their way, a manoeuvre we had often practised successfully. Boelcke and I had just got one Englishman between us when another opponent, chased by friend

Richthofen, cut across us. Quick as lightning, Boelcke and I both dodged him, but for a moment our wings prevented us from seeing anything of one another – and that was the cause of it.'[3]

Manfred Von Richthofen, who was closely engaged in the fight, reported in his autobiography:

The last photograph of Oswald Boelcke, 28 October 1916, 4:30-5:00 pm (Casemate)

'We were six against their two. If they had been twenty we would not have been surprised to receive the signal of attack from Boelcke. The usual battle began. Boelcke went after one and I the other. I had to let go because one of the German machines got in my way. I looked around and noticed Boelcke settling his victim about 200 yards away from me. It was the usual thing. Boelcke would shoot down his opponent and I had to look on. Close to Boelcke flew a good friend of his [Leutnant Böhme]. It was an interesting struggle [fight]. Both men were shooting. It was probable that the Englishman would fall at any moment. Suddenly I noticed an unnatural movement of the two German flying machines. Immediately I thought: collision. I had not yet seen a collision in the air. I had imagined that it would look quite different. In reality, what happened was not a collision. The two machines merely touched one another. However, if two machines go at the tremendous pace of flying machines, the slightest contact has the effect of a violent concussion. Boelcke drew away from his victim and descended in large curves.'[4]

Erwin Böhme continued the description of Boelcke's last battle:

'How am I to describe my sensations from the moment when Boelcke suddenly loomed up a few metres away on my right. He put his machine down and I pulled mine up, but we touched as we passed, and we both fell earthwards. It was only just the faintest touch, but the terrific speed at which we were going made it into a violent impact. Destiny is generally cruelly stupid in her choices; I only had a bit of my undercarriage ripped, but the extreme tip of his left wing was torn away.'[5]

Böhme recovered control of his aircraft and followed Boelcke down. But Boelcke's plane descended into a cloud. When it reappeared, the top wing was gone; it had ripped off. He crashed in the German lines near the French village of Bapaume. Boelcke was killed on impact. His seat belt was found unfastened.

The semi-official German news agency reported an eyewitness account on the death of Boelcke that was cabled to the US and reprinted in the *Dunkirk* (New York) *Evening Observer*, 4 November 1916:

> 'Berlin. Boelcke was precipitated [scrambled for take-off] at five o'clock on the afternoon of 31 October [actually the 28th]. He had a very successful combat. During this action another German machine touched him. Part of his plane was torn off. Boelcke descended immediately in a [n]arrow [sic] spiral line but at a height of 20 yards his machine suddenly fell. His body had not been touched by projectiles. After having defeated forty adversaries an accident ended his life. He died unvanquished.'[6]

The Grief

Leutnant Böhme was beside himself with grief. When he landed, his damaged landing gear collapsed, and the aircraft turned over on its back. He was not hurt, but in the ensuing days he was inconsolable. How could this accident have happened, killing his great mentor?

Böhme, Jasta 2 and the German nation were shocked. First Immelmann and now Boelcke had been consumed by the air war. Oswald Boelcke had no opportunity to return to the ordinary world. He was killed at the height of his career and fame. Now his fate and his legacy would be determined by his comrades, the German air force and the public.

The Memorial Service

Oswald Boelcke's memorial service took place on the afternoon of 31 October 1916, at Cambrai Cathedral, France. That morning his parents and three brothers – all still on active duty – arrived in Cambrai and visited the squadron at Lagnicourt. They wanted to see the place where he had last conducted his valiant business. The body lay in state before the altar of the mighty cathedral. This was the first time that a German memorial service had been conducted in one of the largest cathedrals of northern France. And Boelcke was a Protestant, too. The archbishop was not pleased.

The memorial service was a sombre affair with deep silence pervading the mourners. The hundreds of guests were headed by Crown Prince Rupprecht of Bavaria and General von Below, the commander of the 1st Army. General von Stein had composed a poem, and the crowd sang it as a hymn. Then the 4th Division of Foot Guards chaplain, Pastor Stelter, gave the eulogy,

The memorial service at Cambrai Cathedral with Manfred von Richthofen carrying Boelcke's Ordenskissen, the pillow with his awards and decorations. (Walter Waiss)

taking his text from the heroic words of the First Book of Maccabees, Chapter IX, Verse 10, 'If our time has come, so let us die in knightly fashion for the sake of our brethren and not let our honour be shamed.'[7] As the author, I feel he could have continued on with Verse 21, 'How is the valiant man fallen.'

General von Below gave an oration in the name of the Kaiser. Oberleutnant Stefan Kirmaier, who was to become its commander, spoke on behalf of Jasta 2. In the procession that followed, the coffin was hoisted on a gun carriage and proceeded to the train station. Manfred von Richthofen carried the black velvet awards pillow, the Ordenskissen, which displayed Boelcke's medals and decorations, the Blue Max, two Iron Crosses and a host of other awards. Just as the coffin was carried out of the cathedral, the sun broke out and bathed the proceedings in rays of light. The coffin was carefully laid on a caisson drawn by six black horses. The procession passed through a long honour guard of lancers and footguards.

Front-line soldiers fired volleys. Overhead, dozens of German aircraft, gliding with engines at idle, weaved in criss-crossed patterns to honour the fallen warrior. The coffin was transferred again onto a draped railroad car, and the crowd sang the old hymn, "Good Comrade". Then the train departed slowly, carrying the body across Germany. The cortège stopped in Magdeburg, Germany, and was honoured by pilots and aircraft in the city of Halberstadt, en route to his hometown of Dessau.

The evening of the memorial service, Erwin Böhme wrote a letter expressing his deep grievance:

'A harder blow could not have befallen us. Everything seems so empty here. Only very gradually do we realise what a gap our Boelcke leaves and how the soul of our entity has departed with him. In every respect he was our unique master. He exercised a forceful influence on all who came in contact with him, including his superiors, purely by virtue of his personality and the naturalness of his character. He could lead us anywhere he pleased. When he was with us, we never felt that anything could possibly go wrong, and so we succeeded in practically everything we did. In this last month and a half, he has enabled us to put over sixty enemy machines out of action. The superiority of the English waned daily. Now we others must look to it that his triumphant spirit does not depart from the Staffel.'[8]

The State Funeral

The train arrived in Dessau, Germany, the next evening, 1 November 1916. The coffin was placed on a bier before the altar in St. John's Church, where Oswald Boelcke had knelt for his confirmation. An honour guard was composed of NCO pilots, all of whom had won the Iron Cross First Class. In honour of the dead hero, heads of state and famous dignitaries attended or sent honours and gifts. The Kaiser of Austria sent a medal, the Order of the Iron Crown 3rd Class, a 'war medal, to the Royal Prussian Captain Oswald Boelcke', signed 29 October 1916. Czar Ferdinand I of Bulgaria sent a wreath with a silk ribbon and a crowned monogram. The Pasha of the Ottoman Empire sent a medal as did the head of the House of Coburg and Gotha. Letters of condolence arrived from the Emperor, the Crown Prince, other Prussian royalties, from several of the German states as well as Generals Hindenburg and Ludendorff, the Imperial Chancellor, and many more.

The Kaiser send a telegram to Oswald's father in Dessau, dated 30 October 1916 from the New Palace:

'On this most painful day, I and the entire German people lament the death of our hero son, my bravest and most successful flying officer. My army and especially the air force looked on him with pride; with pride they will keep his memory after his death and strive to emulate his luminous example. God comfort you in your great pain.

Wilhelm IR'[9]

The funeral procession in Dessau, Boelcke's hometown. (Walter Waiss)

The funeral service was in the early afternoon on 2 November. Hundreds of high-ranking generals and royalty attended. The Emperor's representative, General von Lyncker, spoke of his admiration for the dead hero, as he had first seen him perform gymnastic feats as an aspirant in the summer of 1911.

Oberstleutnant Lieth-Thomsen, chief of the general staff of the Imperial German air force, gave the oration in the form of a proclamation:

'Boelcke has fallen. As his comrades received this sad message our hearts were para-lysed. Boelcke had fallen. After a warrior's career filled with incredible success, after forty glorious victories he has gone as an undefeated hero of ours, he, our friend and our master.

'Indeed, the Imperial German army air service has lost much by his early death, but it also has gained much by his life and his work.

'Today, there is no German boy in the homeland who doesn't have the burning desire in his heart: "I want to become a Boelcke!" And there is no one within our young pilots at the front who doesn't have the burning desire: "I want to become a Boelcke!" This is giving us comfort with great pride, which we all, parents and sib-lings, friends and comrades, will take home today from the final resting place of our dear and unforgettable companion.

'And thus, I lay down these words on the grave of our faithful friend as a last farewell; these words should be a solemn pledge to every single German flyer; "I want to become a Boelcke!"

'As long as these words remain as our lodestar; as long as Boelcke's mind and Boelcke's skills remain vivid in our Imperial German army air service; as long: "Dear fatherland, no fear be thine!"

'I proclaim the confident hope and expectation that all members of the Imperial German army air service are anxious to keep this pledge, always and everywhere; that they will never cease to emulate the ideal of our Boelcke with all strength of the mind and body. In order to show our never-ending gratitude for all that Boelcke gave us publicly, and to keep his remembrance alive I have made provisions, for all times; the highest air service command must ensure that fresh laurel will be laid down on Captain Boelcke's resting place on his birthday, his day of death, as well as on prominent national commemorative days.'

Supreme Headquarters
2nd November 1916[10]

The RFC wreath dropped by Lieutenant Thomas Green in honour of Oswald Boelcke. (Walter Waiss)

British Honour Boelcke

The Royal Flying Corps had immediately recognised the accidental death of their leading enemy. In the English officer corps, there still existed a sense of chivalry among "Knights of the Air" that transcended national boundaries. These air pioneers shared the many dangers of flight as well as the uncertainty of war. The RFC commissioned Second Lieutenant Thomas Green of 3 Squadron to carry a message. Green risked his life to fly over the German lines in his Morane-Saulnier Parasol aircraft and drop a wreath of forget-me-nots.

The wreath was accompanied by an envelope with an inscription on a Royal Flying Corps letterhead. The message read:

'On His Majesty's Service
To the Officers of the German Air Corps
'To the officers of the German Air Corps on this front. We hope that you will find this wreath and we are sorry to be so late, but the weather has prevented us to be earlier. We sympathise with his relatives and friends. We all pay tribute to his bravery.
'IN COMMEMORATION OF CAPTAIN BOELCKE, OUR BRAVE AND CHIVALROUS OPPONENT.

FROM THE ENGLISH AIR CORPS'[11]

Lieutenant Green was to achieve five victories and shoot down an observation balloon before he too was killed four months later. He was 21 years old.[12]

British prisoners of war in Germany also heard about Boelcke's accident. Several of them had been victims of Oswald Boelcke, and they felt some pride that they had been shot down by this heroic German pilot. Boelcke had even visited some of them when they were hospitalised, bringing food and refreshments. He treated them as worthy adversaries and always had a kind word. Captain Robert Wilson, the pilot Boelcke had shot down in his twentieth victory a month earlier, was one of these. Wilson made an effort to express their condolences. He sent a telegram to the German authorities requesting permission to lay a wreath on the coffin, describing Boelcke as 'a much admired and honoured enemy'. Wilson's request was granted. Four of the captive English airmen got together and sent a huge laurel wreath that was carried in the funeral procession at Dessau. The wreath was crossed by a satin band with a message in gold letters: 'From the English flying officers who are prisoners of war in Osnabrück, 28 October 1916.'

The wreath ribbon from the British POWs in German. (Walter Waiss)

The accompanying card read to, 'The opponent we admired and esteemed so highly'. As the funeral procession exited the church in Dessau, dozens of aircraft circled overhead and dived with silent engines, to honour their hero. Finally, the procession was met at the entrance to the new war cemetery in Dessau by the reigning Duke of Anhalt. Pastor Finger, who had confirmed Oswald as a boy, gave the final oration. Everyone stood in sadness and shock as Boelcke was interred. He was 25 years old. Twelve days after the accident, Böhme wrote to a friend:

'I have now gained a superficial control over myself. But in the silent hours my eyes see once again that ghastly moment when I had to watch my friend and master fall from beside me. Then the torturing question comes up once more: Why was he, the irreplaceable, doomed to be the victim of this blind destiny – for neither he nor I bore any blame for the calamity?'[13]

National Grief

Oswald Boelcke was mourned by a nation of grieving citizens. One of the expressions of the grief among aviators was printed a week after the funeral in the German aviation periodical, *Flugsport*. The funeral was widely reported in Germany. The *Ahaltischer Staats-Anzeiger* dedicated the front page of its 16 November 1916 edition to "The Heroes' Death and Burial of Oswald Boelcke". Individual columns proclaimed "Our Boelcke", "Young Flier's Death", "Over Captain Boelcke's Lifetime", "The Period of Mourning" and "The Kaiser and Crown Prince Honour the Hero's Death".[14] At least one newspaper in the United States also covered the story. The *Dunkirk (Kentucky) Evening Observer* printed a column, "German Air Hero Buried Today: Highest Honours Shown Him, Chief of Air Fleet Swears to be Second Boelcke".[15]

A 1916 postcard reflects the German national grief. The figure of Germania, the personification of the German people, is shown with the imperial sword (the Reichsschwert),

ermine robe, Imperial Crown of the Holy Roman Empire and bowed head, placing a laurel wreath on a portrait of Oswald Boelcke. The wreath trails a long, black mourning ribbon. At the base of the portrait are an intact propeller and an extinguished Greek torch. Overhead is a black eagle bearing more laurel leaves, and high above fly two aircraft of the German air force, circling in honour. Germania articulates the nation's grief, 'Unser Boelcke' (Our Boelcke).

Oswald Boelcke's family received dozens of telegrams and letters of condolence from German civilian and military officials as well as the general public.

Manfred von Richthofen, his star pupil, sometime later, remarked, 'I am after all, only a combat pilot. But Boelcke, he was a hero.'[16] Shortly after the funeral ceremony, the Crown Prince commissioned a portrait of Boelcke and sent it to the Boelcke family with this caption: 'To the parents of our unforgettable Boelcke.' Ten months later, Manfred von Richthofen wrote a letter to Oswald's father:

A 1916 postcard showing Germania placing a laurel wreath on Boelcke, while repeating the nation's grief, 'Our Boelcke'. (Photo courtesy of Heinz-Michael Raby)

> Rittmstr. Frh.v.Richthofen
> Jagdgeschwader 1
> DFP5
> From the Field, 24 August 1917

'Dear Professor,

The Supreme Commander of the 4th Army includes his compliments with my letter. I am now out of action, having been shot in the head, which is still healing. So I may not fly and therefore want to go on vacation until the wound is healed. With my most sincere condolences, I remain very loyal to you.

> Frhr. von Richthofen'[17]

In 1921, five years after Boelcke's death, the citizens of Dessau dedicated a park to the memorial site. In the centre is a tall granite monument with the image of an eagle. Around the tomb are twenty-two granite pillars in a wide semi-circle with the engraved names of the more than 2,000 Dessau sons who fell in the Great War. Oswald Boelcke's body still lies there today, under the eagle, in that tall, sombre monument that bears his name.

When Max Immelmann died on 18 June 1916, he had seventeen victories; at that time Boelcke had nineteen. Boelcke's death on 28 October 1916 was after his fortieth victory. Von Richthofen on that date had six. When von Richthofen was shot down on 21 April 1918, he

The body of Oswald Boelcke lies in a monument in his hometown of Dessau, Germany. Photo taken 28 October 2014, on the day that the wing commander and personnel from Tactical Fighter Wing 31 Boelcke were there to honour their namesake. (Photo courtesy of Heinz-Michael Raby)

had eighty. Von Richthofen said before he died, that if Boelcke had lived, he would have had over 100.

While he was grieving over the devastating loss, his father collected some of Oswald's letters and co-ordinated with a publisher in Gotha to print them in a booklet. For this, he selected only those letters written after 1 August 1914 and ending with the telegram from his brother Wilhelm, informing the family of his death. The title page reads, 'with an introduction by the hand of his father and twenty photographs'.

Boelcke's Awards and Decorations
Orden Pour le Mérite
Knight's Cross of the Order of the Royal House of
    Hohenzollern with Swords
Iron Cross 1st Class
Iron Cross 2nd Class
Prussian Life Saving Medal
Ducal House Order of Albrecht the Bear Knights 1st
    Class with Swords
Ducal House Order of Albrecht the Bear Knights
    2nd Class with Swords
Anhalt Friedrich Cross 2nd Class

Bavarian Military Order of Merit 4th Class with Swords
Bulgarian Bravery Order 4th Class, 2nd Degree
Knights Cross of the Wurttemberg Military Merit
Order of the Ottoman Empire War Medal
Turkish Imtiaz Medal in Silver with Sabres
Knights 1st Class with Swords of the Ducal Saxe-
    Ernestine House Order
Mecklenberg-Strelitz Cross for Distinction in War
    2nd Class
Pilot's Badge – Prussian (German) Army
Pilot's Badge – Ottoman Empire

Now the squadron would have to tread the long road back, without their leader. The master had trained his pilots, left his mark on them, and they carried his lessons forward.

Hauptmann Boelcke's *Fieldbook* published in 1917. (Author's copy donated by Heinz-Michael Raby, now in the San Diego Air & Space Museum)

CHAPTER XIV

AIR COMBAT AFTER BOELCKE

Combat flying was not the same after Oswald Boelcke died. His organisational genius and leadership established Jasta 2 as the foremost fighter squadron on the continent. His character, his impact on aerial doctrine, and his air-to-air tactics remained with his comrades and influenced other fliers to perform at his level.

Oberleutnant Stefan Kirmaier was promoted to hauptmann and succeeded Boelcke as commander of Jasta 2 on 30 October 1916. He had joined the squadron in early October with three victories. Under Boelcke's leadership he shot down four more aircraft and was a seven-victory ace when he was chosen to lead Boelcke's squadron. In the ensuing three weeks, he extended his victory list to eleven, one ahead of Manfred von Richthofen. Kirmaier led the squadron until 22 November 1916, when he was shot down by D.H.2s of the RFC's 24 Squadron. Jasta 2 had lost two commanding officers in a month.

On the day after Boelcke's memorial service in Cambrai, Manfred von Richthofen shot down his seventh opponent, and six days later he got number eight. He got a double on 20 November, victories nine and ten.[1] Another famous ace joined Jasta 2 in November 1916 – Werner Voss. Voss had joined the light cavalry "Hussars" at age 17 in 1914. After pilot training, he flew two-seater bombers for six months before reporting to Jasta 2. He flew frequently with Manfred von Richthofen for two months and learned many of the ace's tactics.

After Kirmaier was lost, Jasta 2's administrative officer, Oberleutnant Karl Bodenschatz, was appointed interim commander for one week until a new commander could arrive. Passed over in favour of a non-flying officer for Jasta 2's command, Manfred von Richthofen became the de facto leader of Jasta 2 in the air. On the day after Kirmaier's death, 23 November 1916, flying one of the Albatros D.IIs, he became engaged in what was to become one of the iconic air battles of the war. Some writers have noted, 'Richthofen's reputation as Boelcke's star pupil was confirmed on 23 November 1916'.[2] His opponent was RFC Major Lanoe Hawker, 24 Squadron's commander, an ace who had been awarded the Victoria Cross as well as the Distinguished Service Order. He was known to the Germans as the "English Immelmann". Hawker was flying a D.H.2 in an engagement that began with thirty to forty aircraft. Soon he and von Richthofen paired off and fought furiously in a series of fifty or so turns before one of Richthofen's bullets hit home. Hawker's aircraft crashed, becoming Richthofen's eleventh victory. This event was widely publicised in both Germany and Britain. To a limited degree it countered Germany's devastating loss of Oswald Boelcke the previous month. Boelcke's pupil had learned well.

The next week the German air force appointed Oberleutnant Franz Josef Walz, a Bavarian pre-war military pilot, as Jasta 2's new commander. He had previously trained new pilots and commanded both a Kampfstaffel and Jagdstaffel 19 in the German 1st Army area. He had six victories as a two-seater pilot. After a while, it became apparent that Walz was not as aggressive as Boelcke or Kirmaier. He remained as squadron commander for six months, until June 1917, but shot down only one additional aircraft while with Jasta 2. He was awarded the *Orden Pour le Mérite*, but not until two years later on 9 August 1918.[3]

Jasta Boelcke

Six weeks after Boelcke's death, on 17 December 1916, the Emperor renamed Jasta 2, "Jasta Boelcke". A unique honour, the first of its kind and one that remains to the current day. Von Richthofen was immediately identified as a skilled warrior and tactical leader. He was invited to visit and confer with Oberstleutnant Lieth-Thomsen in Upper Silesia in mid-December 1916. In the ensuing months he would be called on to test new aircraft and, like Boelcke, offer recommendations on aircraft design and procurement. He was on course to becoming Boelcke's successor, if not as commander of Jasta Boelcke, then as a pilot, commander and senior advisor with wide-ranging influence on German air force issues.

Air Superiority Reversed on the Somme

The British air superiority of July-August 1916 had been short-lived. As described by the British historian, Barrington J. Gray, and members of the D.H.2 research group:

'The introduction of new German Scouts [especially the Albatros D.Is and IIs] meant that August was to be the last month in which the RFC and their French counterpart could claim to be undisputed masters of the sky over the Somme – for soon the new Jagdstaffeln, after a cautious start, began to exploit the superior performance and armament of their new mounts.'[4]

New confidence had been instilled into the German fighter pilots by the example and tutelage of Oswald Boelcke whose superb tactical command of Jasta Boelcke had cost the RFC dearly.[5] Lieutenant General von Hoeppner, commanding general of the German air force, observed:

'The enemy's superiority in the air that was so oppressive at the beginning of the Battle of the Somme was broken at its end [in November 1916]; the merit is due in no slight measure to Boelcke and the Jagdstaffel he led. Their joyous, vigorous thrustfulness and exemplary teamwork rendered them a model for all German Jagdstaffels. Eighty-seven victories won during the fighting on the Somme testify to their activity. Our Jagdstaffels forced the enemy who hitherto had been so sure of himself to adopt a cautious reserve, the effects of which were gratefully noted by the troops on the ground.'[6]

It was clear that the German air force had reasserted itself and was the dominant air power on the Western Front. The RFC could see that the tide had changed, and their fortitude had been challenged. British historian Christopher Cole writes, 'Clear warnings were now visible that Germany was entering into a second period of air superiority.'[7]

Four factors contributed to this ascendance:

- The introduction of the Albatros D-Series aircraft with their twin machine guns, Fokker's superior interrupter gear, more powerful engine and overall performance. The German aircraft delivered six times the firepower of the RFC's machines.[8]
- The arrival of German reinforcements from the declining Battle of Verdun;
- The reorganisation of the German air service into more efficient fighting units, specialised squadrons; and
- Oswald Boelcke's leadership, tactical doctrine and training of Jasta 2, and who, with his unprecedented flying record, inspired countless other fliers which formed the basis for his enduring legacy.[9]

Another contributing factor was the British dilution of experience in their squadrons. Partly this was due to a rapid expansion of the RFC, and part was due to the personnel policy of "no empty chairs". As one pilot said, a new pilot could 'arrive in the morning and be dead that afternoon, having never had time to unpack his kit'.[10]

Thus, new RFC pilots trickled in singly into squadrons with little thought to how they were to be integrated into the ongoing operations or trained in tactics. A British historian observed that the replacements were 'extremely poorly trained pilots'.[11] For example, spin recovery was only just beginning to be taught in flying schools, and new pilots were being thrust directly into combat with only twenty to fifty hours of flying time.

This contrasted greatly with the German policy of providing operational training and requiring new pilots to undergo a six-month period of combat in two-seaters. Apparently it never occurred to British generals or other officials that the abhorrent and wasteful loss rate was due primarily to the lack of training, both at home and on the Continent. Britain would have been better off in slowing the rate of replacements, providing longer and higher quality flying in the pilot training schools and instituting a thorough operational training course behind the Western Front. These measures would have greatly improved pilot quality before the young, inexperienced pilots and observers were thrown into the meat grinder that existed in the operational squadrons.

The Battle of the Somme Ends

On 18 November 1916, the Battle of the Somme ended. The ground campaign never met its objectives. The deepest penetration of the German lines was less than six miles, with the final British line still three miles west of Bapaume, France. No French town had been liberated; no German line of communications or supply had been cut. The losses were so staggering that, to this day, the Somme symbolises the futility of war. Above the battlefield, the first real air campaign had been fought.

Peter Hart writes that the Somme battle was a success on the ground for the British. John

Cuneo goes much farther. His analysis in Volume II of *Winged Mars* argues that the popular conception of the Somme as being an Allied blunder is a mistake. That even with its huge loss of life, the ground battle made a decisive contribution to the eventual Allied victory. 'The Somme offensive pushed the German army to the brink of defeat. While in the end it managed to stave off the Allied drives, the effort left it in a state of complete exhaustion. The bulk of what had remained of the old highly trained German army of 1914 was sacrificed.'[12]

German losses in the battle were prohibitive, the army's confidence was broken, and it never recovered. Three months later, in February 1917, the German army abandoned the Somme trench system and retreated to the Hindenburg Line. The only political change in Britain that resulted was the replacement of Lord Asquith with David Lloyd George, a critic of the Somme management, as prime minister.

The statistics in the air war tell another story, although the numbers differ according to the source. Professor John Morrow's figures show the Royal Flying Corps began the Battle of the Somme with 410 airplanes and 426 pilots. In the first month, it lost 29 per cent of this force. For the five months of the battle, it lost 499 British aircrew killed, wounded or missing, compared to 359 for Germany. Other figures compiled by John Morrow show the British lost 308 pilots killed, wounded or missing, and another 268 were struck off the lists from sickness or exhaustion, for a total of 576.[13] Slightly more [592] aircraft had been wrecked, shot down, or worn out. An additional 190 were missing, for a total of 782 aircraft losses. The RFC had lost 144 per cent of the aircraft and 135 per cent of its pilots it had at the start of the offensive. The RFC lost 252 pilots killed. These figures support a conclusion that the German air force destroyed virtually the entire British flying corps, nearly one-and-a-half times over. Against these massive losses, the British could claim only 369 German aircraft destroyed and driven down.[14] Denis Winter's analysis reported that the RFC lost 800 aircraft against a German loss of only 359. Similarly, the RFC loss of pilots was 359 to forty-three Germans.[15]

Jasta Boelcke was the leader of the German air campaign. For the four-month period, September-December 1916, its pilots shot down eighty-six opposing aircraft and lost only ten.[16] The ratio was 9:1. The German air force would go on to dominate the skies over the Western Front well into 1917. Its pilots continued to fight outnumbered but imposed unequal losses on the British.

The two biggest battles of 1916, Verdun and the Somme, intensified the war on the ground and in the air. The increase in the numbers of aircraft casualties as represented by RFC losses is dramatic. The five months of August-December 1914 resulted in twenty-two RFC aircraft lost due to enemy action. For the year 1915, they increased sixfold, to 137. The next year, 1916, with its bigger battles, saw an increase to 519, a further near fourfold jump. It would multiply by more than three in 1917.

Although many in the Allied air forces disparaged the German pilots, this was not the case with some of those who had been in close contact with them in air battles. The English ace James McCudden penned three paragraphs of insightful comments on the calibre of German pilots, with a particular note about young Werner Voss, *Pour le Mérite*, who joined Jasta 2 in November 1916:

'I think it is my duty, in conclusion, to give the reader my views on the German aviators who have been my enemies since 4 August 1914. The German aviator is disciplined, resolute and brave, and is a foeman worthy of our best. I have had many opportunities of studying his psychology since the war commenced, and although I have seen some cases where a German aviator has on occasion been a coward, yet I have, on the other hand, seen many incidents which have given me food for thought, and have caused me to respect the German aviator. The more I fight them the more I respect them for their fighting qualities. I have on many occasions had German machines at my mercy over our lines, and they have had the choice of landing and being taken prisoners or being shot down. With one exception they chose the latter path.

'Further, it is foolish to disparage the powers of the German aviator, for doing so must necessarily belittle the efforts of our own brave boys, whose duty it is to fight them. The marvellous fight which Voss put up against my formation will ever leave in my mind a most profound admiration for his, and the other instances which I have witnessed of the skill and bravery of German pilots give me cause to acknowledge that the German aviators as a whole are worthy of the very best which the Allies can find to combat them.'[17]

The Rest of the Albatros Story

In January 1917, Albatros D.I and D.II aircraft constituted 67 per cent of the German fighters at the front. Improved D.III models were deployed in March. The Albatros D-Series fighter aircraft continued to be the best fighters over the Western Front after Boelcke died. The D.III was followed by the D.V later in 1917.

The central problem with the Albatros aircraft over the long run was that it was the victim of its own success. Entering the air battle in August 1916, the type continued to be the dominant fighter until the arrival of the Fokker Dr.I in mid-1917 and Fokker D.VII in 1918. This was a problem of the German war ministry and its inspectorate. In October of 1916, these officials had ordered a drastic reduction in the number of different types of aircraft so industry could concentrate on the mass production of a selected few. Among those favoured were the Albatros factories. In late October, the inspectorate awarded Albatros for 400 planes the largest aircraft contract to that date. The problem was that the inspectorate in the spring of 1917, continued to award Albatros production contracts for the later versions (D.V and D.Va) instead of putting out a requirement for a more advanced aircraft.

This was a problem repeated by the German Luftwaffe in 1938-1940 when they delayed in issuing a technical requirement for an advanced aircraft to replace the Messerschmitt Bf-109. In contrast, the British continued to modify the Spitfire, and later models had improved performance. The US set higher requirements for the P-47 and P-51, and both of these aircraft outperformed the Bf-109.

The Albatros works continued to operate until 1931, when, under government pressure, it was merged into the Focke-Wulf aircraft corporation (Focke-Wulf Flugzeugbau AG). After several further mergers, the firm became the European Aeronautic Defence and Space Company N.V. (EADS), which was later reorganised and continues today as Airbus Group.

Boelcke's Star Pupil: Von Richthofen

Manfred von Richthofen continued to fly Albatros D.II 491/16 through the end of 1916. On 14 January 1917, he got his sixteenth aircraft, one of the new Sopwith Pups of 8 Squadron, Royal Naval Air Service.[18] Von Richthofen was amazed at his own success.

'That I should succeed in this I did not believe myself. Other people also did not expect my success. Boelcke is supposed to have said, not to me personally – I have only heard the report – when asked: "Which of the fellows is likely to become a good chaser?" – "That is the man," pointing his finger in my direction.'[19]

Boelcke had personally mentored von Richthofen through victory number six on 25 October 1916; barely nine weeks later he had sixteen. This resulted in two dramatic events: a transfer and a medal.

'One fine day a telegram arrived, which stated, "Leutnant von Richthofen is appointed Commander of the Eleventh Chasing Squadron" [Jasta 11]. I must say I was annoyed. I had learnt to work so well with my comrades of Boelcke's squadron and now I had to begin all over again working hand in hand with different people. It was a beastly nuisance. Besides I should have preferred the *Orden Pour le Mérite*.

'Two days later, when we were sitting sociably together, we men of Boelcke's squadron, celebrating my departure, a telegram from Headquarters arrived. It stated that His Majesty had graciously condescended to give me the *Orden Pour le Mérite*. Of course my joy was tremendous.'[20]

This was to be his last victory with Jasta Boelcke. Von Richthofen took command of Jasta 11 on 14 January 1917. He immediately began training his new pilots in the lessons he had learned from Oswald Boelcke and insisted they learn Boelcke's Dicta. The new unit also received new aircraft – the just-off-the-line Albatros D.III. This model had the same Mercedes 160-hp engine as the D.II, but the upper wing had an increased span and the lower wing dramatically reduced in chord. The bottom wing had the rear spar removed and the configuration converted to a sesquiplane design (literally "one-and-a-half wings"). The German air force had seen the French Nieuport design and was convinced that the narrow wing increased manoeuvrability.

One week later, on 23 January 1917, von Richthofen shot down his seventeenth aircraft flying a new Albatros D.III. His eighteenth victory fell the next day. In his autobiography, *The Red Battle Flyer*, published in 1918, he related his motivation in Jasta 11, his new command:

'I was trying to compete with Boelcke's squadron. Every evening we compared our bags. However, Boelcke's pupils are smart rascals. I cannot get ahead of them. The utmost one can do is to draw level with them. The Boelcke section has an advantage over my squadron of 100 aeroplanes downed. I must not allow them to retain it.'[21]

Three more victories followed in February. Then in March, von Richthofen downed ten British aircraft, for a total of thirty-one. On the last day of this month, 30 March 1917, Jasta 11 and von Richthofen lost its first pilot, Leutnant Eduard Lubbert. Von Richthofen was disconsolate, but paid him what he considered to be his highest praise. He wrote in his diary: '... this outstanding officer had the stuff to become a Boelcke [and] died a hero's death for the fatherland.'[22]

Bloody April 1917

Jasta 11's Flight Line of Albatros D.Vs at Roucourt, near Douai, early 1917. In this famous shot the Baron's Albatros D.III is second from the front, its black crosses barely visible against the red overspray. (Don Holloway)

Six months after Boelcke's death, in April 1917, the Allies launched another joint ground offensive, with the British attacking near Arras in Artois, northern France, while the French Nivelle Offensive was launched on the Aisne River. The British offensive was actually a diversion away from the major French push. The air forces on both sides were called on to provide support, predominantly in reconnaissance, artillery spotting, ground support and tactical bombing. The Germans continued their defensive air campaign against the French on the Aisne, using the tactic of keeping on their side of the front.

The more intense German action was against the British. The Battle of Amiens began on 9 April 1917. In support, the Royal Flying Corps deployed twenty-five squadrons, totalling 385 aircraft, about a third of which (120-130) were fighters. There were initially only five German Jastas in the region, but this rose to eight as the battle progressed (some 114 or so operational fighter aircraft in total). The Germans were outnumbered, as they were during most of the war.

In January 1917, the German fighter force was predominantly composed of Albatros D.Is and IIs. By March, 137 Albatros D.IIIs had arrived, and the majority of fighter pilots were flying D.II and D.III aircraft in April. The British had not yet deployed any fighters more advanced than they fielded in 1916. They suffered the consequences. The Germans had a field day. The German air force downed 275 aircraft in the month of April 1917 alone.

Jasta Boelcke, still commanded by Oberleutnant Franz Walz, was heavily engaged. Its pilots shot down twenty-one British aircraft in April, led by Werner Voss. The 20-year-old Voss got his twenty-third and twenty-fourth in the first week of April. On 8 April, he was awarded the *Orden Pour le Mérite*. The immediate reward for this honour was a well-deserved extended leave, and Voss left on a publicity tour around Germany. He missed the rest of the battle and did not return until May 1917. As an aside, Lieutenant General Hoeppner and Oberstleutnant Lieth-Thomsen were both awarded the *Pour le Mérite* the same day as Werner Voss, 8 April 1917. They were the only two non-combat aviators to win that award throughout the First World War.

Leutnant Fritz Otto Bernert, who was to command Jasta Boelcke in June, developed a hot streak. With the onset of the Battle of Amiens, Bernert scored nineteen victories by 11 April and was awarded the *Pour le Mérite* on 23 April. The next day, he celebrated by downing five aircraft in a single action – a record.[23]

Manfred Von Richthofen's Jasta 11 downed more than 100 per cent of two French Nieuport Squadrons 29 and 60, which lost twenty-seven pilots, dead, missing or taken prisoner.[24] On the Saturday after Easter, Jasta 11 downed thirteen aircraft.[25] For the month, Jasta 11 accounted for eighty-nine of the German victories. Von Richthofen alone got twenty victories that month, including three on April 13, raising his score to forty-three, ahead of his mentor, Boelcke. Von Richthofen's overall score in April zoomed from thirty-two to fifty-two.[26]

However, Peter Hart reminds us that the air contest was not fought in isolation. It was conducted to support the ground armies locked in the Battle of Arras. As in most ground battles of the time, the primary mission of British airpower was air observation, and in this mission they did rather better than in air combat. The artillery of the British Expeditionary Corps was devastating.

There are many sets of numbers for the air results of Bloody April 1917, but they mainly differ in degree. The most reliable appear to be from the extensive database collected by authors Franks, Guest and Bailey in *Bloody April...Black September*. The authors cite RFC losses as 316 British aviators killed or missing with 245 aircraft destroyed by direct enemy action. To those numbers can be added French losses as seventy-four airmen killed, missing or prisoners of war and fifty-five aircraft downed. Totals are 390 Allied airmen and 300 aircraft. These numbers correspond almost exactly with German claims of 298 aircraft shot down or forced down.[27] Known German losses were seventy-six aircraft, but only twenty-four personnel dead, missing or wounded.[28]

Over the broader period between March and May 1917, the RFC lost 1,270 aircraft destroyed or failed to return. In seven days alone (8-14 April), they lost forty-seven aircraft of which thirty-one fell within German lines.[29] British losses were well known throughout the RFC, with brief accounts of day-to-day fighting published in the *Weekly Communiqué* which everyone called the "Comic Cuts". The month was so disastrous for the RFC that it is still known as "Bloody April".

The German success was even more remarkable given the fact that in April there were only six Jastas operating in the Arras battle until 12 April when they were increased to eight. They averaged seven serviceable aircraft per Jasta.[30] British officers knew they were in trouble. Analysis would show that Germany had maintained this superiority since the introduction of the Albatros fighter in late August 1916.

One of the significant outcomes of the April and May 1917 air battles was that General Trenchard finally recognised that his policy of offence would have to be modified. Accordingly, on 10 June, he instructed his brigade commanders:

'To avoid wastage of both pilots and machines, for some little time. My reserves at present are dangerously low, in fact, in some cases, it barely exists at all. It is of the utmost importance, however, that the offensive spirit is maintained.'[31]

Why was the German air service so successful? The author believes from his research that the most prominent reason was that the German pilots were much more experienced. The German pilot training system recognised, valued and developed experienced fighter pilots. The components of this system were:

- The use of advanced tactical training schools behind the fronts;
- The German practice of assigning new pilots to lower-risk units of two-seaters until they built up their flying time and obtained combat experience.
- The Jastas had been in existence for some nine months and had developed discipline and combat tactics that worked. This included attacking in larger numbers – not the huge numbers of the Jagdgeschwader that would appear in June, but large enough to be dominant in the air battle.
- German pilots flew in loose, tactical formations that maximised the capabilities of each pilot and gunnery machine.
- The German pilots were equipped with what we might call "third generation" WWI fighters: Albatros D.IIIs and Halberstadts that were superior in performance to their Allied counterparts. The lesson for aircraft developers is not to focus on who has air superiority at the moment in the campaign, but what does the next generation need to look like to maintain supremacy, however defined.

British Air Vice-Marshal Arthur Gould Lee was especially critical of the British performance, claiming that quantity was given preference over quality, in both men and machines. He titled Appendix A to his 1968 book, "Failure of the High Command". In it he detailed the set of decisions to allow the government-run Royal Aircraft Factory at Farnborough a monopoly of aircraft production under the advice of its superintendent, Mervyn O'Gorman, who was a favourite of the Air Ministry. Under his guidance the firm produced single-designed, stable machines that could be flown "hands off" for aerial observation. The result was the mass production of the B.E.2C/D/E and the B.E.12 and the severe restriction of growth of private industry. He cites as final proof of his accusation the fact that of Manfred von Richthofen's eighty victories, forty-six were over Royal Aircraft Factory products.[32] The end result of this early RFC decision was even worse. When the Air Ministry finally turned to the private aircraft industry for aircraft, they found that virtually all of the firms were already locked up under contracts to the Royal Naval Flying Service under the First Sea Lord, Winston Churchill.

Lee's Appendix B was no less direct. Entitled, "Trenchard's Strategy of the Offensive", he faulted the coupling of the "offensive spirit" to an offensive strategy that was interpreted to mean a "territorial offence". Thus, if one mile across the front was offensive, ten miles across was more offensive. The daily flying orders featured distant offensive patrols and numerous standing patrols at regular intervals throughout the day. This pattern of offensive tactical doctrine allowed the Germans to mount superior numbers and equipment at times and places of their own choosing. The cumulative result was British losses exceeding German by a ratio of about four to one. Lee concludes, 'For the high command to persist, despite the loss in life and machines, in continuously patrolling the Lines, and in sending obsolescent machines deep into German territory, was incomprehensible even at the time'.[33]

Organisation of the Jagdgeschwader (Fighter Wings)

The trend to larger units, begun by the consolidation of the KEKs into Jagdstaffeln, continued in mid-1917. On 24 June, Richthofen's army group commander, Crown Prince Rupprecht of Bavaria, ordered Jastas 6, 7, 11 and 26 to be reorganised into a larger combination of squadrons called Jagdgeschwader 1 (Fighter Wing 1). Manfred von Richthofen was chosen to be its first commander, and under his leadership it became known as the Flying Circus due to the colourful paint schemes of their aircraft. Subsequently, two other fighter wings were established, with Jasta Boelcke assigned to Jagdgeschwader 3.

The Fokker Dr.I Triplane

The British and French would produce better designs after April 1917, but they were late in coming to the front. The Germans would counter in August 1917 with the Fokker Dr.I. Anthony Fokker designed the new fighter around the 110-hp Le Rhône rotary engine since there was no more powerful rotary available, and he designed it for manoeuvrability. In his words:

'I sacrificed speed for climb and manoeuvrability, and the Fokker triplane was the result. It proved to be one of the most remarkable ships that had ever been built. They [the Allies] never had an opportunity to realise how slow the triplane was because of the way it climbed, flipped, and stunted in a fight. In the turmoil of combat, with its extraordinary climb and manoeuvrability, it proved almost invincible under able piloting .... Richthofen flew it with consummate skill, as did some of his brother pilots. Voss, a leader of one of Richthofen's Staffel's, won twenty-two victories in three weeks in his triplane.'[34]

The Fate of Erwin Böhme

Meanwhile, Leutnant Erwin Böhme continued to fly in Jasta Boelcke. By February 1917, he had twelve victories, but on the 11th he was wounded in the arm and hospitalised. In early April 1917, Böhme wrote home that only he and Manfred von Richthofen were left alive from the original Jasta 2 founder members of 1916. By 8 April, Böhme was well enough to be posted back to flying as an instructor at the advanced fighter training unit, Jastaschule I, at Valenciennes aerodrome. On 2 July, he was given command of Jagdstaffel 29 based at Bersee, north-west of Douai and covering the German 4th Army. Böhme was again wounded in his hand on 10 August while attacking an observation aircraft, and was attacked by a SPAD fighter of SPA 3, possibly flown by the famous French ace, René Fonck.

While recovering, Böhme was posted as commanding officer to Jasta Boelcke, effective 18 August 1917. On 19 September, Böhme began his final series of claims, scoring twice in September and five more in October, bringing his total to twenty victories. On the first anniversary of Boelcke's fatal accident, 28 October, he attended memorial ceremonies in Dessau, Germany, to honour his hero's death. The next day he travelled to Hamburg to propose marriage to Annamarie Bruning. She accepted despite her father's fear that her fighter pilot fiancé might not survive the war.

On 31 October 1917, Böhme visited Manfred von Richthofen at Jasta 11. On his flight home, he was interrupted by an attack from an 84 Squadron S.E.5A, which he quickly downed for his twenty-first triumph. He scored two more victories on 6 and 20 November 1917. On the 24th, he was awarded the *Pour le Mérite*. On the morning of 29 November, he downed a British Camel for his twenty-fourth victory, although there is some mystery about the events of that day. There were no Camels reported lost. The record shows that in the afternoon, Böhme attacked a British Armstrong Whitworth two-seater and was killed by machine-gun fire from the observer – thirteen months after Boelcke died.

Another famous Boelcke pilot was Leutnant Max Ritter von Müller, a Bavarian from Rottenburg. He was one of the first non-commissioned officers to join the squadron in September 1916, at age 29. He had first flown with Field Section 1b (Bavarian) where he earned both classes of the Iron Cross and the Bavarian Military Merit Cross 3rd Class with Crown and Swords and the Bavarian Bravery Medal. With Jasta 2, Müller scored rapidly in October, and by 1 December 1916, he was an ace with five victories. In January 1917, he was transferred to Jasta 28, and while there had extended his score to twenty-nine victories and was awarded the Blue Max. Müller received a battlefield promotion to leutnant in the regular army, the first time this had ever happened. In the same month, he was awarded the Bavarian Gold Bravery medal. Already having the Bavarian Bravery Medal, Müller is the *first* and *only* aviator to receive both during the First World War. He returned to Jasta Boelcke in late autumn. He continued to score until his string ran to thirty-five. When Leutnant Walter von Bülow was shot down on 6 January 1918, von Müller was appointed squadron leader *in the air* and acting commander on the ground. Unfortunately, he was shot down and killed three days later, on 9 January 1918.

Fokker D.VII

The Fokker D.VII was a response to the Allies fielding the S.E.5 and SPAD fighters. After their dramatic losses in Bloody April, the new British S.E.5 and the French SPAD XIII allowed the Allies to regain air superiority. As a desperate counter, the German government invited aircraft manufacturers to deliver two prototype single-seat fighter designs (one for inline engines and one for rotary) for a flying competition at Aldershof airfield in Berlin in January 1918. Industry responded with thirty-one airplanes from ten companies. The evaluation criteria were: speed; manoeuvrability; diving ability; pilot's view; climb rate; and high-altitude performance. The Fokker design bureau used a metal-tube fuselage structure and internally-braced cantilever wings that were so well built that the wings needed no wires for support.

Anthony Fokker wisely asked Manfred von Richthofen to test fly their model V.11. Richthofen did and commented that while the aircraft was very manoeuvrable, it was directionally unstable in a dive. Fokker, who was also an intuitive test pilot, immediately lengthened the fuselage, added a fixed vertical tailfin and modified the rudder shape. Richthofen flew the aircraft again, found the controls delightful and recommended it to the other pilots in the evaluation.

The result was that Fokker won both contests. The rotary engine design did not pan out, but Idflieg awarded Fokker a contract for 400 D.VIIs. However, the inspectors were also concerned that the Fokker factory would not be able to produce the fighters on a timely schedule, so they ordered Fokker to license the Albatros factory to build the aircraft. Subsequently, the Albatros-built aircraft were considered to be of higher quality. Albatros built approximately 1,000 of the aircraft, which began to be delivered to the field in April 1918, replacing for the most part Fokker Dr.Is. Initial D.VII aircraft incorporated the 160-hp Mercedes engine, but by the summer, BMW's 185-hp model was in use and dramatically improved performance. Speed with the 160-hp version was 120 mph, and with 185-hp version, it increased to 124 mph.[35]

Leutnant Ernst Udet standing in front of his Fokker D.VII, 4253/18, 1918 (Wingnutswings)

One of the features of the craft was its good stall characteristics, which in combat allowed the aircraft to be pulled into a steep climb and virtually "hang on its prop" while the pilot fired at the underside of an enemy plane. Manfred von Richthofen did not live to see the Fokker D.VII in action.

Dicta Updated

Boelcke's Dicta became well known around the German air service. Manfred von Richthofen had learned Boelcke's lessons at the hand of the master. In 1918, he expanded on the original dicta, sometime between 8 April and his death on 21 April 1918. His principal topics were: (1) unit organisation; (2) rules for the employment of single and multiple squadrons and (3) techniques for combat with emphasis on the leader's signals. A summary of von Richthofen's dicta is included in the Appendix.

Von Richthofen said he developed his spirit of attack with Boelcke as his idol. His string of victories continued through 1917 and did not end until his eightieth victory in April 1918. Of these, sixty-three were gained flying the Albatros. He became the ace of aces in the First World War. He was shot down and killed flying a Fokker Dr. I triplane on 21 April 1918, when he was 26 years old. There ensued a long controversy over whether Richthofen was shot down by Canadian Captain Roy Brown in a Sopwith Camel, or from the ground by Australian machine gunner, Robert Buie. Analysis of the bullet trajectories seem to confirm that the deadly rounds came from the ground. Meanwhile, the air battle continued. By September 1918 Jasta Boelcke was entirely equipped with Fokker D.VIIs.

Black September

Lieutenant Generals Jack Merritt and Pierre Sprey noted in their iconoclastic 1972 article that outnumbered forces tend to extract very high exchange ratios on their enemies.[36] Nowhere was this truer than in the air war in September 1918. While April 1917 had been disastrous for the Royal Flying Corps, the most devastating month of the entire war was September 1918. With the German army demoralised and in retreat and the German navy having mutinied in 1917, the German air force was still flying and potent. The situation on the ground was set by the British, Canadians and Australians pushing forward on both sides of the Somme River and breaking the front at Amiens. The French and Americans were battling fiercely in the south, opposite Verdun and Sedan in the battles of Château-Thierry and Saint-Mihiel. The German army was retreating to fortified positions on the Hindenburg Line. In the air, the situation was different. The German air force had replaced virtually all the Albatroses and other fighter types with Mercedes and BMW-powered Fokker D.VIIs.

The RFC had grown into the Royal Air Force (RAF) in April 1918, but its planes were suffering obsolescence. The Sopwith Camel was now obsolete. The Bristol F.2B two-seat fighter was performing satisfactorily, but the English S.E.5A could barely hold its own against the German D.VII. The only 1918-designed fighter the British fielded was the Sopwith Dolphin, but there were only four squadrons of them. The RAF had suffered badly in August 1918, but its pilots were continuing its aggressive policy of flying over the German lines and attacking virtually everything in sight. The Americans had joined the war in force, and their squadrons supported the French portion of the front.

The German air force was also having difficulties. Throughout 1918, the Germans were short of replacement pilots and planes, and aviation fuel was scarce.[37] Twelve Jastas had been consolidated into three Jagdgeschwader wings; those opposite the British Front were JG I and JG III, plus Jasta 5. Jasta Boelcke had been assigned to JG III along with Jastas 26, 27 and 36. Both Jasta Boelcke and the JG III wing were major players in the September slaughter.

The difference between April 1917 and September 1918 was one of scale. The numbers of aircraft on both sides had doubled. With more squadrons, the numbers and types of missions increased, with many more becoming specialised (e.g., night bombing). Both the German and the French air force were flying in larger numbers. The French introduced the Groupe de Combats, its designation for assembling multiple squadrons into wings. The RAF did not follow suit but continued to fly by squadrons. Its wing-level organisations were mainly administrative, not operational, and the British had difficulty in coordinating the operations of different squadrons. Where the British excelled was in army cooperation: close air support, protection of reconnaissance, mapping, aerial photography, artillery spotting, smokescreen laying and armoured tank support. The Americans followed the pattern of the French, often grouping multiple squadrons on patrols.[38]

Other Jastas may have been short of pilots, but Jasta Boelcke on 1 September 1918, had thirteen, led by thirty-one-victory ace, Leutnant Karl Bolle. This was only one short of the planned number of fourteen. The battle for Jasta Boelcke began on the first day of the month when Ernst Bormann knocked down a Bristol of 62 Squadron, RFC. The next day the Boelckes flew against the 148th Squadron of the American Expeditionary Force (AEF) flying Sopwith Camels. Elliott White Springs, experienced with the RFC and an AEF flight commander, tells the story when his flight met Jasta Boelcke:

'The Huns meant business and so did we. As soon as I would get on the tail of one, another would get on me and as soon as I would shake him off there would be another. My lower left wing buckled. I went into a spin. I thought the machine was falling to pieces and reflected with pleasure that I had forgotten my pocketbook. I thought of Mac [a dead friend] and how glad he would be to see me. But my plane held together. I got out of the spin in time to hop a Hun. I don't know how many Huns we got out of it. I'm the only one of my flight who returned.'[39]

Elliott Springs' squadron, the American 148th Aero, lost four aircraft and pilots that day, 2 September 1918. Jasta Boelcke claimed seven Camels. The next big day was on the 4th, when the German wing downed four but lost Kurt Jentsch (seven victories), who never saw his attacker until he was wounded and limped back to base. Paul Bäumer had a sensational run of good fortune. He had victories on 5, 6, 14, 16 and 20 September and three on the 21st. In one of these engagements, his aircraft was set on fire, but he saved his life by using his parachute.[40] He went on to collect a double on 24 September. The next big day was the 27th, when the British attacked the Hindenburg line directly. Jasta Boelcke claimed nine victories, which brought the squadron to the 300-victory mark. Paul Bäumer got three each on the 27th and 29th. The next few days netted more engagements, with the Jasta ending September 1918 with forty-six victories, which brought the squadron's cumulative total to 309.

The top-scoring German pilots were: Ltn Paul Bäumer with sixteen; Ltn Otto Löffler with nine; and Ltn Ernst Bormann with eight. Together these top three aces accounted for thirty-three aircraft, fully 72 per cent of the Jasta's total of forty-six for the month. With this bag of victories, Jasta Boelcke led not only JG III, but the entire German air force for recorded claims during the month.

The Americans

The United States declared war on Germany on 6 April 1917. Unready for war, the AEF had only landed 14,000 troops by June. Their first role in combat was in late October 1917, but by May 1918, the Americans had over one million men on the continent. Originally labelled the Aviation Section, Signal Corps, on 24 May 1918, the organisation was redesignated the Army Air Service, with forty-five squadrons serving in France. They were assigned 85 miles of the French sector, which became known as the American Sector. Although they participated in the spring 1918 Second Battle of the Marne at Château-Thierry and Belleau Wood, their first offensive action was at the Battle of Saint-Mihiel, beginning in the middle of Black September. Their first day in this combat was 12 September, where the Americans lost fifteen aircraft and claimed seven victories, including a balloon by Frank Luke.[41]

The Americans contributed fully for the first time in this high-scoring month. Some participants were surprised at their effectiveness. Historians credit the performance to their tactical leadership, which was derived from individual participation with the RFC, Lafayette Escadrille and the Armée de l'Air. The squadrons also demonstrated a high degree of teamwork, often with large numbers of aircraft from many squadrons. Their borrowed pursuit aircraft were very good with the Nieuport 28 and SPAD XIII, but the pilots were even better. This was due to the fact that well-educated young men in excellent physical condition flocked to the air service in large numbers. This was no different from other combatants, except that the American cadre had not been thinned by four years of arduous combat. Noted Australian historian, Russell Guest, added that the American aviators were all officers, and they had no inborn class hang-ups such as the British and French.[42]

Between 12 and 30 September, the American squadrons claimed 135 aircraft downed to a loss of eighty-seven. In the 18 days of fighting, Frank Luke scored eighteen of these victories, and Eddie Rickenbacker was well on his way to becoming the American ace of aces. Among the American units was the 90th Aero Squadron, which in Black September was assigned to Ourches aerodrome on the Somme River and scored seven confirmed aerial victories.

Opposite the Argonne Forest, the American 11th, 13th, 22nd, 28th, 94th, 95th and 96th Aero Squadrons were heavily engaged. Eddie Rickenbacker shot down a Fokker D.VII on 1 September and scored eleven more in the rest of September 1918. He would go on to gain twenty-six victories to become the American ace of aces. Major Carl Spaatz (future general) was flying with the 13th Aero when he downed one Fokker and damaged another. Overall, the box score for Black September can be estimated:

Best Estimates for Claims and Losses, Black September 1918

Nationality	Claims	Opponents Lost	Best Estimate
German	715	560	560
British	885		
French	90	107	107
US	135		
Allied Total	**1,110**	**107**	**107**

Source: Russell Guest, "Black September," in *Bloody April . . . Black September*, pp. 245-247

At the End – November 1918

German Karl Bolle returned from leave to Jasta Boelcke in mid-September 1918. On 1 November, he scored again and brought down an S.E.5. The last great air battle of the war was fought on 4 November, and the Jasta's Fokker D.VIIs scored six victories. The members of the squadron and their scores at war's end were: Karl Bolle (thirty-six); Ernst Bormann (sixteen); Otto Löffler (fifteen); Alfred Lindenberger (twelve); Gerhard Bassenge (seven); Hermann Vallendor (six); Karl Fervers (four); Paul Blunck (three); Johann Heemsoth (two); and Kurt von Griesheim (one). Leutnant Mynereck, Leutnant Schlack and Eberhard Fr von

Gudenburg had not yet scored.[43] Ten of the thirteen pilots had victories, and six were aces. The total of 102 victories of these ten pilots was 30 per cent of Jasta Boelcke's total for the war.

Then the pilots were told that as part of the negotiated ceasefire agreement, each squadron had to turn their aircraft over to the Allies. This was too much! The pilots decided that if they were required to give up their planes, they would make the ceremony memorable. Karl Bolle, their leader, describes the scene:

'[Jasta Boelcke] could be proud of the results of the first four days [of November], with nine aerial victories. According to the conditions of the ceasefire, its aircraft were to be given up to the Englishmen. It was not easy to convince the Staffel that this order was to be complied with. Yet it had to be carried out. The handover followed: each aircraft carried the glorious name of its pilot and the number of his victories. Thus they gave witness to the deeds which were accomplished by them.'[44]

With this one final act of defiance, Jasta Boelcke ended the war. The British pilots who received their aircraft must have been astounded. Jasta Boelcke was demobilised in 1919 with the rest of the German air force.

CHAPTER XV

Boelcke's Legacy

Oswald Boelcke's legacy was both immediate and long lasting. The immediate legacy was the impact on his men, the superior performance of Jasta Boelcke, the aviators of his period, his personal record of forty victories and the effect on the public. The longer-lasting legacy was his character and the contributions he made to the organisation of the German air force. To these must be added the continued influence of his men, many of whom later became commanders and aces with outstanding records. The fifth-ranking German ace in WWI, Joseph Jacobs, reminisced in a 1968 interview with Edward Sims, about the most famous scout pilots:

> 'We heard more about Coppens, Guynemer, Nungesser, Navarre, Ball and McCudden than the rest. Of ours, Voss was very good. Boelcke was probably the best. He taught us much and Richthofen learned from him.'[1]

Boelcke's Character
Oswald Boelcke was aggressive in the air, but modest and quiet on the ground. Ian Mackersey stated his conclusion about Oswald Boelcke's character:

> 'Boelcke, still regarded as one of the greatest fighter pilots of all time, wore his fame lightly. His great celebrity was said not to have affected him in the smallest way.'[2]

Boelcke's character was also noted by his opponents. Gwilym Lewis, 32 Squadron, RFC, wrote, 'I didn't like Germans as a whole, but I had respect for certain of them. The great commander Boelcke. I respected him tremendously. He was a splendid chap, and in an enemy sense, he was a gentleman.'[3]

A Colorado cowboy, Frederick Libby, went to Canada during WWI to join the RFC and had this to say about Boelcke, 'Every week Boelcke has one of his pilots drop over a list of our fellows who are prisoners and also the names of the ones who are wounded or killed. Damn decent chap, this Boelcke.'[4]

The Jasta Boelcke squadron commander at the Armistice, Oblt Karl Bolle, *Pour le Mérite*, was philosophical, 'Boelcke's lessons and Boelcke's spirit should be kept holy to the last bitter end.'[5]

Anthony Fokker, among many others, included Oswald Boelcke in a long list of heroes with chivalry. In 1931, Fokker wrote in his autobiography:

'What could Fonck, Nungesser, Guynemer, Bishop, Fall, McCudden, Boelcke, Richthofen, Immelmann, Udet, Lufbery, Bert Hall, Luke, Rickenbacker, or Landis ever do to equal their superhuman exploits under a shining sun for all the world to witness? If there is anything left of chivalry in modern warfare, they are the knightly ones.'[6]

Boelcke's Victory Record

Oswald Boelcke compiled a record of air-to-air victories that was unmatched in WWI history. From July 1915 to October 1916 he flew almost daily and downed twenty-seven British, eleven French and two unknown aircraft. There is a story behind every one of those exploits. There are some interesting features that can be derived from reviewing the list, however. He flew and scored in four types of aircraft:

Boelcke's Victories by his Aircraft Type

Type	Victories
LVG	1
Fokker E-Series	18
Fokker D.III	8
Albatros D.II	13
Total	**40**

It was a characteristic of WWI aviators, that if they lived through the first few weeks, they were destined to fly many different kinds of machines due to the rapid development of aviation technology. The aircraft he shot down also varied:

Boelcke's Victims by Aircraft and Nationality

Type	Victories	Nationality	
		British	French
B.E.2C/D	9	9	
F.E.2B	5	5	
D.H.2	4	4	
Sopwith 1½	4	4	
Voisin	3		3
Farman	3		3
Morane	3	2	1
Nieuport	2		2
Caudron	1		1
2-seat Pusher	1		1
B.E.12	1	1	
R.E.7	1	1	
Martinsyde	1	1	
Unknown	2		
Total	40	27	11

Boelcke's Impact on his Men

Oswald Boelcke made a deep impression on virtually everyone he came in contact with. The leadership of his men can be demonstrated by quotes from three pilots. Hauptmann Hans Ritter is a good example, as he wrote in retrospective:

'Under the leadership of a Boelcke, the German Jagdstaffels accomplished the wonderful feat of gradually checking the activities of the enemy aircraft to such an extent, despite their numerical superiority, that our own reconnaissance machines were eased of their burdens and could work again; at the same time they had sufficient forces left to put a very perceptible check on the activities of the enemy artillery planes that had hitherto worked practically unmolested. The attacks of the Entente [Allies] lost a considerable amount of thrust when their unconditional supremacy of the air was abolished. In the late autumn of bloodstained 1916, the Battle of the Somme slowed down to its end.'[7]

The second is Erwin Böhme (Boelcke's closest friend in Jasta 2) who wrote to his girlfriend, Annamarie, on 18 October 1916:

'It is somewhat unique [also translated "most remarkable"[8]] how Boelcke conveys his spirit to each and every one of his students, how he carries all of them away. They follow him wherever he leads. Not one would leave him in the lurch. He is a born leader. No wonder that his Staffel blossoms! We presently have received as reinforcements a number of excellent young men.

'Every victory which I achieve is counted not only for me, but also for my Staffel, and in its service we strive to achieve successes. It is called *esprit de corps*. That prevails the more so in the Boelcke Staffel and our outstanding young men are totally committed to it. It may indeed seem strange that I, an old character, have been so set on fire – but it is a holy flame.'[9]

The third is Vizefeldwebel Karl Friedrich Kurt Jentsch who arrived at Jasta Boelcke on 13 August 1918. In contrast to many of the new arrivals in that year, he had a great deal of combat experience. He started combat flying in Macedonia and was already an ace who had downed seven confirmed and seven unconfirmed aircraft. He was recommended to the Staffel by Leutnant Alfred Lindenberger, who had been his observer in FA234, and they had obtained two victories together. Lindenberger later became a pilot and served with Jasta Boelcke. Lentsch's interview and introduction to Jasta Boelcke is instructive on the subject of Boelcke's legacy:

'Today, shortly before lunch, I was called on the telephone. My old observer, Leutnant Lindenberger, was on the line. Upon his invitation, I flew to Chambry. Immediately after landing I was introduced to the pilots of Jagdstaffel Boelcke, which Lindenberger is a part of.

'Jagdstaffel Boelcke is led by Leutnant Bolle and belongs to Jagdgeschwader III, whose commander is Oberleutnant Loerzer, a knight of the *Pour le Mérite*. Under his energetic leadership the Geschwader has developed splendidly. It holds, thanks to the number of its victories, a prominent position in the army.

'Leutnant Lindenberger took me to the mess for coffee. The rectangular room made an impression of picture perfect cleanliness. Tablecloths as white as blossoms, uniform coffee service and flowers in vases, cleverly spread about, gave the tables a friendly look. Staffelführer Bolle sits at the head of the table.

'Next to his place stands the telephone, which is indispensable to a successful air service. On the walls hang pictures of the fallen. First was Hauptmann Boelcke and Oberleutnant Kirmaier, then came Leutnant Voss, Oberleutnant Bernert, Leutnant Ritter Max von Müller, Leutnant Walter von Bülow and many others.

'At one time our most important combat pilots began their careers in this Jagdstaffel: they absorbed Hauptmann Boelcke's teachings which brought about their unforeseen blossoming. Rittmeister Manfred Freiherr von Richthofen greatly excelled his teacher and master through his exemplary number of victories. I have to think of all of these things because they immediately come involuntarily to mind when one is a guest here.

'It was mentioned that two shot-down enemy aircraft were in possession of the Staffel, a SPAD and a Sopwith. If I wanted to, I could take them up, said Leutnant Bolle. I accepted this opportunity with joy; firstly, one would not be the dumber for it, and secondly, it excited me, just for military reasons, to put these two enemy machines through the motions.

'Lindenberger informed me, as we bade farewell, that Leutnant Bolle would apply for my transfer to Jagdstaffel Boelcke. I was very happy about this. Hopefully, Jagdstaffel 61 will not cross out the request.'[10]

Kurt Jentsch's time with the Jasta was limited as he was shot down and wounded in action on 4 September 1918. But he lived to survive the war. His former observer, Leutnant Alfred Lindenberger, also joined Jasta Boelcke in 1918 and was credited with sixteen victories. He too survived WWI. He joined the Luftwaffe prior to WWII, attained the rank of major and downed four aircraft in air defence of the Reich in 1944. He lived until 1973.[11]

Jasta Boelcke's commanders

After Oswald Boelcke's death on 28 October 1916, there were seventeen other officers who commanded Jasta Boelcke. Of these, seven were in an acting status, commanding only for a few days or weeks while a current commander was ill or on leave or a new commander was being appointed. Three commanders resumed command after a brief absence. Thus, between October 1916 and November 1918, Jasta Boelcke had seven permanent commanding officers. Of these seven succeeding Boelcke, three had served under the "master" while he was its commander. They were: Stefan Kirmaier, who joined the squadron in October, 1916, followed Boelcke in command but was shot down in November; Erwin Böhme, who joined on 1 September 1916, already with two victories, was involved in the tragic accident with Boelcke, and commanded for four months in 1917 until he was shot down; and Walter Höhne, who joined way back in August 1916, and commanded the squadron for a month in 1918. In addition, Max Ritter von Müller joined in September 1916 as an enlisted pilot and was appointed acting commander in January 1918. Boelcke's Dicta and training regimen were transferred to these men directly, and the lessons they learned at his feet (or cockpit) served them well as commanders and flight leaders. This was one of the first legacies of the great Boelcke.

Boelcke's Effect on the German Air Force

Oswald Boelcke's effect on the German air force was monumental and sequential. As soon as he began by downing aircraft in the summer of 1915, he was mentioned in dispatches to higher headquarters and among the flying sections. The effect was both motivational and instructive. It was motivational to the entire German air service as his fame spread, and it was instructive to other pilots and crew members who learned from his tactics. Of course, when he and Max Immelmann were awarded the Blue Max in 1916, their popularity and fame expanded exponentially.

The next increment of effect was in his articulation and documentation of the dicta. This contribution to tactics of air warfare had a direct effect on those pilots in his squadron, but the effect was multiplied by Lieutenant General Hoeppner's distribution of the dicta to other units.

A fourth increase in effect was realised when Boelcke organised and led Jasta 2 to the outstanding success in its first two months (September and October 1916). His death at the end of October extinguished any expectation of future accomplishments, but it neither diminished his fame nor his inspirational contribution.

Another legacy from Boelcke was a formal Jastaschule at Fomars, near Valenciennes. At that aerodrome, newly-graduated pilots who were to be assigned to fighter squadrons received formal training in acrobatics and aerial combat tactics, what we would now call "operational training". The effect here was the saving of lives, as the recipients learned and applied the lessons Boelcke had so painfully gained over his two years of combat flying.

A further legacy was the one left with his commanders and other members of the air force. Lieutenant General von Hoeppner compared the airmen of the Great War in an interview in 1917 that was published in the *Fort Wayne (Indiana) Sentinel*:

COMPARES AIRMEN OF THREE BELLIGERENTS
German Flying Commander Says His Birdmen Are Best for War.
The HAGUE, Netherlands-6 July 1917.
'In their Spad [sic] aeroplanes of 200-horsepower and the British Sopwith triplanes, they possess splendid machines which mostly equal our best machines. More important, however, than the superiority of the machines is that of the crews.

'To the British, flying is a sport, the climax whereof is a fight. They seek the combat regardless of the question whether the carrying out of the charge entrusted to them renders this necessary or not. The German is first of all soldier, who looks upon every flight as a military operation, and that decides his line of conduct. Our proportionately small losses, therefore, show that our commanders are too good soldiers to set their airmen impossible tasks. Moreover, the airmen are not sent out singly, for the fulfilment of military tasks is more important than all spirit of sport and bravery. The century-old German military traditions cannot be caught up by the three years' warfare of the British. With us, every soldier wants to be a Boelcke – the death of his comrades does not frighten him.'[12]

The organisational evolution from sections to squadrons was a major contribution. This concentration of similar type aircraft and crews into larger fighting units had a dramatic effect. As H.A. Jones wrote, 'The formation of these pursuit squadrons was to have a profound influence on the whole future air war on the Western Front.'[13] A lasting effect on the German air force and aviation history was articulated by author John Killen, in his book, *A History of the Luftwaffe*:

'Oswald Boelcke [is] the man responsible for turning a collection of men and machines into efficient fighting squadrons, and then outlining the tactics that would regain Germany the air supremacy that her defensive policy so badly needed. His instructions – the famous Dicta of Boelcke – were the most valuable legacy any airman could leave to his successors, and perhaps his greatest achievement was the way in which they so unfailingly stood the test of time.'[14]

Boelcke's Effect on the German Public

The Prussian high command made a conscious decision to broadcast the successes of Kurt Wintgens, Max Immelmann, Oswald Boelcke and many other successful pilots while they lived and to memorialise their exploits after their death. They had postcards – called Sanke cards (much like US baseball cards) – printed and distributed. These cards enhanced enthusiasm, were in high demand and rapidly became collectors' items. When the famous pilots depicted on the cards died, their memorials and funerals were covered in great detail by newspapers and radio. Sanke cards were even issued after their deaths. On the international scene, the American ace, Quentin Reynolds described the effect of Boelcke's exploits on the German people:

'Boelcke soon earned the love of the whole German people and the ungrudging respect of his foes, not only because of his ability but because of his nature. Generous, warm-hearted, he shrank from killing, and when he shot down a British aircraft without meeting death to the pilot, he invariably visited the defeated pilot in the hospital or prison camp. He would arrive laden down with wine, cigarettes and food, and long after the war British pilots spoke warmly of this generous enemy.'[15]

Boelcke, Immelmann, von Richthofen, and other famous fliers remained very popular in Germany into the 1940s. After the disastrous outcome of Germany's participation in the Second World War, most of its citizens underwent a long period of national guilt, reflection and the rejection of things military. The famous names of the two world wars fell into obscurity. As Colonel Gert Overhoff, former commander of the Boelcke Wing, 1980-1985, relates in the afterword, for many years following the war, it was not possible to learn to fly in Germany. Today, there are many German people who have never heard of Manfred von Richthofen, the Red Baron, let alone Oswald Boelcke. Claus Wollhaf, owner of the Red Baron restaurant at Berlin's Tegel Airport, estimates that less than one third of Germany's citizens have heard of the restaurant's namesake. An unscientific sampling by an editor of the US *Wall Street Journal* in 2015 suggests the proportion is even lower.[16] As time passes, the horrors of wars pass away, and it will be possible once again for Germans to honour the honourable men and women who contributed to their legacy of aviation.

Boelcke's Effect on the American Public

Archival research indicates that Oswald Boelcke was also well known to the American public. Beginning with his fame achieved by June 1916, US newspapers started picking up news of Boelcke's exploits and printing them. One of the earliest reports was in *The New York Times* on 30 June 1916, which claimed that Boelcke had shot down Victor Chapman, one of the original Lafayette Escadrille pilots. The article was written in London and provided by cable to New York. It read, in part:

> 'Boelcke, their pet enemy, was flying a small, fast machine painted entirely in black. He is extremely active and while no one fan disputes his courage, he takes no more unnecessary risks than advertising his presence by the colour of his machine.'[17]

The facts of this news article are wrong; he never flew a black airplane. But the article shows the awareness of Boelcke, and it amplified his name recognition to US readers. Also, Boelcke could not have shot down Chapman because he was not near Verdun on 22 June. He was at Douai attending the funeral of Max Immelmann. He remained there, flying several times, until he reported to the German air service headquarters at Charleville on 27 June. He did not return to Sivry on the Verdun Front until that evening.[18] Norman Franks comments that it was Kurt Wintgens who battled Chapman north of Verdun.[19] The truth we can derive from this article is that Boelcke was the most famous enemy to the British, and that he took no unnecessary chances.

Another news flash was printed in the *Dunkirk Evening Observer (NY)* on 4 November 1916 under the headline, "German Air Hero Buried Today: Highest Honours Shown Him, Chief of Air Fleet Swears to be Second Boelcke". The article added that the funeral was 'like that of a prince'.[20]

On 28 January 1917, *The New York Times* reported on a last interview with Oswald Boelcke on the day he died (see Chapter XIII). A search of other newspaper archives in the US alone revealed there are at least 180 articles on Oswald Boelcke in 114 different newspapers. Several of the articles were published during the First World War, and many of the columns were printed afterward. There was a spate of lengthy articles in 1927, many written by Milton Bronner from Berlin under the title, "The War Heroes of Germany".

One such article was written only four months after Charles Lindbergh's famous solo flight across the Atlantic. In July 1927 G.P. Putnam's Sons published Lindbergh's autobiography,

We: The famous flier's own story of his life and the transatlantic flight, together with his views on the future of aviation (New York, 1927). Bronner's readers in Charleston, SC, would have been familiar with the book, *We*, so the writer cleverly subtitled his column, "The First We". Several excerpts from this article about Oswald Boelcke are instructive:

'After his eighth victory he had won the *Pour le Mérite*, highest German reward for bravery. After his twelfth victory he had been made a captain, though he was only twenty-four, and though the German regulations do not permit captains to be younger than thirty.

'It was Boelcke and his plane "Wir" [We] who began German aggressiveness in the air and made the British admit that the German fliers were their equals.

'Boelcke was the man who brought knighthood into flower again. As his victims went to earth in their flaming coffins, he would tilt his wings – a last salute to those vanquished in the skies of battle. It was not a boast; it was tribute to his enemy.

'A Boelcke myth sprang up, in spite of his reticence, and nowhere did this myth spread more than among British airmen. There was glory unlimited for the knight of the air who could bring down Boelcke. It was an honour no allied airman ever won, for Boelcke was never defeated.'[21]

In 1935, several US newspapers including the *Charleston Gazette* published a multi-section cartoon of Oswald Boelcke, written by none other than the American ace of aces, Eddie Rickenbacker, with figures drawn by Clayton Knight. The title of the cartoon was "Hall of Fame of the Air". One of the sections depicted Boelcke visiting a comrade in a hospital ward, with the caption: 'Among friend and foe, Boelcke has a reputation for bravery and chivalry. He devoted many of his best hours to visiting wounded men he had brought down.'[22]

The most popular of the German flyers in WWI in US media is undoubtedly Manfred von Richthofen. Charles Schulz's cartoons of "Snoopy and the Red Baron" have delighted readers since their introduction on 4 October 1950. Snoopy's challenges, aerial dogfights and frustration with the baron are legendary. Frank Tallman, III, Orange County, CA's, most knowledgeable aviation historian, credits much of the Red Baron's fame to 'his teacher, Oswald Boelcke, who was considered the father of German combat aviation.'[23]

Boelcke's Effect on Other Fliers

There is a brotherhood of pilots and other aircrew members around the world which began with Oswald. They share the call to adventure, the challenge of crossing the threshold into the special world of flying, and the thrill of facing the ordeal. There is an enthusiasm in slipping 'the surly bonds of earth' and flinging one's 'eager craft through footless halls of air' as artfully described by John Gillespie Magee, Jr. in *High Flight*. The art of flying combines the skills of academic study and coordination of arm and leg movements. Expert pilots are said to 'have good hands'. Good eyes are essential for pilots to see other aircraft at great distances as well as their instruments. Flying by instruments alone requires focused concentration. Flying in close formation requires courage and intimate controls.

Boelcke's Effect on the Ground War

Oswald Boelcke's exploits were broadcast widely and had a huge following in the German army. That his success motivated the soldiers was inevitable. But assessing the effect of air power on ground operations has always been a controversial issue. Some air power advocates claim that air alone can win wars. Others claim that air forces exist only to assist the ground battle. From the experience of the First World War, General Erich von Ludendorff reportedly said that Manfred von Richthofen's presence at the front was worth three divisions.[24] John Cuneo cited the impact of the Fokker Eindecker and it famous pilots on the air service and the army:

'As the victories over enemy airplanes increased [in late 1915] and particularly as publicity suddenly exaggerated the accomplishments of Lieutenants Boelcke and Immelmann, the morale of the German air force began to soar and ground forces again began to have faith in it.'[25]

And again in the Battle of the Somme:

'Flying alone on 2 September [1916], Captain Boelcke scored his twentieth victory (a D.H. 2) and the reappearance of his name in the communiqué acted as a tonic to the ground forces.'[26]

John Cuneo mentions the effect of Boelcke's performance on the ground war for the third time:

'At the time of the attack [on 20 September 1916 in the Battle of the Somme] the Germans attained a local air supremacy. While the contact patrols followed the ground progress other German machines even attacked ground troops and artillery positions. Again the failure of the attack could not be laid to the lack of air support. Heavy air reinforcements poured into the Somme area and the stiffening of German morale by the widely publicised successes of Fighter Flight [Jasta] 2 (Captain Boelcke alone obtained twenty victories between September 8 and October 28 when he was killed in the crash following a collision in midair with a member of his flight) were only two of the factors contributing to the growing power of the German air service in the sector.'[27]

In the middle of WWII, British Field Marshal Bernard Montgomery is quoted as saying, 'First of all you must win the battle of the air. That must come before you start a single land or sea engagement.'[28]

Jasta Boelcke's Record of Claims & Losses

Jasta Boelcke was one of the most successful squadrons in the history of air warfare. From its inception in September 1916 to the Armistice in November 1918, the squadron compiled an air-to-air record that far surpassed anything previously established and is unique in aviation history. (See Appendix D)

The initial record is the period when Boelcke actively led the squadron – September and October 1916. Squadron pilots shot down twenty-one aircraft in September and thirty in October, with losses of only three each month. The "exchange ratio" for these two months is calculated by dividing the sum of the victories (21 + 30 = 51) by the number of losses (6), which is 8.5:1, a remarkable achievement. The remaining two months of 1916 yielded thirty-five claims against only four losses. When looked at individually, in the two months October and December 1916, the ratio each was 10:1.

1917 can be divided into three periods: January-March, Bloody April, and May-December. In the first three months, when there was bad winter weather, Jasta Boelcke shot down thirty-two aircraft, but lost eight of their own. January 1917 was their worst month in the entire war. They scored only three and lost five as several of the most experienced pilots were drawn off to join von Richthofen's Jasta 11.

In Bloody April Jasta Boelcke got twenty-one victories and lost only two, for a 10.5:1 ratio. The remaining part of the year was less dramatic: only forty-one claims against fifteen losses. The record would have been much higher, but after Bloody April, headquarters staff broke up the squadron with the rationale that there was too much first-class talent in one unit. The squadron commander was reassigned to the Palestine Front, and aces Bernert and Voss were transferred to other squadrons.[29] The dispersion of talent resulted in Jasta Boelcke's victory ratio decreasing from 1916's 8.6:1 to 4.1:1 for 1917. This was still outstanding and better than virtually all Allied squadrons.

The first six months of 1918 were undistinguished: claims of forty-five aircraft versus seven losses. July was a different story. In that month alone they shot down eighteen aircraft and only lost one – a record exchange ratio of 18:1. August was also good with eleven victories and no losses. September was truly "Black" for the Allies as Jasta Boelcke downed forty-six aircraft and only lost three for the month's third highest exchange ratio of 15.3:1. October was the banner month with eighteen victories and no losses. November's short month produced nine claims and one loss. Overall, the 1918 record shows 147 victories with only twelve losses; a 12.3:1 exchange ratio.

The total number of victories in the period of Jasta Boelcke's existence in the Great War was 336, including three balloons. The squadron lost only forty-seven aircraft for an overall exchange ratio of 7.1:1. However, many of the pilots shot down landed within the German lines and were only slightly injured or not at all. Franks, Bailey and Guest in *Above the Lines* recorded only forty-four casualties: thirty-one dead; nine wounded; two prisoners of war; and two killed in non-combat flying accidents.[30] This record of 336 victories was the second highest in the German air force, and was only exceeded by von Richthofen's Jasta 11 with 350.

The overall results from the air war in WWI are revealing and somewhat controversial. The official British history shows the relative statistics as 6,166 British dead as opposed to 5,853 German. However, these numbers probably understate the actual situation. British pilots flew mainly on the Western Front while Germans flew on both east and west. Germans fought the French and the Americans as well. The British historian H.A. Jones contacted the German Potsdam archives and received relative numbers relating just to the Western Front. His data showed 4,726 British deaths to 1,052 German. Jones is a 'competent and critical historian' who came to the conclusion that the British losses were about four times those of Germany.[31]

Jasta Boelcke Aces and Air Superiority

Jasta Boelcke produced twenty-five aces in the twenty-seven months of its existence. Ltn Paul Bäumer scored the most victories while serving in Jasta Boelcke by gaining forty (forty-three total). The highest-scoring ace overall, of course, was Manfred von Richthofen, who was one of the first pilots to join the squadron and scored his first sixteen victories in Jasta 2. The second highest was a young 19-year-old, Werner Voss, who flew with Jasta Boelcke from November 1916 until May 1917, scoring twenty-eight of his forty-eight total victories while in the squadron.

Oswald Boelcke's legacy directly influenced eight of the twenty-five Jasta Boelcke aces and indirectly motivated and helped train the seventeen others. The eight were: Böhme, von Richthofen, von Müller, Kirmaier, König, Höhne, Immelmann and Reimann, all of whom served directly under Boelcke while he commanded the squadron. They received his dicta and direct training in private conversations, squadron meetings, pre-flight briefings, in-flight formations and engagements, and post-flight debriefings. They obviously learned their lessons well.

There is a further point to be made about aces in general. It is fashionable in some circles of historians to claim that there has been too much attention paid to kings, generals and aces. Such focus on individual efforts – especially high-ranking ones – they say is not warranted given the large bodies of ordinary men and women who participated in making history. Nowhere is this more evident than in the history texts of the former Soviet Union, which systematically ignore individual heroes and glorify collective actions. With regard to the aces, these revisionist historians argue that the downed aircraft can be attributed to a large number of participants, and that elevating the role of the aces and the air war neglects the contributions of reconnaissance, bombing and ground support crews. Without tackling the importance of "air superiority" directly, they tend by inference to downplay the significance of winning the air war and its contribution to the ground campaign and overall victory.

The focus of this book has been on Oswald Boelcke and Jasta 2. As a final piece of analysis, we can interpret the detailed data on aces collected by Norman Franks, published in Jasta Boelcke, and the list of aces published by Franks, Frank W. Bailey and Russell Guest in *Above the Lines*. For Jasta Boelcke, the overwhelming majority of victories were conducted by a relatively small number of pilots – the aces. Twenty-five German aces flew at least part of their career in Jasta Boelcke. They are credited with 304 victories while flying in the squadron. If the overall squadron total of 336 compiled by Franks is correct, the squadron's aces accounted for 90 per cent of Jasta 2's victories. Surely, this is not a minor contribution to the overall effort. The quotations by German and Allied leaders noted in these pages confirm what the participants thought at the time about the importance of air superiority, the difficulties in achieving it and the men who made it possible.

Boelcke Wing in World War II

After WWI, the Versailles Treaty severely restricted German rearmament, and it prohibited the development of an air force. Hitler became chancellor in 1933, and in 1934 he started activities to rebuild the Luftwaffe. Kampfgeschwader (Battle Wing) KG154 was secretly commissioned at Fassberg near Hannover, Germany. In the spring of 1935, after unmasking the wing, it received the name "Boelcke" in line with the extensive Nazi propaganda campaign. In 1939, the wing was renumbered KG27. The unit had three squadrons and flew Heinkel 111 medium bombers. The wing was based at Tours, France, in 1940-1941, flew in the Battle of Britain, and was transferred to the Eastern Front in June 1941, where it fought 1942-1944. In late 1944 it was re-equipped with Messerschmitt Bf-109s and Focke-Wulf 190 fighters, which flew in air defence of the Reich until the end of the war.

Boelcke in the Modern Luftwaffe

The long-term legacy of Jagdstaffel Boelcke began with the Federal Republic of Germany (West Germany) inaugurating the new Luftwaffe in 1956. On 20 June 1958, Fighter Bomber Wing 31 was officially commissioned at Nörvenich air base, near Cologne, with F-84F Thunderstreak jet fighters. These aircraft had been provided to the Federal Armed Forces of Germany (Bundeswehr) as part of NATO's Mutual Defence Assistance Programme. It was the first operational jet wing to be assigned to NATO on 19 January 1959.

On 21 April 1961, the 43rd anniversary of the death of Freiherr Manfred von Richthofen, four jet wings of the new German air force received the honour to carry traditional names. Fighter Bomber Wing 31 at Nörvenich was one of this select few and received the name "Boelcke". The three other wings were named after: Max Immelmann, Manfred von Richthofen and Johannes Steinhoff. Later that year, the Boelcke Wing was the first to transition to the F-104 Starfighter. Twenty-two years later, in 1983, the wing was the first German air force unit to convert to the tri-national (UK, Germany and Italy) multi-role combat aircraft, Tornado. The wing operated the Tornado until 2010, when it was replaced with the EF 2000 Eurofighter Typhoon.

In October 2013, a reorganisation of the German air force brought Richthofen back to his old squadron leader, Boelcke. Jagdgeschwader 71 Richthofen (FW71 R) from Wittmund, was downsized to a Taktische Luftwaffengruppe (Group) Richthofen and put under the command of Taktisches Luftwaffengeschwader 31 Boelcke at Nörvenich, forming the

German air force's largest fighter wing. After the conversion to the Typhoon, starting in 2016, 100 years after Jasta Boelcke, Taktische Luftwaffengruppe R was upgraded again to a full wing, and Richthofen will become independent once more from his great teacher, Boelcke.[32]

Visit to Nörvenich

In August 2015, the author was privileged to visit the Boelcke Wing at Nörvenich air base, near Cologne, at the invitation of the wing commander, Colonel Stefan Kleinheyer. Besides the author, the visiting group consisted of: Colonel Gert Overhoff, commander of the Boelcke Wing from 1980-1985; Heinz-Michael Raby and Walter Waiss.

Eurofighter, the current steed of 31 Wing Boelcke at Nörvenich air base. (Heinz-Michael Raby)

As the author, I wanted to see how the legacy of Oswald Boelcke was being kept alive by the wing. I sat in the cockpit of a Eurofighter on static display, observed take-offs and landings, visited the Boelcke Traditionraum (tradition room), and had lunch with the Boelcke staff and pilots. The traditionraum is a base museum with hundreds of artefacts from the Boelcke family, government records and model aircraft showing the several types of aircraft Boelcke and the wing have flown, starting with the Fokker Eindecker.

Not surprisingly, the young pilots of the Luftwaffe were acquainted with the Boelcke name and recorded fame, but they were not aware of his specific historical achievements. Some of them, especially the more senior, knew Boelcke had been the author of the first set of air-to-air tactics. There is no special briefing to welcome new personnel to the 31st Wing, but new pilots are invited to become acquainted with Boelcke's exploits on their own. All of the personnel are proud to be a member of such a distinguished unit and consider themselves to be "Boelckianer".

Boelcke's presence is felt throughout the base. The street on which wing headquarters is located is named "Boelcke Allee". There is a bust of the master in the headquarters entryway. Portraits of Boelcke and his aircraft are hung in offices and hallways. Artistic renderings (some quite large) adorn the outsides of several buildings. The bright blue tail section of a Tornado aircraft with Boelcke's portrait sits adjacent to the main road. The Boelcke heraldic

Emblem of the Luftwaffe's Tactical Air Force
Wing 31 Boelcke. (Heinz-Michael Raby)

shield of the unit with its red wings and gleaming sword is found everywhere.
The base's monthly magazine is titled *The Boelcke Echo*. One of the summer events was labelled, "Girls Day bei Boelcke". The base football team's name is "Team Boelcke". The main ceremony in which the wing honours Oswald Boelcke is the annual pilgrimage of the wing commander and staff members to the Boelcke burial plot and memorial at Dessau, near Berlin, on the anniversary of his death.[33]

In appreciation of my visit, I wrote an article, "Where is Boelcke Today" which was published in the base magazine, *The Boelcke Echo*, under the title, "*Wo Finden Wir Oswald Boelcke Heute?*"[34] In summary, Boelcke's legacy is sustained to the current day in the Luftwaffe and around the world.

The author, Brigadier General R.G. Head, with Colonel Stefan Kleinheyer, Boelcke wing commander, in front of a Tornado tail section featuring a drawing of Boelcke's Fokker. (Heinz-Michael Raby)

CHAPTER XVI

Conclusions

'Oswald Boelcke is not remembered because he was a great pilot,' said Colonel Gert Over-hoff, a former wing commander of the Boelcke Wing. 'No, he is remembered because of his character.'[1]

One of the best examples of his character and humanity is recorded in the newspaper interview published first in Berlin and then in Salt Lake City, Utah. When he was asked by the reporter which of the honours showered upon him had pleased him the most, Boelcke answered:

> 'I was, of course, proud when I received the *Pour le Mérite*, and my elevation to the rank of a captain also made me happy, but my proudest moment was when I re-ceived a gold lifesaving medal for snatching a little French boy who had fallen into the Meuse from death.'[2]

Oswald Boelcke's character was formed from his birth into a middle-class German family, although one that had travelled and lived abroad. Arriving as the fourth child, he had none of the advantages of the first born or the nobility. He was small: five feet, seven inches tall. (Manfred von Richthofen was five feet, four inches.) Oswald contracted whooping cough in his early years and frequently suffered from its lasting symptoms: dry cough; tightness in the chest; difficulty breathing; wheezing; shortness of breath after exercise and lingering colds. It is commendable that he would seek to overcome these deficiencies in his school years. What is even more remarkable is that he chose to tackle this illness head on – by throwing himself into the vigorous sports of swimming, gymnastics and mountain climb-ing.

He was not a great scholar. There was little in his academic performance that would have predicted an outstanding career, although he was recognised on the school play-ground as a "leader". What comes across in the reading of his early life is the application of willpower, what Viktor Frankl called, "The Will to Meaning".[3] He obviously inherited much of his personality, even perhaps the tendency to introversion that was a common characteristic of WWI pilots. But he also learned that he was, to a large degree, the master of his own destiny. He willed himself to participate in sports; he forced himself to ignore or minimise the symptoms of his asthma. He pushed himself to analyse his situation when flying in WWI, and to relate it to the larger strategy and tactics of early aviation combat fly-ing. He also willed himself to get out in public. The tour to the east undoubtedly improved his ability to meet strangers and to speak to them on their own terms. In writing down his thoughts in letters, he practised his logic and descriptive capability. His set of fighter tactics were cogent and persuasive. Whatever the combination of introversion and extroversion he possessed, the result was a balance that supported his extraordinary skill as a fighter pilot and the leader of others as an outstanding squadron commander.

Individualism vs Teamwork

Single-seat fighter pilots are, by nature, individualists with a streak of daredevilry. The drive to volunteer, enter pilot training, master the techniques of formation flying and learn the aerobatics that are the essence of combat, are inherently individualistic. The student pilot is alone with an instructor. When they are subjected to a check-ride with an examiner, they feel very alone. No one can advise them, and no one can substitute for the person sitting in the seat. Many, many of the most famous pilots have been renowned – often infamous – for their individualism. Englishman Albert Ball was a loner and called his own technique 'going mad dog'. He flew alone and attacked formations of German aircraft in almost a desperate rush to get the next kill. Sometimes he would close to point-blank range, less than ten metres, fire and then dive away from the formation to escape. He reportedly would fly as many as twelve sorties a day. Ball had lots of company in the ranks of individualism. James McCudden, Billy Bishop, Roland Garros, Georges Guynemer, Arch Whitehouse and Frank Luke also were individualists. Often individualists defy regulations. And, they tend to die alone.

Individualism thrived in all of the air forces in the early war years. Max Immelmann and Oswald Boelcke achieved many of their victories by flying alone in either early dawn or late dusk. Flying alone was fostered somewhat by the dispersement of the few primitive fighter aircraft among many different units. For example, the first Fokker Eindeckers were allocated one to each of a dozen different sections. Immelmann and Boelcke started as individualists but ended up working as a team. They flew together on several occasions. Their Fokker monoplanes would be in a loose two-ship formation, and they found it to be a useful tactic in combat. Four eyes looking for enemy aircraft were better than two, and there emerged a kind of rough mutual support. The air services soon recognised the value of massed energy, which was implemented first in the creation of temporary sections of the same aircraft, and then in formal squadrons of fighters, reconnaissance and bombers. The KEKs were the first German organised units of multiple fighters. The Jastas followed with their larger concentrations of talent, technology and firepower.

Boelcke's professional life is a microcosm of this trend. In the first two weeks of September 1916, when Jasta 2 had fewer than six aircraft, he flew alone and scored seven victories. After the Albatroses arrived in mid-September, he organised and led flights of three to five then scored another fourteen victories.

Oswald Boelcke is studied in this book partly because of his character and partly because he was one of the first aviators to write down the principles of his action and teach and train his squadron pilots in their implementation. Boelcke is famous for his dictum, 'It is not the individual that counts, it is the Staffel.' As the technology improved, aerial combat intensified, and the massing of airpower increased. The culmination of this trend is found in the June 1917 reorganisation of Jastas 6, 7, 11 and 26 into Jagdgeschwader 1 which became the Flying Circus. Formations as large as eighty aircraft were the result. The idea of this massing tactic reasserted itself in fighters in the Battle of Britain's "Big Wing" formations and in bombers with the Eighth Air Force offensives.

Unifying Factors

Fighter squadrons in WWI and today embody a fundamental dichotomy. The components are individualists, sometimes extreme, often introverted, but they live and operate as comrades and professionals, under a collective set of tactics, techniques and procedures. Denis Winter points out that in WWI, the individualist impulse was moderated by three supportive institutions: rigid insistence on obedience to flying orders; total relaxation on the ground; and the creation of a corporate entity of teamwork, symbolised by the flying schedule, the dining hall (the mess) and squadron rituals. Let me explain.

I will never forget my first deployment in F-100s from Homestead AFB, Florida, to Itazuke air base, Japan. At Homestead we had four fighter squadrons, but massed wing maintenance – Strategic Air Command-style. One maintenance organisation repaired and maintained all four squadrons' airplanes. Our 306th Tactical Fighter Squadron was housed in one half of a building, sharing the facility with another squadron. In contrast, when we deployed to Itazuke, we had our own building, our own squadron maintenance and a separate table in the officers' club with a red squadron tablecloth! Years later, when I was stationed at Udorn, Thailand, we had squadron tables with squadron table cloths. A ritual? Yes, but a visible symbol of teamwork.

The same urge to collective distinction is found in the flying uniforms of pilots and other crew members. The baggy, fire-retardant flight suit and flight jackets are universal, but the outfits are personalised by the wearing of name tags and distinctive unit patches. The US Navy had the most distinctive jacket, made of soft leather with a fur collar. The distinction of aircrew members is maintained by the regulations that prohibit non-flying personnel from wearing flight clothing.[4] In Thailand, during the Vietnam War, each of the flying squadrons had colourful "party suits" which were full-length, cotton outfits that were informal, but had the aircrew's name, rank and wings embroidered. Powerful social forces operated to reduce and eliminate these "class" distinctions. However, some of them were permitted in the informality of combat. Within weeks after the end of the Vietnam War, non-flying personnel complained to the Inspector General, and higher headquarters issued orders that all military symbols of rank had to be removed from these social outfits. However, all military services still maintain degrees of separation and distinction among the ranks.

Boelcke's Dicta Revisited

Chapter VIII listed and discussed the principles that Oswald Boelcke wrote down and taught to his squadron and other pursuit pilots. Their development, distribution and application were the origin of air-to-air tactics, the first tactics manual. Since then, there have been numerous studies that have clarified, revised and expanded these "rules". The value and contribution of these tactics endure both as historical examples and current doctrine, modified as necessary by recent experience, advancing technology and circumstances.

The Hero as Myth

Oswald Boelcke was a hero of WWI. His character has been verified by countless colleagues. From his earliest days as a schoolboy, his contemporaries commented on his leadership abilities. He prepared himself for the adventurous life, and when the war came he was positioned in a small group of fliers whose exploits caught the public imagination. He, von Richthofen and others were catapulted into fame. The French started the publication of aerial exploits; the Germans followed; and the British very reluctantly gave in to the trend. It is not surprising that their real-world actions would become mythic projections, as the "collective wish" of the public. Sigmund Freud had said, 'Myths are public dreams; dreams are private myths'. Karl Jung expanded the thought when he wrote, 'Myths represent the wisdom of the species by which man has weathered the millenniums'. Oswald Boelcke and many other fliers were genuine heroes, but their mythic elements magnified, inspired and lifted the spirits and motivation of millions of people, young and old. That their actions were publicised and exploited for public relations purposes needs to be recognised, but this does not detract from their accomplishments. What matters is how we think about their accomplishments in the light of what we know, and their impact on our lives.

In reviewing the life of Oswald Boelcke, I am struck by the degree to which he characterises Air Force General Ron Fogleman's core values: 'Integrity First; Service above Self; Excellence in all we do'. (see the foreword.)

Air Superiority

The term air superiority has been mentioned frequently in this book, and its attainment and meaning deserve some attention. The US Department of Defense (actually the Joint Chiefs of Staff) define air superiority as, 'that degree of dominance in the air battle by one force that permits the conduct of its operations at a given time and place'.[5] Other definitions add the capability of denying this to the enemy.

The analysis in this book suggests that the Fokker Eindeckers were the first to establish air superiority, even if it was on a small scale. Then superiority transferred to the French by massing aircraft in the early phases of the Battle of Verdun (February-March 1916). As the KEKs with their experienced pilots were concentrated opposite Verdun, air superiority switched back to the Germans from April to June. The period of German dominance ended with Immelmann's death in June 1916. The British undoubtedly held clear air superiority in the first phase of the Battle of the Somme (from July until the middle of September 1916). In addition to having more airplanes, the British employed a new tactic of extensive and repeated mission of bombing the German fighter air bases. This destroyed many German fighters on the ground and kept the remaining few involved in air defence battles well behind the front. The combination of tactics thus opened the door for relatively unopposed Allied offensive reconnaissance, photography and bombing missions. The British also dominated in fighter quality, tactics and quantity, and they were able to prevent the German air service from interfering.

However, the British lost air superiority to the Germans under Oswald Boelcke from 17 September 1916 until Bloody April 1917. This was due to four primary factors:

1) Better German fighters;

2) Superior organisation with the Jastas;

3) Better tactics;

4) Boelcke's leadership and influence.

As we have seen after their beating in April 1917, the Allies introduced faster and more manoeuvrable fighters and vastly outnumbered the German air force, regaining air superiority which they maintained until the end of the war on 11 November 1918.

However, the full meaning of air superiority and its effect on war is more nuanced than just who is winning the air battle. The French commandant of aviation of the Vaux-Douaumont sector noted in a report on 3 May 1916, that despite one side's control of the air, it was impossible to prevent the opponent from gaining temporary air superiority at a chosen point by the concentration of his forces. It is this inherent flexibility that is, after all, a key feature of airpower. The ability to mass, disperse and focus is a powerful capability. The conclusion to be drawn from history is that air superiority is a useful concept to characterise large trends, but it is not absolute and can be gained for specific periods for focused purposes.[6]

In the Battle of the Somme, the British learned that obtaining air superiority was necessary in support of trench warfare as a prerequisite for effective artillery fires. Air superiority was required to permit the virtually unhindered use of reconnaissance and aerial direction of artillery. Thus, the British lesson was that air superiority must precede the artillery battle, even in a situation where air is not the primary military arm.[7]

The German reacquisition of air superiority under Lieutenant General von Hoeppner and the Jastas presents another interesting feature. The Germans attained air superiority in the third month of the Battle of the Somme (September 1916) almost exclusively by the success of their fighter pilots. The conception of the German leaders was that air superiority needed to be won by air combat alone. This conception neglected the potential contribution of "offensive counter-air" missions, bombing and strafing enemy airfields and aircraft on the ground. Although both world wars and Vietnam have shown this mission to be of high risk, with large losses, the mission has high pay-off to achieve an overall objective.

Jasta Boelcke's Missions

Virtually every nation's air force began in its army. It is both natural and inevitable that the first missions and flying units were closely connected to army missions. Thus, the earliest air missions were reconnaissance and artillery spotting. The German air service policies of using its force sprang from its army origins and evolved as technology improved the quality of the aircraft and the needs of the air service became more apparent over time. The initial mission assigned to the biplanes and Fokker monoplanes of Field Aviation Section 62 was that of "escort" – to provide armed protection for slower aircraft, who themselves were performing reconnaissance, artillery spotting or bombing. An example was demonstrated in Boelcke's letter to his parents of 30 June 1915:

'As the French tried to obstruct our reconnaissances round Arras by means of fighting machines, we have now got a few of them to protect the section machines when out reconnoitring. When the others take off on artillery flights, etc., I go up with them, fly about in their neighbourhood and protect them from enemy attacks. So if a Frenchman comes along, I pounce on him like a hawk, while our other machine goes on calmly flying and observing. Meanwhile I whack the Frenchman by flying up to him and giving him a good hammering with our machine gun. Those chaps bolt so quickly that it is really glorious. I have whacked about a dozen Frenchmen in this way. It is great fun for me.'[8]

Note that this mission, which we call at this time "escort" is not dependent on a particular type of aircraft. Boelcke was flying an LVG biplane. Fokker's timely construction of the Eindecker was one of the first examples of an aircraft built for a specialised mission. The mission of escort is, 100 years later, one of the functions of offensive counter-air, which the US defines as a mission of 'operations aimed at destroying, disrupting, or limiting enemy air and missile threats'.[9] Even at this early time [1915] Oswald Boelcke, Kurt Wintgens and Max Immelmann departed from this army-derived and relatively passive function, to perform what we would call "fighter sweep" – the hunting and killing of enemy aircraft wherever they are to be found. Again Boelcke's own words describe the change in mission, *which he developed*. This mission of fighter sweep was not assigned from higher headquarters; he developed it on his own initiative. His letter of 16 July 1915 is an example of how technology enables doctrinal innovation:

'*Douai. 16.7.15.* In addition to its technical points my little single-seater [Fokker Eindecker] possesses the advantage of giving me complete independence; I can fly when, where, how long and how I will. I have not caught anyone else over our lines – the event of 4.7 [4 July] has given the French a mighty scare and they treat my single-seater with holy respect.'[10]

This letter documents the freedom that as a German junior officer, Boelcke felt free to exercise with his little monoplane. Later in the same letter, he describes the essence of offensive counter-air:

'Most of the other gentlemen flying Fokker fighters – there are only eleven all told so far on the Western Front – think differently and do not intend to attack anywhere but behind our lines, because they can fight to a finish there only. That is certainly true, but the consequence is that they do nothing but go for joyrides round our lines and never get a shot at the enemy, whereas I have the pleasure of getting a good smack at the fellows over yonder. *One must not wait till they come across, but seek them out and hunt them down.*' [emphasis added][11]

No clearer definition of offensive counter-air is needed.

When Boelcke's section was moved to Jametz opposite the Verdun battlefield early in 1916, the three KEKs were assigned the mission of "barrage" or "barrier patrol". This is a "*defensive* counter-air" mission, which is, 'to protect friendly forces and vital interests from enemy air and missile attacks and is synonymous with air defence'.[12] Barrier patrol is one of the most inefficient and ineffective methods of defence.

The reason this mission is inefficient is that fighter aircraft tend to be small and have a limited fuel supply. It takes many, many aircraft sorties to maintain a constant barrier as the (usually) two-ship flights have to be replaced on station every hour or so, and they have a limited range of sky they can cover. The German leaders quickly realised this strategy required more airplanes, and they diverted several two-seater squadrons from their bombing missions to barrier patrol. Modern-day air-to-air refuelling has made this tactic more practical, but it is still very expensive. It is also ineffective because the routine of a constant patrol allows attacking aircraft to spot and gain a height advantage in initiate an attack or to penetrate into a neglected area. Barrier patrol is also – like guard duty – deadening, as boredom quickly sets in, and the bored aviator is not likely to spot an attacker until he is close by. Being on the receiving end of the first volley is not a position the fighter pilot wants to be in.

Between February and June 1916, Boelcke's missions varied from offensive to defensive counter-air as opportunities presented themselves. Defensive when intruders were spotted penetrating the German lines and offensive when he and his comrades flew westward to find targets.

When Boelcke returned from his inspection trip to the east, he established Jasta 2. When the Albatroses arrived, he intuitively led the squadron mostly on "fighter sweeps". These were independent actions, in flights of three to six aircraft, seeking enemy planes whenever and wherever they could find them. Boelcke's tactics – his dicta – are oriented on this offensive, aggressive use of airpower, which he used so successfully.

It must be noted, however, that the RFC's use of numerous bombing raids on German air service airfields was also a mission of counter-air, offensive counter-air (OCA). As air force doctrine states, 'most OCA operations will prevent the launch of aircraft and missiles by destroying them and their supporting systems on the ground.' If they can't take off, they can't beat you in the air. As the Allied air forces increased in numbers, and the Germans declined, this mission was increasingly effective for the Allies. Boelcke's journal is full of notations that the squadron had to move its location because they were being bombed or shelled effectively. While there were only four aerodrome moves in 1916, Jasta Boelcke moved eight times in 1917 and 17 times in 1918.[13]

A Final Note

Boelcke's biographer, Professor Werner, provides a thoughtful summary of this young pilot's contribution to aviation and history:

'Boelcke's letters also show the enthusiasm which he gave to the training of his Staffel. His skill in the air, his mastery of the tactics of aerial warfare and above all his inspiring and yet tranquil steady personality made him a leader and instructor who remains second to none. He picked out his pupils with unfailing discrimination, grounded them thoroughly in all technical details, imbued them with the spirit of unselfish teamwork and welded them into a fighting unit with thrusting powers that had never before been seen in the air. Through his foundation of a school which turned out a large number of brilliant scout aces Boelcke rises above his personal masterly achievements to grow into a figure of historical importance in war aviation. For a master of aerial single combat, he developed into a masterful instructor of organised teamwork in scout flying.

'What Boelcke taught his pupils was no blind, headlong thrustfulness but a combination of daring and deliberation. He held that an attack should only take place after a careful deliberation of the circumstances which might motivate an avoidance of combat or even a direct retreat; once an attack had been decided upon, however, it was necessary for the leader to carry it through with an impetuous obstinacy while still keeping a cool head. That is the principle which Boelcke adopted from the very beginning of his war flying – the combination of vigour, audacity and prudent restraint with which his firm, resolute, balanced nature endowed his entire personality.'[14]

Secrets of Boelcke's Success –a Summary

- Positive attitude. Oswald Boelcke set high goals for himself and worked to achieve them. He was not deterred by his middle-class social standing, his stature or his health.
- Character. He developed a moral character of integrity. He respected others and treated them fairly. He maintained a humble countenance despite his growing fame and celebrity status. His character is apparent in his frequent letters to his family and the many efforts he took to visit and honour the opposing airmen he encountered.
- He looked for opportunities. Writing to the Emperor at age 10 was a bold move that paid off in his appointment to the military academy. He flew often and voluntarily. Boelcke flew when he didn't have to. No squadron commander in the Royal Flying Corps was expected to fly with his men. Boelcke led from the front.
- He became physically active and strong, despite his chronic asthma, which allowed him to withstand the rigors of open cockpit flying.
- By the time fighter combat began in 1915, he had accumulated experience through many hours of flying time, and he developed more in the Fokker Eindecker.
- Boelcke developed, followed and taught a strict, disciplined regime of flight briefing-flying-debriefing. His insistence on this routine is an example of the discipline with which he balanced freedom of flying. He was a true leader to his men.
- He observed the situation of the moment, developed tactics and taught them to his colleagues. He was a master tactician and became a leader who influenced the first organisation of fighter squadrons.
- He was a talented flier and a gifted gunner. These are the reasons he became famous, but not the reasons he became important to the history of aviation. Other pilots scored higher; he had the character to look out for others, teach them from his experience and thus develop a lasting legacy.

Oswald Boelcke started flying in 1914, achieved forty victories and was killed at age 25 in a freak accident with his own wingman. He tends to be overshadowed by aces who flew later in WWI and had more victories. Examples include Manfred von Richthofen (eighty victories), René Fonck (seventy-five), Billy Bishop (seventy-two), Ernst Udet (sixty-two), Mick Mannock (sixty-one), and James McCudden (fifty-seven). These men flew at a time when more aircraft were being produced and more targets were available in the sky. Their armament was no better than the two Spandau machine guns that Boelcke fired, but their engines had more power and drove the aircraft faster and higher. At the same time, their two-seater victims were not much faster, so the faster fighters had a higher overtake rate, which added to surprise and lethality. In fairness, it should be acknowledged that the later aces on both sides were also fighting against pilots who were more skilled and better trained than Boelcke's victims. Even though Oswald Boelcke did not fly in the last two years of the war, his final record of forty victories places him tenth among the list of top German aces, a remarkable achievement.

In Boelcke's time, everything involving aviation was new, untried and tentative. The separation from ground forces and army commanders was not clear, and every change was controversial. What should be the organisation of this new force? What should pilot training teach? What were the features of the best airplane? What were the best tactics for fighter aircraft in combat? Boelcke answered these questions in his time. We are left to do the same in ours. Aviation has evolved to address these questions and others. But these were the early days of aviation, and the men and women who participated were real pioneers.

Oswald Boelcke did not invent air-to-air tactics, the squadron organisational system or the German air force. Still, because his contributions to air warfare were so profound, he is considered the father of all three. He is the central figure in air warfare across the spectrum of history.

Ode

He shall not grow old, as we that are left grow old
Age shall not weary him, nor the years condemn.
At the going down of the sun and in the morning
We will remember him.

From "For the Fallen"
Robert Laurence Binyon

Tornado of 31 Wing Boelcke, Nörvenich,
Germany, 2015 (Heinz-Michael Raby)

AFTERWORD

The author, Brigadier General (ret.) R.G. Head, has made a remarkable effort to answer all questions as correctly as possible, which might come up when looking at the person of Oswald Boelcke. The appendices and bibliography alone testify to that. The result of his searches is an astonishing book with two aspects, in my view. The first is the fact that it shows our complete knowledge about Oswald Boelcke; the second, however, more important to me, is that it has been written by an air force officer of a former enemy nation without ideological prejudices, which might generally be expected under these circumstances.

The question today is certainly legitimate: What is so fascinating about the person of Oswald Boelcke 100 years after his lethal mid-air collision with his wingman when in a pursuit situation? It's neither the number of his aerial victories – other pilots accumulated higher numbers – nor the observation that he was particularly daring and courageous. No, it was the sum of his characteristic features. Beyond his military virtues Oswald Boelcke was a man who paid respect to everyman, always keeping their dignity in mind. That was also true towards his wartime opponents, which he had to fight against. He considered them as "victims of politics" just like himself. There was no negative or any hostile perception. Instead, he always proferred his hand in mutual understanding. Above that he was the first German flyer recognising the tremendous potential of a fledgling aviation for wartime purposes. He worked constantly for the improvement of military aviation in all aspects. He developed tactical rules, the importance of which is still valid today.

What does Oswald Boelcke mean to me?

When I was a child, I used to build aircraft models of all types. I was very interested in aviation in general, military models in particular. So I tried to gather aviation publications of all kinds. In this way I also learned about WWI, the fledgling development of fighter aircraft and their pilots. I also read about Boelcke, Richthofen, Immelmann and others. Of course, I was too young to understand everything about the meaning of that time period. At the age of 12, I decided for myself that I wanted to fly, no matter how. Since at that time, flying in Germany was not possible so soon after WWII, I planned to go to Switzerland to become a pilot. As time went by, just before I finished Gymnasium (German term for high school) Germany became a new NATO partner, so consequently I joined the Luftwaffe. It never crossed my mind that I might fail during the pilot training. Well, I was right not to care about that. My first operational aircraft for the first two years was the Republic F-84F, serving as a fighter-bomber. The following Lockheed F-104G became my main tactical aircraft for some 20 years, thereafter the Panavia Tornado. My last "little bird" was the E-3A NATO AWACS. In all the years of active military duty and private flying, sixty-one different aircraft types are in my logbooks.

During the first flying years, I was simply too busy to enjoy the fulfilment of my dream. Philosophical thoughts came up later, when I got an assignment as commander of an F-104 squadron and started to develop tactical models to safeguard against Russian weapons systems like the ZSU-23/4 [the four-barrelled anti-aircraft gun] (quite successfully by the way). After initially and obviously naively trying to get higher command levels to support my idea, I learned from reading about such problems in WWI. Without really recognising it, I was following Oswald Boelcke's path right there. From the first silly answers from higher headquarters, I stopped asking permission for anything, but did what had to be done without asking further questions. No weapon is sharper than the plain truth. It was then that I started to follow the good reasoning of an exceptional person like Oswald Boelcke.

When I was lucky enough to get an assignment as commander of Luftwaffe Wing 31 Boelcke I started to think about the heritage of Oswald Boelcke. I sensed a certain pride within my troops, very similar to 71 Richthofen Wing and 51 Immelmann Wing. After the fall of the Iron Curtain in Europe, we were immediately on the way to Dessau [which had been in Soviet East Germany] to visit the Boelcke Memorial. From then on we keep travelling to Dessau each year to visit the place on 28 October, the date of his lethal collision with his wingman. This has developed into a lasting tradition. We try to remind everybody again and again to measure up to Boelcke's personality. It does not work on everybody, though. There are always people who don't care. But the majority are thoughtfully listening and – hopefully – following.

The wing at Nörvenich was my little "kingdom". It was a pleasure to observe my men and their spirit. There were almost no disciplinary actions necessary within four years of high activity. In my period there, we had our conflicts with peace movement demonstrations, but we simply won the "battle"; it was fun to see how it worked.

There is no doubt in my mind that the example of Oswald Boelcke in combination with my experience in and with NATO has changed my view of the world. Today, no one would get me to point a gun at a Brit, a Frenchman or an American. Thus, a man of WWI becomes a good example over the past generations and those to come in the future.

Therefore, I am rather happy that the author characterised the personality of Oswald Boelcke so well and published an excellent book. I hope that all readers will follow Boelcke's example; certainly it would be a great benefit for this crazy world.

Gert Overhoff

Colonel (ret.) Luftwaffe

former commander Tactical Air Force Wing 31 Boelcke

St. Augustin, Germany

2016

APPENDIX A:
OSWALD BOELCKE CHRONOLOGY

19 May 1891	Oswald Boelcke is born in Giebichenstein, Germany, near Halle, a small town of Saxony-Anhalt, the fourth child of six.
1901	At age 10, Oswald writes to the Emperor, asking for an appointment to the military academy.
Summer 1908	Boelcke masters mountain climbing in the Austrian Alps.
Early March 1910	Boelcke graduates gymnasium with abitur distinction.
15 March 1910	Boelcke joins the Third Telegraph Battalion at Koblenz as an aspirant.
January 1912	Boelcke enters the military academy at Metz.
July 1912	Boelcke commissioned as an ensign in the Telegraph Battalion.
2 August 1912	Promoted to "swordknot ensign".
1 October 1912	The German Fliegertruppe (Flying Force) is established.
Late August 1913	Boelcke promoted to leutnant (2nd lieutenant).
2 June 1914	Begins pilot training at the Halberstädter Fliegerschule (Halberstadt Flying School).
28 July 1914	World War I begins as Austria-Hungary declares war on Serbia.
1 August 1914	German army mobilises for WWI.
3 August 1914	France and Belgium enter WWI when Germany invades Belgium and declares war on France.
4 August 1914	The United Kingdom enters World War I, declaring war on Germany.
15 August 1914	Boelcke graduates from pilot training, earns his Prussian pilot's wings. His initial assignment is to a replacement section at Darmstadt, flying an Aviatik B.I.
1 September 1914	While ordered to fly from Trier to Sedan, he 'inadvertently' lands at Montmédy, the field of Flying Section 13 and visits his brother, Wilhelm.
Sept-Dec 1914	The two brothers fly numerous reconnaissance missions in two-seat LVG V and Albatros B-Series biplanes.
12 October 1914	Boelcke awarded the Iron Cross, 2nd Class, for flying fifty missions.
December 1914	Boelcke first flies unarmed Fokker M8 monoplane.
January 1915	Boelcke awarded Iron Cross, 1st Class.
April 1915	Section commander transfers Wilhelm to Aviation Reserve Section in Posen, eastern Germany.
25 April 1915	Boelcke transferred to Flying Section 62 at Döberitz.
Spring 1915	Boelcke hospitalised, but 'escapes'.
May 1915	Meets Max Immelmann in Flying Section 62.
	Fokker invents the synchronised machine gun and demonstrates in several locations, including at Section 62 in Douai.
1 July 1915	Fokker Scourge begins when Leutnant Kurt Wingtens shoots down a French Morane-Saulnier L two-seat Parasol while flying the Fokker Eindecker E.5/15, M.5K/MG prototype, achieving the first

aerial victory using a synchronisation gear. The victory is unconfirmed because the aircraft fell beyond German lines.

4 July 1915	Boelcke and his observer flying an LVG-VI, shoot down a French Morane-Saulnier Parasol monoplane. The ace race is started.
7 July 1915	Boelcke's first flight in the armed Fokker E.I monoplane.
Summer 1915	Boelcke is promoted to oberleutnant (first lieutenant).
1 August 1915	Max Immelmann shoots down French plane for the first official Fokker Eindecker victory.
19 August 1915	Boelcke shoots down his second aircraft, a Bristol biplane, while flying Fokker E.3/15.
28 August 1915	Boelcke saves a French boy from drowning.
September 1915	Boelcke develops the two-ship tactic of flying together for mutual protection, shocking his opponents.
9 & 25 September	Boelcke scores third and fourth victories over French opponents.
1 October 1915	Boelcke meets Manfred von Richthofen on a train.
16 October 1915	Boelcke shoots down a French Voisin, his fifth victory; becomes an ace although this term is not recognised in the German air service at this time.
30 October 1915	Boelcke downs victory number six. Boelcke and Immelmann's success leads the other Eindecker pilots to become increasingly aggressive, causing great concern among the RFC and French units. Allies forced to add escorts for reconnaissance missions.
1 November 1915	Receives award of Knights Cross of the House of Hohenzollern, with Swords.
24 December 1915	Receives Ehrenbecher goblet.
12 January 1916	Oswald Boelcke and Max Immelmann gain their eighth victories and are awarded the *Pour le Mérite*, the Blue Max.
21 February 1916	German army launches a battle of attrition at Verdun.
February 1916	The German air service establishes *Kampfeinsitzer Kommando* (single-seat battle units, KEKs) consisting only of fighter aircraft at Vaux-en-Vermandois, Jametz, Cunel, and other strategic locations to act as *Luftwachtdienst* (aerial guard force) units.
	Boelcke is hospitalised with intestinal problems at Montmédy; then transferred to KEK Jametz, near Verdun.
11 March 1916	Boelcke allowed to command small section, KEK Sivry-sur-Meuse, close to the front.
24 March 1916	Boelcke writes technical document, "Report on the 160 HPE Machine".
April 1916	German air service begins to fly in pairs with a section leader and wingman.
21 May 1916	Boelcke shoots down number seventeen and the Emperor promotes him to hauptmann. This makes him the youngest captain in the history of the Prussian army. He departs on leave to Dessau.
May-Jun 1916	Boelcke develops drafts of his dicta.

12 June 1916	Boelcke is informed he is to get command of his own Staffel.
18 June 1916	Max Immelmann gets two victories, for total of seventeen, but is killed in an E.III Eindecker.
24 June 1916	Boelcke reports to headquarters and learns he is grounded. He negotiates an inspection tour.
27 June 1916	Boelcke flies twice over Verdun and shoots down his nineteenth.
1 July 1916	British and French launch the Somme offensive.
10 July 1916	Boelcke begins his tour to Austro-Hungary, the Balkans and Constantinople in the Ottoman Empire.
8 August 1916	Boelcke is recalled, receives orders to form and command Jasta 2.
10 August 1916	German air service orders two-seater units to consolidate into permanent bomber units, Kastas, and single-seat scouts into Jagstaffeln or Jastas.
20 August 1916	Boelcke ends his tour of the east and returns to Dessau.
27 August 1916	Boelcke reports to Jasta 2 at Bertincourt and begins the unit's war diary.
29 August 1916	Field Marshal von Hindenburg replaces General von Falkenhayn as chief of the general staff. His first decision is to terminate the offensive at Verdun and concentrate forces to defend the Somme.
1 September 1916	Jasta 2 receives its first aircraft: one Albatros D.I and two Fokker D.IIIs.
2 September 1916	Boelcke takes off on Jasta's first sortie and shoots down his twentieth.
8-15 September	Boelcke flies frequently, getting double victories on both the 14th and 15th; total score on September 15 is twenty-six.
16 September	Six new Albatros aircraft arrive; Otto Höhne downs the first non-Boelcke aircraft.
17 September	Boelcke flies Albatros D.II No. 387/16, shooting down number twenty-seven. Leutnants von Richthofen and Hans Reimann get one each.
22-23 September	Boelcke is grounded with an asthma attack; relinquishes command of Jasta 2 for two days.
30 September	Jasta 2 completes its first month with twenty-five victories; Boelcke's total is twenty-nine.
8 October 1916	The Emperor declares the transition of the German air service to the German air force; Liuetenant General von Hoeppner, chosen to be the commanding general.
1-25 October 1916	Boelcke flies the Albatros and gets ten more victories, numbers thirty to thirty-nine. Von Richthofen gets his number six on 25 October.
26 October 1916	The date of Boelcke's last victory, bringing him to a total of forty.
28 October 1916	Oswald Boelcke is killed when he and his wingman, Erwin Böhme, collide and Boelcke's Albatros spins out of control.
30 October 1916	Oberleutnant Stefan Kirmaier promoted to hauptmann and is appointed commander of Jasta 2.

31 October 1916	Oswald Boelcke's memorial service is conducted at Cambrai Cathedral, France. His parents, three brothers, Crown Prince Rupprecht of Bavaria and hundreds of mourners attend.
	Jasta 2 records thirty-two victories for the month, for a September-October total of 53-57.
2 November 1916	Oswald Boelcke's state funeral is held in Dessau, his hometown, where the coffin was placed on a bier before the altar in St. John's Church.

APPENDIX B:
THE VICTORIES OF OSWALD BOELCKE

Sources: Norman Franks, 1991 Appendix to Professor Werner's *Knight of Germany*, pp. 272-275, with the column on "Boelcke's Aircraft" added by the author. Reprinted by permission of Casemate Publishers. Data cross-checked with Trevor Henshaw's *The Sky Their Battlefield II Expanded and Updated* (Fetubi Books, London, 2014).

No.	Date	Boelcke's Aircraft	Victim	Notes
			1915	
1	4 July	LVG C-1 biplane	Morane-Saulnier Parasol	Lt Tetu and Lt de la Rochefoucauld of MS15, both KIA. Crashed near Valenciennes.
2	19 Aug	Fokker E.I	Bristol biplane B.E.2C?	2 Sqn British Capt J.G. Hearson DSO/Capt W.R. Barker. Forced-landed beyond front lines with shot-up fuel pipe.
3	9 Sept	Fokker E.II	Morane-Saulnier 2-seater	Crashed near French front trenches. Douai: evening. Two killed. (No French casualties recorded.)
4	25 Sept	Fokker E.II	Voisin?	Crashed in front lines near Pont-à-Mousson. (MF29 lost two Farmans on this date.)
5	16 Oct	Fokker E.II	Voisin B1	Crashed near St Souplet, AM. (VB110 lost one aircraft on this date.)
6	30 Oct	Fokker E.II	2-seat pusher?	Crashed near Tahure, AM. (MF8 lost a Farman on this date.)
			1916	
7	5 Jan	Fokker E.IV	B.E.2C (1734)	2 Sqn RFC 2/Lt W.E. Somervill. Loyal North Lancs Regt/RFC, WIA/POW. Lt G.C. Formilli, Royal Garrison Artillery/RFC, WIA/POW. Near Harnes, Hénin-Liétard.
8	12 Jan	Fokker E.IV	R.E.7 (2287)	12 Squadron RFC, 2/Lt Leonard Kingdon, Worcs Regt & RFC. KIA. (Aero Cert No. 1533, 4 Aug 1915) Lt K.W. Gray, 3rd Wilts Regt/RFC, WIA/POW north-east of Turcoing, AM.

No.	Date	Boelcke's Aircraft	Victim	Notes
9	14 Jan	Fokker E.IV	B.E.2C (4087)	8 Sqn RFC, 2/Lt Justin Howard Herring, RFC MC (SR), wounded by three bullets in small of back. From Surrey. Aero Cert No. 1430, 13 July 1915. Capt Ralph Erskine, Royal Scots Fus/RFC, from Glasgow, wounded in the leg, but died in captivity 1 Jan 1918. Forced-landed in front-line trenches near Flers. Aircraft destroyed by artillery fire.
10	12 March	Fokker E.IV	Farman	Forced-landed in front trenches E of Mare, AM. No French aircraft reported lost but several airmen were wounded on this date.
11	13 March	Fokker E.IV	Voisin	Crashed 1 PM. Malincourt, Verdun. One crew of BM113 wounded this date.
12	19 March	Fokker E.IV	Farman	Crashed near Cuissy, 1 PM. MF19, Lt Libman and Sgt Galiment, both killed.
13	21 March	Fokker E.IV	Farman	Forced-landed Fossers Wood, 11:15 AM. From either VB109 or VC111 Escadrille.
14	28 April	Fokker E.IV	Caudron	Crashed, Verdun Front, near Vaux. No French two-seaters reported lost.
15	1 May	Fokker E.IV	Biplane	French front lines, evening. Two French airmen wounded this date.
16	18 May	Fokker E.IV	Caudron 2 engine	Forced-landed, evening near Ripont. C56 lost one aircraft this date.
17	21 May	Fokker E.IV	Nieuport	Crashed, AM, near Morte Homme. Two French Nieuport pilots wounded on this date.
18	21 May	Fokker E.IV	Unknown French	Crashed, evening at Bois de Hesse. AL209 and C42 each lost an aircraft this day.
19	27 June	Prob. Fokker E.IV	Unknown French	Crashed evening. Douaumont. No known French losses this date.
20	2 Sept	Fokker D.III biplane 352/16	D.H.2 (7895)	First victory in Jasta 2. 32 Sqn. Capt Robert E. Wilson, Hamps Reg & RFC, POW. Controls and engine hit; forced-landing on fire near Thiepval.

No.	Date	Boelcke's Aircraft	Victim	Notes
21	8 Sept	Fokker D.III	F.E.2B (4921)	22 Sqn. Lt Eynon Berorge Arthur Bowen, RGA & RFC. Served in France with artillery and later as air observer. Aero Cert No. 2541, 6 June 1916. Lt Robert McCallum Stalker, 5th Seaforth Highlanders, att'd RFC. Both killed when they fell from their spinning and burning machine, near Flers.
22	9 Sept	Fokker D.III	D.H.2 (7842)	24 Sqn, Lt Neville Philip Mansfield, N'ton Regt & RFC. Aero Cert No. 2384, 22 Nov 1915. Fell in flames over front lines near Bapaume.
23	14 Sept	Fokker D.III	Sopwith 1½ Strutter (A1903)	70 Sqn, 2/Lt John High Gale, RFC (GL). From Oxford, KIA. Sapper J.M. Strathy, 2nd Canadian Div, Sig. KIA. Machine fell and disintegrated south of Bapaume.
24	14 Sept	Fokker D.III	D.H.2 (A7873)	24 Sqn 2/Lt J.V. Bowring, 5th Lancers Regt & RFC. POW after forced-landing near Driencourt.
25	15 Sept	Fokker D.III	Sopwith 1½ Strutter (A895)	70 Sqn, Capt Guy Lindsay Cruikshank DSO, MC, RFC. French Aero Cert No. 1520, 9 Aug 1913. KIA. Lt Rudolph Arthur Preston, MC Lincs Regt. Att'd RFC, KIA. Fell near Hebecourt, Ypres.
26	15 Sept	Fokker D.III	Sopwith 1½ Strutter (A1910)	70 Sqn 2/Lt F.H. Bouyer, WIA, POW. 2/Lt W.B. Saint, RFC, died of wounds.
27	17 Sept	Albatros D.II 386/16	F.E.2B (7019)	First use of the Albatros D.II aircraft in which Boelcke shot down Capt David Benjamin Grey, 11 Sqn. 48th Pioneers, Indian Infantry/RFC, POW. Aero Cert No. 2263, 10 Jan 1916. Lt L.B. Helder, Royal Fus, POW. Forced down near Equancourt and crew set the machine on fire. Jasta 2 brought down a total of four 11 Sqn F.Es in this fight.
28	19 Sept	Fokker D.III	Morane V Bullet (A204)	60 Sqn, Capt Hugh Christopher Tower, RFC (SR), aged 30, KIA. Aero Cert No. 486, 23 April 1913. Fell in flames into Grevilliers Wood, early evening.

No.	Date	Boelcke's Aircraft	Victim	Notes
29	27 Sept	Albatros D.II	Martinsyde G 100 (A1568)	27 Sqn, Capt Henry Arthur Taylor MC, Royal West Kent Regt/RFC. KIA. Aged 18 from Wimbledon. Aero Cert No. 2306, 18 Jan 1916. Went down over Ervillers.
30	1 Oct	Albatros D.II	D.H.2 (2533)	32 Sqn Capt H.W.G. Jones. Aircraft crashed in a shell hole and abandoned, NW Flers.
31	7 Oct	Albatros D.II	Nieuport 2-seater	Crashed in flames at Morvai. Possibly a Nieuport XII of F24, lost this date.
32	10 Oct	Albatros D.II	D.H.2 (A2539)[1]	32 Sqn, 2/Lt M.J.J.G Mare-Montembault, uninjured. Controls shot away. Crashed just inside British lines at Mouquet Farm. German artillery destroyed aircraft.
33	16 Oct	Albatros D.II	B.E.2D (6745)	15 Sqn, Sgt F. Barton, KIA; 2/Lt Edward Mervyn Carre, Lincs Regt/RFC. KIA. Carre was 22, served in the Artist' Rifles in 1914 and was commissioned into the Lincolnshire Regt in 1915. Transferred to RFC May 1916. Elder brother killed in 1915. Crashed into front trenches near Hebuterne.
34	16 Oct	Albatros D.II	D.H.2 (A2542)	24 Sqn, Lt Patrick Anthony Langan-Byrne, DSO, Royal Artillery/RFC. KIA. Fell east of Bullencourt.
35	17 Oct	Albatros D.II	F.E.2B (either 6965 or 7670)	One of two F.E.2Bs lost this morning by 11 Sqn in fight with 20 German aircraft. A/C 6965 also claimed by Ltn Leffers, Jasta 1, but victory awarded to Boelcke. 6965 piloted by 2/Lt C.L. Roberts, crash-landed in no man's land, hid until night, walked in fog, but captured, POW. 2/Lt Pulleyn, RFC, KIA. A/C 7670 shot down in same fight. 1/Lt W.P. Bowman, RFC, KIA. 2/Lt G. Clayton, RFC, KIA. Victory awarded to Oblt S. Kirmaier, Jasta 2.

No.	Date	Boelcke's Aircraft	Victim	Notes
36	20 Oct	Albatros D.II	F.E.2B	11 Sqn, Lt Robert Parsons Harvey, 4th Norfolk Regt/RFC. Aero Cert No. 2766, 10 Apr 1916. WIA. 2/Lt George Keith Welsford, RFC, KIA. Welsford was 25, educated at Harrow. School champion lightweight boxer. Dispatch rider 1915, commissioned June 1916. Crashed inside British lines west of Angy although Welsford was thrown out during the descent, falling into the German lines.
37	22 Oct	Albatros D.II	B.E.12 (6654)	21 Squadron, 2/Lt W. I. Wilcox, W. Yorks Regt/RFC. POW. Fell on fire south of Bapaume.
38	22 Oct	Albatros D.II	Sopwith 1½ Strutter (A7777)	45 Sqn, one of four lost during an air battle this AM. A1061, 7777 and 7786 all fell to Jasta 2, over Grevillers Wood/Bapaume. 2/Lt G.B. Samuels, RFC, KIA.
39	25 Oct	Albatros D.II	B.E.2D (5781)	7 Sqn, 2/Lts William Fraser, KIA. Bernard Tarrant Collen (GL). POW 26 October. Crashed east of Puisieux-au-Mont mid-morning.
40	26 Oct	Albatros D.II	B.E.2D (5831)	5 Sqn, 2/Lt J.S. Smith, WIA. Lt John Cedric Jervis, RFC, KIA. Smith, age 26, had previously served with the Royal Fusiliers. Jervis was killed in the air, and the B.E. fell into British second-line trenches where it was shelled on the ground.

Appendix C:
Jasta Boelcke Aces

Source: Compiled from Norman Franks' data, *Jasta Boelcke*, Appendix E.

Name	Victories w/Jasta 2	Total Victories
Ltn Paul Bäumer	40	43
Ltn Karl Bolle	30	36
Ltn Werner Voss	28	48
Ltn Erwin Böhme*	22	24
Haptm Oswald Boelcke	21	40
Ltn Otto Bernert	20	33
Ltn Ernst Bormann	16	16
Ltn Manfred von Richthofen*	16	80
Ltn Otto Löffler	15	15
Ltn Max Ritter von Müller*	12	36
Ltn Hermann Frommherz	10	32
Ltn Alfred Lindenberger	9	12
Oblt Stefan Kirmaier*	8	11
Ltn Karl Gallwitz	8	10
Ltn Richard Plange	7	7
Ltn Gerhard Bassenge	7	7
Ltn Erich König*	6	6
Ltn Otto Walter Höhne*	6	6
Ltn Hans Imelmann*	6	6
Ltn Hermann Vallendor	6	6
OffzSt Leopold Rudolf Reimann*	4	5
Oblt Adolph Ritter von Tutschek	3	27
Ltn Dieter Collin	2	13
Haptm Franz Walz	1	7
Ltn Theodore Camman	1	12
Totals	304	538

*Trained by Oswald Boelcke in Jasta 2

APPENDIX D:
JASTA BOLECKE'S RECORD OF VICTORIES & LOSSES

Source: Compiled from Norman Franks, *Jasta Boelcke*, Appendices C and E

Year	Month	Victories Month	Victories Cum	Losses Month	Losses Cum	Ratio Month	Ratio Cum
1916	Sep	21	21	3	3	7	7
	Oct	30	51	3	6	10	8.5
	Nov	25	76	3	9	8.3	8.4
	Dec	10	86	1	10	10.0	8.6
Totals		86	86	10	10		8.6
Year	**Month**	**Victories Month**	**Victories Cum**	**Losses Month**	**Losses Cum**	**Ratio Month**	**Ratio Cum**
1917	Jan	3	89	5	15	0.6	5.9
	Feb	14	103	3	18	4.7	5.7
	Mar	15	118	0	18	Inf	6.6
	Apr	21	139	2	20	10.5	7.0
	May	5	144	3	23	1.7	6.3
	Jun	1	145	1	24	1.0	6.0
	Jul	0	145	0	24	Inf	6.0
	Aug	1	146	2	26	1.0	5.6
	Sep	6	152	4	30	1.5	5.1
	Oct	11	163	2	32	5.5	5.1
	Nov	18	181	2	34	9.0	5.3
	Dec	8	189	1	35	8.0	5.4
Totals		103	189	25	35		5.4
Year	**Month**	**Victories Month**	**Victories Cum**	**Losses Month**	**Losses Cum**	**Ratio Month**	**Ratio Cum**
1918	Jan	6	195	2	39	3.0	5.3
	Feb	5	200	1	40	5.0	5.3
	Mar	10	210	2	42	5.0	5.3
	Apr	3	213	1	43	3.0	5.2
	May	8	221	1	44	8.0	5.3
	Jun	13	234	0	44	Inf	5.6
	Jul	18	252	1	45	18.0	5.9
	Aug	11	263	0	45	Inf	6.1
	Sep	46	309	3	48	15.3	6.7
	Oct	18	327	0	48	Inf	7.1
	Nov	9	336	1	49	9.0	7.1
Totals		147	336	12	49		7.1
Grand Totals		336		49			7.1

Appendix E:
Evolution of the Albatros fighter

The Albatros fighter was the most famous aircraft of 1916 and remains an iconic symbol of its time. It was designed by Albatros technical director Robert Thelen, a rated pilot, as a single-seat, one-bay biplane in the spring of 1916 with the factory designation of L.15. The aircraft was designed around the Mercedes/Daimler engine and featured two Maxim machines guns. The aircraft included five different models as the war continued through 1918.[2]

Albatros D.I Design

Robert Thelen's design contained three innovations: 1) The plywood fuselage combined longitudinal strength with light weight; 2) The aircraft's lightness and its 160-hp Mercedes engine gave a top speed of 109 mph, among the fastest of the period, with an amazing ceiling over 15,000 feet; 3) The twin Maxim machine guns provided concentrated firepower that was double that used previously on either side. Although the second and third of these features are the most commonly mentioned, the plywood construction of the fuselage was a major contributor to the aircraft's success. The Russian designer, Steglau, built the first aeroplane made entirely of plywood in 1913. Robert Thelen borrowed these techniques and fashioned the fuselage with longerons over plywood bulkheads. He then enclosed the frame with plywood sheets that gave the aircraft flat sides, but the top and bottom of the fuselage were formed by thin sheets, molded to provide curves. The plywood sheets were fastened to the longerons and bulkheads with screws or nails. The surface sheets became an integral part of the structure and made it light and streamlined. The resulting fuselage was completely free of internal bracing – a semi-monocoque technique. The fuselage was not painted, but varnished.

The design was sleek and aerodynamic with streamlined struts. There were two Windoff "ear" radiators, one on each side of the fuselage. The cabine struts were set in an inverted "V" configuration, with the top wing positioned high above the fuselage. The D.I underwent static and dynamic testing beginning on 6 June 1916. Static-load test results were mixed until the top rear wing spar was strengthened. The aircraft was cleared for production in July. The first D.Is were delivered to Jasta 1 in August of 1916 and Jasta 2 in September. The airplane was an immediate hit. It was well built, sleek, rugged, fast, heavily armed and easy to fly.

The Airframe

The fuselage featured a round nose, which tapered back to the two flat sides. The design of the fuselage was semi-monocoque, which meant that the stresses were shared between the external skin and the internal frame. This resulted in great strength with minimum weight. The frame was made of spruce wood. The forward longerons up to the cockpit were of ash, and those from there to the tail were also of spruce.

The two wings were of constant chord with slightly unequal span, the lower being somewhat shorter than the upper. They were framed with basswood ribs, capped with ash, and two wooden spars held in alignment with compression bars parallel to the ribs. Metal crosswires with turnbuckles were fastened internally between the ribs to provide rigidity and strength. The entire frame was covered with linen fabric sewn to each of the ribs and covered with multiple applications of dope to weatherproof the fabric.

The Cockpit

The pilot was seated immediately behind the two machine guns in a deep and spacious cockpit. The stick was topped with a spade grip, composed of two wooden hand grips that straddled the two machine-gun triggers, which were operated by the pilot's thumbs. The engine throttle was also on the stick, with an alternate on the left quarter panel. The controls had no trim tabs, but there was a locking lever that could hold the stick fore and aft. The rudder was conventional, except that there were no pedals, just a bar with two metal straps over the pilot's boot toes. There were no brakes, only the metal tail skid shoe that dug into the ground to slow the machine on landing.

Instruments were meager – there was no instrument "panel" as such. The only gauge directly in front of the pilot was a tachometer, mounted to the metal bar holding the machine-gun breeches. There was a fuel-pressure gauge tucked behind a wooden former and a fuel-quantity gauge mounted on the right-hand cockpit wall. Altimeter and airspeed indicators were not included in the factory machines, but some were retrofitted. There was no clock. Some pilots strapped their pocket watch to their wrists. The only navigation instrument was an alcohol magnetic compass mounted in a pedestal on the floorboard – similar to those in boats and ships. There was a map case and flare holders.

There were numerous engine and fuel controls. The left cockpit wall held an engine magneto switch key, attached to a chain, a spark-retarding level, and a starting magneto crank. The engine was not started by the ground crew swinging the propeller; they would only prime the engine, following which the pilot would engage the magneto and hand-crank the magneto lever creating a spark that ignited the fuel in the cylinders.

The right-hand quarter panel contained four valves: a fuel-pressure gauge valve control; an air pump selector; a fuel tank air pressure lever and a fuel-tank flow selector. Finally, the right-hand cockpit wall held a hand-operated air pump to pressurize the fuel tanks and a water pump grease gun that the pilot had to twist a half-turn every 10 minutes to keep the water pump lubricated.[3]

Another unusual feature of the Albatros was its landing gear. The axle was not mechanically attached to the landing-gear struts. It was held in place only by wrappings of bungee cord, which acted as a shock absorber upon landing. Steel restraining cables limited axle travel and acted as a safety feature in case of bungee failure.

The Machine Guns

The Albatros fighter carried two Maxim machine guns of 7.92 mm mounted atop the fuselage and firing through the propeller. Ammunition was 1,000 rounds, 500 for each gun. The guns were manufactured at the Spandau arsenal outside Berlin; hence the term, "Spandau machine gun". The design for the gun was invented by Hiram Maxim, an American, in 1883 as a recoil-operated, belt-fed machine.[4] Maxim settled in London in 1900 and became a

British citizen. His gun appeared in Germany in 1908 and was designated the MG.08, using the 7.92 rifle cartridge. The infantry version used a water jacket for cooling, but the air-craft-mounted one used a perforated jacket for the barrel. Anthony Fokker used the Maxim for his synchronized gun experiments in 1915. Actually, the design for an interrupter gear was patented by Swiss inventor, Franz Schneider in 1913, but it had not been tested. The engineers at the Fokker factory modified, machined and tested the design and produced the model MG.08. Barrett Tillman in the USA's current magazine, *Flight Journal*, notes this was one of the first 'system aircraft' because the result was a 'weapon system' combining the aircraft and gun. Fokker integrated the gun on his Eindecker E.I, and the Fokker Scourge began.

The Engine

The Mercedes D.III engine was a marvel of its time. The D.III ("D" for Daimler and III for >150 hp) engine was a six-cylinder, water-cooled, in-line design that developed 160 hp at 1,450 rpm. In reality, at altitude the output varied between 130 and 180 hp.[5] First produced in 1914, it was so powerful that few airplanes could be designed to handle it before 1916. By then, the horsepower had been increased to 160 and would increase to 217 by the end of the war. The remarkable design featured many items common to other Daimler engines: over-head camshaft; steel cylinders (at a time when many others were cast iron or aluminum); dual ignition and dual spark plugs driven by two Bosch magnetos; cast-iron pistons with drop forged steel domes; self-starting utilizing the Bosch hand-starting magneto situated within the cockpit; one dual Mercedes twin-jet carburetor; carburetor mixture pre-heating; and a decompression setting to facilitate starting.[6]

Mercedes D.III Engine with 160 hp (Mark Miller)

These early Mercedes engines ran at a much lower rpm than modern engines. The 160 hp was measured at 1,450 rpm, with a slightly higher maximum speed. Current reciprocating engines perform between 2,000-2,700 rpm. (Above that speed the propeller tips became supersonic.) Current automobile engines reach 7,000 rpm and motorcycles top 10,000. The Mercedes aircraft engine had a very short stroke with a correspondingly low compression ratio (4.73:1), but responsive to the low octane fuel of the time. For comparison, the compression ratio in a current automobile is 9.0-9.5:1, featuring small pistons and long strokes. All the engines of WWI were limited by the fuel available. Aviation fuel was mainly benzene and produced almost exclusively by distillation – separating chemical components by weight. The octane rating of 1916 aviation fuel was never above 70, and American manufacturers were producing gas with gasoline with octanes in the range of 45-50. Oil companies had not worked out how to introduce additives to their product to increase the octane rating and thus eliminate "knocking" in the cylinders at higher revolutions. There was no firewall between the engine and the pilot.

Engine Characteristics: Mercedes D.III (Source: John Weatherseed, "Mercedes Engine History", *The Vintage Aviator*)

Power/ weight	Horsepower	Cylinders	Rated RPM	Bore (mm)	Stroke (mm)	Compression	Weight
.64	160	6	1450	140	160	4.73:1	660 lb

Anthony Fokker was exceptionally impressed with the Mercedes engine. The vast majority of his aircraft used rotary Gnome and Le Rhône engines produced by the Oberursel firm, where Fokker bought a controlling interest, but he was clear in his praise of the Mercedes:

'From the front came the constant cry for more power. Manufacturers worked day and night to answer that demand, but it was not until early in 1916 that a really splendid engine was adapted in Germany to combat flying. That was the 160-hp water–cooled Mercedes, which remained the outstanding aviation motor, with the later developed 185 BMW, during the final period of the war.'[7]

The best objective evaluation of the Mercedes D.III was published in England in January 1917. The RFC examined a captured Albatros D.I and produced the following report:

'If we are not altogether enamoured of the design ... the workmanship and finish embodied on the Mercedes are, on the other hand, such as to excite admiration, for they are certainly of the very finest. Moreover, it is very evident that reliability almost to the exclusion of all else has been the object sought after. This is revealed by the "heftiness" of every internal working part; even in the reciprocating members little or no effort seems to have been made to cut down weight to an extent likely to influence reliability. On the contrary, it is clear the designers have, as we suggested above, been content to limit revolutions, and by doing so take the advantage permitted to increase the factor of safety, the result being that the Mercedes – as it undoubtedly is – is an engine comparable with an ordinary car engine in the matter of infrequent need for attention and overhaul, long life, and unfailing service except for accident.'[8]

Albatros D.II

The D.II was designed and constructed simultaneously with the D.I in the summer of 1916. It was not the result of operational feedback. Nevertheless, the D.II contained several improvements over the D.I, and these were retained with subsequent

The production Albatros D.II with "cheek" radiators, 1916.

models. They included the inversion of the cabine struts in an "N" configuration, which were splayed *outward* from the side of the fuselage to the upper wing. The builders also lowered the upper wing by 250 mm (9.8 inches). Both of these changes greatly improved the pilot's visibility. On the prototype D.II, the Windoff radiators were replaced with a Teeves & Braun design that fit smoothly into the centre of the upper wing, providing a streamlined surface. In later models, the radiator was shifted to the right to prevent scalding water from the radiator falling on the pilot in case of battle damage. The Teeves & Braun versions were retained in all subsequent aircraft of the D-Series.

The company completed production of the D.II at the Johannisthal facility, the East German (Ostdeutsche) Albatros Werke (OAW) and under license by LVG. In December 1916, the Austrian Aircraft Factory (Oeffag) received an order for twenty D.IIs to support the Austro-Hungarian army and Imperial air service. The Oeffag machines had an upgraded 185-hp Mercedes.

Albatros D.II Features (R. L. Rimell, *Windsock Datafiles*)

Wingspan	27 ft, 10 in (top wing)
Length	24 ft, 3 in
Engine	Mercedes D.III, 160 hp
Armament	2 Maxim (Spandau) 7.92mm machine guns, w/ 1,000 rounds
Gross Weight	1,980 lbs fully loaded
Maximum Speed	109 mph
Rate of Climb	600 ft per min.
Ceiling	15,250 ft
Weight Empty	1,484 lbs

The D.III Design[9]

The third model, D.III, retained most of the features of the D.II, but the wings were changed dramatically. In the autumn of 1916, while the Albatros factory was rolling D.IIs out of the door, the inspectorate provided French Nieuports to three firms and requested designs of improved aircraft using a thinner lower wing (less chord). The Nieuports featured a sesquiplane design (literally "one and a half wings"), which the officials believed made their aircraft highly manoeuvrable. Robert Thelen immediately set about to redesign the D.II's lower wing, using only one main spar. He also rounded out the after fuselage with its traditional plywood covering. This extended the curved sheets to both sides of the airframe, making the fuselage oval or virtually round in many places.[10] This made the aircraft even more streamlined. The upper wing was lengthened by nearly 2 feet, and the chord decreased by 4 inches. The lower wing was lengthened by 2½ feet, and the chord reduced by 2 feet. In aeronautical engineering terms, the aspect ratio (the relationship of the wing's length to its chord) on the D.III's top wing was increased from the D.I/II's 5.32 to 6.00. The lower wing was much more dramatic as its aspect ratio was increased from 5.00 to 7.95 (long and narrow).

During the production run, the Mercedes engine was upgraded by redesigning the pistons, and the horsepower increased from 160 to 170. Between April and August 1917, Albatros received contracts for 840 D.IIIs. About 500 were built at Johannisthal airfield,

Berlin. Then it shifted production to its subsidiary, Ostdeutsche Albatros Werke (OAW), where more than 1,300 were built.

The result was the Albatros D.III, perhaps the highest performing model of the entire series. The top speed remained the same at 109 mph, but the rate of roll and of climb was greatly increased. The time to 1,000 metres (3,281 feet) was decreased from 4 minutes to 2 minutes, 30 seconds, a decrease of 37.5 per cent. Albatros D.IIIs began arriving at the front in January 1917, but structural failures of the wing resulted in the aircraft being grounded from 27 January to 19 February. Strengthened the wings did not eliminate the structural problems, but the D.III remained an outstanding performer. It was well respected by the pilots and became the dominant aircraft in Bloody April 1917.

The D.IV

The D.IV was a test bed for an improved, higher compression ratio Mercedes engine, and only three were built.

The D.V Design

The D.V dimensions were virtually the same as the D.III, and the Mercedes engine remained the same at 170 hp. The most notable difference was the change to a fully elliptical fuselage, making the aircraft lighter and more streamlined. The aileron cables were rerouted to run from the fuselage up to the upper wing and then out to the wing-tip control surfaces. It also incorporated a different wing/fuselage interface that eliminated the fairing where the lower wing attached to the fuselage. This difference turned out to be critical. Since the wings were unchanged from the D.III, Idflieg performed tests only on the fuselage and missed a fatal flaw. When the D.V arrived at the front in May 1917 there were numerous wing failures, mostly of the lower wing. The upper wing also suffered failures of the outer wing panels. Performance also suffered. The rate of climb to 1,000 metres *decreased*. The time to higher altitudes also increased over the D.III, but was still faster than the D.I/II.

The inspectorate was caught in a trap of its own making; having not advertised for more advanced aircraft in the nine months since August 1916, its officials had no choice but to order more D.Vs. They contracted for 200 in April 1916, 400 in May and alluded to contracts for 1,500 over the next six months. Ultimately, only another 300 of the D.V design were built because the design shifted to the next version.

German pilots became distraught over the D.V, many of whom favoured the older D.III. Manfred von Richthofen was especially irate. In a July 1917 letter, he described the D.V as 'so obsolete and so ridiculously inferior to the English that one can't do anything with this aircraft'. Albatros responded to this feedback with the D.Va.

The D.Va Design

The first design requirement was to correct the deficiencies of the D.V. This resulted in stronger wing spars, heavier wing ribs and a reinforced fuselage. This added weight, and the D.Va was 50 lbs heavier than the D.III. The added weight was compensated for by using a high compression 180-hp Mercedes D.IIIa engine. Both wings of the D.Va and D.V were within inches of those of the D.III, and they were, in fact, interchangeable. The aileron cable linkage was also changed and reverted back to the D.III's design where the aileron cables ran out through the lower wing and then over pulleys and upward to the top wing. This was to increase the responsiveness of the ailerons in a roll. The D.Va's struts were fitted with a small diagonal brace where the strut connected onto the lower wing.

Idflieg contracted for 262 D.Va aircraft in August 1917, 250 additional in September and 550 in October. Initial deliveries to the field began in October 1917 and continued through the winter and spring of 1918. But the design had outlived its utility; it was obsolescent. The Allies had superior aircraft in front-line squadrons. The British introduced the amazingly manoeuvrable Sopwith Camel (115-125 mph) and the S.E.5 (130-138 mph). The French deployed an advanced version of the Nieuport 17 (110 mph), the rugged SPAD VII (119 mph) and SPAD XIII (138 mph).

The German air force hoped the Fokker Dr.I Triplane would replace the Albatros, but top wing failures of the triplane, also in October 1917, resulted in two dramatic crashes that grounded the aircraft. The Ostdeutsche Albatros Werke, which had built many of the D.III model, received orders for 600 of the D.Va in October, the same month as the grounding order. Production ended in April 1918. The German air force had no alternative but to keep flying the Albatroses until the Fokker D.VII arrived at the front in the summer of 1918. By that time, there were 131 Albatros D.Vs and 928 D.Vas still flying on the Western Front. They continued to be active until the Armistice on 11 November 1918.

Production numbers for Albatros D-Series were:[11]

Prototype D.I/II	12
D.I Production	50
D.II	291
D.III	1,340
D.IV (Test models)	3
D.V	700
D.Va	1,605
Total	4,001

Appendix F:
Four Views on Aerial Tactics

The Red Baron's Dicta – Manfred von Richthofen[F]

Geschwader [Wing] Flights. In the autumn of 1916, Boelcke divided his twelve pilots into two Ketten, each five to six aircraft strong, six or seven aircraft being the most that one leader can effectively manage.

Before taking off, I discuss my intentions, such as initial direction, with my pilots. This discussion before take-off is at least as important as the one on return.

He gathers his Staffel, at a low altitude (100 metres) over a specified point to right or left of the previously announced. The commander flies slowly until the Staffel leaders have occupied their prescribed positions.

I like to lead Jagdstaffel 11 like the field of a mounted hunt for then it does not matter how I manoeuvre, dive or climb. If, however, the Staffel is not so experienced, a placement is recommended. The Staffel leaders who fly nearest to the Geschwader commander must not fly so close that it is impossible for the commander to make a sudden U-turn. This would hinder his attacks and possibly spoil the success of the group.

The aim of strong Geschwader flights is to destroy enemy squadrons. In this case, attacks on single pilots by the commander are ineffective.

From the moment the attack begins, everyone should know where all of the enemy planes are. The enemy squadron should be ripped apart by the impact of the first attack and through the absolute determination of each individual to get into the battle. If this has succeeded, then the shooting down of an enemy is only a single battle. If such a battle is successful and has split up into individual combats, the Geschwader becomes dispersed. It is not easy to reassemble it, and in most cases it will be possible to find only individual separated aircraft. To avoid unnecessary losses, individual members of the formation who are not able to rejoin the Geschwader should fly home and should not remain alone at the front.

It is important, and instructive, that a discussion be held immediately after each Geschwader flight. During this, everything should be discussed from take-off to landing and whatever has happened during the flight should be talked through. Questions from individuals can be most useful in explaining things.

The Commander. I require the following of a Kette, Staffel or Geschwader commander: he must know his fliers well. Even as the unit works on the ground, so it is in the air. Thus conditions must be: 1) friendship and 2) strict discipline.

[F] Extracted from "Dicta-Richthofen: The Last Will & Testament," translated by Stephen T. Lawson. *Cross & Cockade*, Vol. 23, No. 2 (1992), pp. 65-74, by permission. The full account of this document is found in *Rittmeister Manfred Frhr von Richthofen: Sein militärisches Vermächtnis.* Verlag von E.S. Mittler & Sohn: Berlin, 1938. This testament was originally made public in 1918 in a German book, and this paper was reportedly distributed to chiefs of aviation detachments, Geschwader and Jagdstaffel commanders with one copy going to the general of the air force, von Hoeppner.

The Attack. I distinguish between attacks on squadrons and on single planes. The latter is the simplest. [On single planes] whoever reaches the enemy first has the privilege to shoot. The whole flight goes down with him.

Formation flights on the other side are the most difficult, especially with an east wind. Then, the commander must not stick rigidly to his plan, for he will face great losses. As long as I can remain offensive, I can engage in squadron battle also on the other side. With an especially well trained Staffel I can attack a superior enemy from above, as well as on the other side. To see clearly is the prerequisite and the principal requirement of the flight leader.

How I Train Beginners. Under my leadership, six *Pour le Mérite* knights have shot down their first twenty kills. Before I allow a beginner to fly against the enemy, I ensure that he has adjusted the interior of his plane so that he is comfortable in it. The main concern for a fighter pilot must be his weapons. He must understand them so that he can immediately diagnose and rectify the cause of an ammunition jam. When a pilot has personally practised in this way he must next practise on targets in the air until he has become expert.

I pay considerable attention to flying ability. I had shot down my first twenty whilst flying itself caused me the greatest trouble. If someone is a "flight-artist" it does not hurt but, in general, I would rather have the poor pilot but who attacks the enemy, than the expert pilot from Johannisthal [the factory] who attacks too carefully. I prohibit the following exercises over the airfield: looping, spinning and manoeuvring at low altitudes. We do not need aerial acrobatics but go-getters. Orientation flights, in good and in bad weather, should be practised far more on our side of the line. If he answers all of these requirements, then he flies forth first time 50 metres on my port quarter and observes his leader. It is at least as important for a beginner to know what he should do, in order not to be shot down.

The One-to-One Battle. Every formation battle dissolves into individual combat. The subject "Aerial Battle Technique" can be explained with one sentence, namely, 'I approach the enemy from behind to within 50 metres, I aim carefully, fire and the enemy falls'. These were the words used in explanation by Boelcke when I asked him his trick. Now, I know that this is the whole secret of aerial victory. When I am attacked by a one-seater from above, in principle I never reduce speed, but make all my turns and dives with full throttle. I bank towards the opponent and seek, by climbing in the turn, to climb above him. In doing this, I must never allow the enemy to get behind me.

General Principles. It is never wise to stick obstinately to an enemy you were unable to shoot down through bad shooting or his manoeuvreability when the fight takes place far across on his side of the front line and one faces a large number of opponents alone.

The Sortie. In my opinion, a sortie can be judged only by a participating pilot. Therefore, we also need older experienced officers as fighter pilots. During a defensive battle I consider it best that each Armee group be given support of a fighter group. The fighter group should not be bound to a narrow group sector, but its main task is to provide immediate protection to the close support pilots to allow them to carry out their tasks without interruption. These should be granted absolutely free range and their function is to respond to enemy flight activity.

During Penetration Battles and Actual War. For the purpose of an attack, all fighter pilots of an army should be under one command. The only thing which should be dictated by the Armee each day to the next is:

1) Detailing of pilots for the first flight of the day. The reason for this is to give the other pilots the opportunity to sleep in;

2) Detailing of pilots for the afternoon flight. The reason for this is to ensure that pilots (who may be in constant action against the enemy) get at least an hour during the day to rest;

3) The third detailed flight is the last one before darkness falls.

In between these detailed start times, "free hunting" is encouraged as this gives the opportunity to provide relief for the infantry. By "free hunting" we mean not the attack of neighbouring armies or the enemy's airfields, but low altitude attack of enemy infantry on the battlefield. If possible, this is best carried out with the support of the whole squadron.

MICK MANNOCK'S PRACTICAL RULES OF AIR FIGHTING
Source: *The Aerodrome, Aces and Aircraft of World War I*, Internet.

Edward (Mick) Mannock, an Irishman, was a British fighter pilot in WWI. When the war started he was in Constantinople. Since the Ottoman Empire sided with Germany, he and other British citizens were thrown into prison, where he developed a hatred for the Turks and Germans. Repatriated in 1915, he joined the Royal Army Medical Corps and then the Royal Engineers, where he was commissioned a second lieutenant. He transferred to the RFC in 1916, and when completed with pilot training in April 1917, joined 40 Squadron flying Nieuport 17s. He made an awful first impression, detesting the clubby atmosphere of the public school boys, and breaking all sorts of pilot etiquette (e.g., by sitting in a chair that had belonged to a pilot who had been killed). In his first combat sorties, he displayed some fear, and he voiced a consummate dread of being set on fire. He even carried a service revolver to use in case he was flamed.

Despite having an injured eye, Mannock rapidly developed into a flight leader. He became a flight commander in June 1917 and issued his set of air-to-air tactics to his pilots. By the end of 1917 he had fifteen victories. He became a wonderful teacher, a selfless leader and inspired all who flew with him. In July 1918, he was given command of 85 Squadron flying S.E.5As. He increased his string of victories to sixty-one, although he deserved many more since he refused to claim over a dozen. After the war, his admirers got the number raised to seventy-three, one ahead of Billy Bishop. Mannock was shot down on 26 July 1918 by troops on the ground, with his aircraft catching fire and crashing in flames. In 1919, he was awarded the Victoria Cross posthumously.

Mick Mannock's practical rules were:
- Pilots must dive to attack with zest, and must hold their fire until they get within one hundred yards of their target.
- Achieve surprise by approaching from the east. (*From the German side of the front*).
- Utilise the sun's glare and clouds to achieve surprise.
- Pilots must keep physically fit by exercise and the moderate use of stimulants.
- Pilots must sight their guns and practise as much as possible as targets are normally fleeting.
- Pilots must practise spotting machines in the air and recognising them at long range, and every aeroplane is to be treated as an enemy until it is certain it is not.
- Pilots must learn where the enemy's blind spots are.
- Scouts must be attacked from above and two-seaters from beneath their tails.
- Pilots must prastice quick turns, as this manoeuvre is more used than any other in a fight.
- Pilots must prastice judging distances in the air as these are very deceptive.
- Decoys must be guarded against – a single enemy is often a decoy – therefore, the air above should be searched before attacking.
- If the day is sunny, machines should be turned with as little bank as possible; otherwise, the sun glistening on the wings will give away their presence at a long range.
- Pilots must keep turning in a dogfight and never fly straight except when firing.
- Pilots must never, under any circumstances, dive away from an enemy, as he gives his opponent a non-deflection shot — bullets are faster than aeroplanes.
- Pilots must keep their eye on their watches during patrols, and on the direction and strength of the wind.

ALBERT BALL'S NOTE ON ATTACKING A FORMATION WITH A LEWIS GUN AND FOSTER MOUNTING

Source: Albert Ball, "Comments by Captain Ball on a lecture on aerial tactics from the point of view of a single-seat pilot". Notes attached to papers of Robin Rowell, Imperial War Museum document 85/28/1, cited in Peter Hart, *Somme Success: The Royal Flying Corps and the Battle of the Somme*, pp.151-152.

Lieutenant Albert Ball was the first ace idolised by the British public and became a national hero. He was an engineering student when the war broke out, but enlisted and was promoted to sergeant in October 1916. He transferred to the Royal Flying Corps in 1917. He was a loner with strong religious convictions, a fearless pilot and an excellent marksman. In just three months over the Somme, he shot down thirty aircraft. He had a total of forty-four victories when he was shot down by Lothar von Richthofen in May 1917. He was only 21 years old. His death caused a period of national mourning, and he was awarded a posthumous Victoria Cross. Albert Ball wrote:

'If a scout attacks a large formation of HA [hostile aircraft], I think it is best to attack from above and dive in amongst them, getting under the nearest machine. Pull gun down [from the top wing] and fire up into HA. If you get it, a number of HA will put their noses down and make off. Don't run after them, but wait for a bit and look out for a straggler. One is nearly always left behind. Go for that and give it a drum, at the same time keeping your eyes as much as possible on the other machines, as they may get together and get round you. If fighting on the Boche's side (as you mostly are), never use your last drum, unless forced to do so. Keep it to help you on your way back. A Hun can always tell when you are out of ammunition and he at once closes with you, and if they are in formation, you stand no chance. Keep this last drum and when you want to get back, manoeuvre for a chance to break away, and if they follow you, as they mostly do, keep turning on them and firing a few rounds at long range. When this is done they nearly always turn and run. This gives you a chance to get on the way home.'

DICTA HARTMANN

Source: *The Aerodrome, Aces and Aircraft of World War I*, Internet.

Erich (Bubi) Hartmann was a German pilot in WWII who flew 1,456 missions with JG52 and JG53, engaged in air combat approximately 850 times and scored the most recorded air-to-air victories of any conflict, 352. He survived the war and died in Schönbuch, Germany, in 1993. His rules for combat were simple: See-Decide-Attack-Coffee Break.

1. **See** You have to see your prey first. Ninety per cent of all kills are made against pilots who never saw the threat.
2. **Decide** Is it safe to attack? Can you get away with it, or are there factors that should induce caution? Can you attack from your current position or must you manoeuvre?
3. **Attack** Make it swift and merciless. Fly close to your victim, from dead astern or slightly below if possible, and shoot only when you are certain to score an immediate kill. This means closing to minimum distance – your sight should be black with the enemy.
4. **Coffee Break** If you can't attack safely or without the enemy taking drastic action to evade you, take a coffee break, i.e. disengage and look for an easier victim. If you do attack, make it in one single pass and immediately disengage to a safe altitude or a safe area to regain situational awareness.

APPENDIX G:
HOW THIS BOOK CAME TO BE WRITTEN

I had just completed a homemade model of Manfred von Richthofen's Fokker Dr.I Triplane and had donated it to the Coronado, California, public library. Looking around for another project, I was determined that this one was going to be of museum quality. The six-foot wingspan of the Dr.I fascinated me because that was the largest model I could make in my garage. I was also intrigued by WWI models since one could duplicate their building materials of wood and fabric. After consultation with Jaime Johnston of Arizona Model Aircrafters, Al Valdez and Terry Brennan of the San Diego Air & Space Museum (SDASM) California in Balboa Park, we settled on an Albatros D.II.

The Albatros D.II is made in a kit by Arizona Model Aircrafters. The best thing about the kit is the marvellous set of plans (nineteen in all) that Jaime Johnston provided in 3 x 6 foot dimensions. The second best feature is the high quality wood, metal rods and smaller pieces. The kit is oriented toward a flying semi-scale version, but if one uses the factory plans, the conversion to a scale replica is doable. However, the builder has to constantly avoid the shortcuts that are offered by the flying model plans.

The size of the model is quarter scale, that is ¼ inch to the inch. Thus, the 28-foot wingspan of the full scale Albatros contracts to seven feet for the model. The fuselage is approximately six feet long. While the kit was being produced, I took the opportunity to build a 1:72 scale plastic version to acquaint myself with the aircraft's features and colour scheme. I also started research on the original aircraft, its colours and its most famous pilot, WWI German ace, Oswald Boelcke. While researching in the SDASM's archives I found an article that detailed the original colours, "The Camouflage and Markings of the Albatros D.II Aircraft," by Dan-San Abbott, published in *WW1 Aero*. Abbott referenced the definitive work on WWI colours, the *Methuen Handbook of Colour*, first published in Copenhagen and later in London shortly after the Armistice.

SDASM has an excellent set of archives of plans, books and articles, which produced an initial cache of research materials. But I wanted to go beyond that and began research on the internet and in libraries. After learning that the Luftwaffe's 31st Tactical Air Force Wing was officially named after Oswald Boelcke, I wrote to the wing commander and introduced myself and the project. Soon I got a reply from a German historian, Heinz-Michael Raby, who is a prominent member of the Boelcke Tradition Association. He had been contacted by Lt Col Ulrich Metternich, GAF (Ret.), to respond to my letter. Raby was so gracious that we corresponded frequently after that initial contact. He immediately sent an original 1916 postcard of "Captain Oswald Boelcke" and information from German archives. In the ensuing months, he answered dozens of technical questions about Oswald Boelcke and his prototype Albatros D.II as well as identifying numerous memorabilia.

During the progress of the model construction, I took completed sections to the curators of the SDASM to show them the status and get their comments. During one of these early sessions, they recommended leaving the left side open for public viewing and covering only the right half. This would allow viewers to see the internal construction. In exchange for this construction technique, the curators said they would build a display case to house the model and its accompanying artefacts.

Inspired by the German tradition of the Ordenskissen, the fallen warrior's medals on a velvet pillow in his funeral procession, I determined to create one to accompany Boelcke's model in the display case. I immediately purchased a replica of the Blue Max, the *Pour le Mérite*, which heads the pillow display. Raby followed with purchases and gifts of an Iron Cross Second Class, an Iron Cross First Class and Prussian Pilot's Wings. I added a Royal Order of the House of Hohenzollern Knights Cross with Swords. The completed Ordenskissen was presented to the SDASM with the model, and we have since added copies of more of Boelcke's medals.

On Armistice Day, 11 November 2014, my wife, Carole, and I invited about fifty friends to the museum and officially presented the model. The event included a champagne toast and a 45-minute briefing titled, "The Albatros D.II and its Famous Pilot." The briefing was well received, the audience was enthusiastic, and there were many questions and answers. James Kitrick, president and CEO of SDASM, accepted the model and prepared to have it displayed. Coming home to Coronado, I was greeted by all the research material I had collected, and with the encouragement of my wife and Heinz-Michael Raby, decided to write a book on this amazing German aviator. Subsequent trips to Europe provided opportunities to continue my research at the RAF Museum's archives at Hendon and at the 31st Wing at Nörvenich, where their Boelcke Tradition Room houses a host of original artefacts.

My wife even thought my life was similar to Boelcke's – middle-class families, military academy, love of flying, and even a crash landing. Fortunately, I survived mine but Boelcke didn't make it. Incidentally, a film of my crash landing and I were featured on *The Ed Sullivan Show*.

ENDNOTES

PROLOGUE

[1] Source: Michael Seamark. The full caption is: 'Dropping a line: The chivalrous German visited the British observer Lieutenant Geoffrey Formilli in hospital, and then incredibly undertook a perilous mission to drop a note from Formilli over his English squadron's HQ to let them know he was alive.'

INTRODUCTION

[1] Franz Immelmann, *Immelmann: The Eagle of Lille* (Greenhill Books, London, 1990), pp.ix-x.

[2] Richard Hillary, *The Last Enemy* (Read Books Ltd, Oxford, first printed in 1942 and reprinted in 2011), p.16.

[3] The term "victory" as used in this volume means a claim confirmed by an official agency. The best description of the records, the confirmation process and construction of the victory lists is in Norman L. R. Franks, Frank W. Bailey & Russell Guest, *Above the Lines: A Complete Record of the Fighter Aces of the German Air Service, Naval Air Service and Flanders Marine Corps, 1914-1918.* (Grub Street, London, 1993), pp. 5-8. See especially the quote on page 4 noting that 'generally speaking, the German claims are very good [accurate]'. The numbers of German victories used in this book have been cross-checked from *Above the Lines*, *Jasta Boelcke* by Norman Franks and *Bloody April … Black September* by Norman Franks, Russell Guest and Frank W. Bailey. Where there are minor variations, the most recent data has been used. Allied powers had a more difficult time verifying pilots' claims when they occurred behind the German lines, as they were not in position to verify that a plane seen falling or spinning actually crashed. Many of these victories were frequently claimed as "driven down", "forced to land", or "out of control". These were counted in British lists of victories. In WWII and later wars these were classified as "probables" and were not included as victories.

CHAPTER I

[1] Denis Winter, *The First of the Few: Fighter Pilots of the First World War* (University of Georgia Press: Athens, Georgia, 1983), p. 36.

[2] Air Education and Training Command, email communication from Capt Jennifer M. Richard, AETC Public Affairs Officer, 19 March 2015.

[3] Winter, op. cit., p.30.

[4] Ibid., p.20.

[5] Derek Robinson, *Piece of Cake* (Maclehose Press, London, 2008), p.178.

[6] Winter, op. cit., p.30.

[7] Ibid., p.24.

[8] Ibid.

[9] Ibid.

[10] Ibid., p.38.

[11] Ibid., p.39.

[12] Cited by John H. Morrow, Jr., *The Great War in the Air: Military Aviation from 1909 to 1921* (Smithsonian Institution Press. Washington, D.C., 1993), p. 184.

[13] Ibid.

[14] Major James T.B. McCudden, *Flying Fury: Five Years in the Royal Flying Corps*, (Doubleday & Co. Inc, 1968), p. 125.

[15] Arch Whitehouse, *Decisive Air Battles of the First World War.* (Duell, Sloan and Pierce, New York, 1963), p. 173.

[16] Interview, Major Nathan G. Martens, USAF Altitude Chamber, Peterson AFB, CO, 20 January 2015. Documentation is provided in Roy L. Dehart, M.D. and M.P.H. and Jeffrey R. Davis, M.D., M.S., *Fundamentals of Aerospace Medicine, 3d Ed.* (Lippincott Williams & Wilkins, New York, 2002), pp. 36-37.

[17] Winter, op. cit., p.147.

[18] David Rice, "The Observant Quirk: The Rice Brothers, A Family History of WW1" *Cross & Cockade*, Vol. 20, No. 4 (1989), p. 196.

[19] Herbert Molloy Mason, Jr., *The Lafayette Escadrille* (Random House, New York, 1964), p. 67.

[20] Oswald Boelcke, *An Aviator's Fieldbook: Being the*

Field Reports of Oswald Boelcke, from August 1, 1914, to October 28, 1916, pp. 138-139. Translated from the German by Robert Reynold Hirsch, M.E., with a Foreword by Joseph E. Ridder, M.E. (National Military Publishing Co., New York, 1917). The original was *Hauptmann Boelckes Feldberichte*, with an introduction by his father Professor Hermann Boelcke, Dessau [in German] (Friedrich Andreas Berthes A.-G. Gotha, Berlin, 1917).

[21] Winter, op. cit., p.159.

[22] Boelcke's letter of 16 March 1916, *Fieldbook*, op. cit., pp. 105-108.

[23] Ibid., p.143.

[24] Oswald Boelcke, letter to his parents, 17 September 1916, *Fieldbook*, op. cit., pp.185-186.

[25] Professor Werner's biography is *Knight of Germany: Oswald Boelcke, German Ace*, (Casemate, Havertown, PA, 2009), p. 245. Werner uses Boelcke's *Fieldbook* as his main reference, but he includes many letters that precede 1914. However, the wording of Werner's quotations and the *Fieldbook* versions published by the National Military Publishing Company in New York in 1917 are sometimes quite different. Where Werner is more explanatory, the author has used his edition.

[26] Quote from Boelcke's batman, cited at length in Werner, op. cit, p, 256.

[27] Cited in Winter, op. cit., p. 173.

[28] Winter, Ibid., p. 190.

[29] Ian Mackersey, *No Empty Chairs: The Short and Heroic Lives of the Young Aviators Who Fought and Died in the First World War* (Orion Publishing Group, London, 2012), pp.67 and 75.

[30] Winter, op. cit., p. 191.

[31] Quoted in Winter, op.cit., p. 163.

[32] Ibid., p.164.

[33] Undated letter cited by Winter, *The First of the Few*, op.cit., pp. 159-161.

[34] Air Vice-Marshal Arthur Gould Lee, *No Parachute* (Grub Street, London, 2013), p. 229. The memorandum was discovered by Lee in the WWI War Office aeronautical records at Kew, UK. He had flown 120 combat sorties over the lines in WWI, and was determined to find who had disapproved the use of parachutes in the RFC. The memorandum was written by the assistant director of Military Aeronautics when he forwarded the proposal for continued tests by Mervyn O'Gorman, then superintendent of Farnborough. Also cited in Mackersey, op. cit., pp 296-297.

[35] Lee, op.cit., p.231.

[36] The best description of this evolving process of counting victories is in Norman Franks, *Sharks Among Minnows* (Grub Street, London, 2001), pp. 12-14.

[37] Ibid., p. 13.

[38] John R. Cuneo, *Winged Mars: Volume I: The German Air Weapon 1870-1914* (The Military Service Publishing Company, Harrisburg, PA, 1942), p. 3.

[39] Cited in Peter Kilduff, *Billy Bishop VC* (Grub Street, London, 2014), p. 133.

[40] Jack Merritt and Pierre Sprey, "Negative Marginal Returns in Weapons Acquisition," in *American Defense Policy*, 3rd ed. (The Johns Hopkins University Press, Baltimore, 1973), p. 493.

CHAPTER II

[1] Cuneo, op. cit. p. 132. The author is indebted to Charles Dusch, Jr., deputy command historian at the USAF Academy for this insight.

[2] Ibid., pp. 162-168.

[3] Lieth-Thomsen had been born in Prussia in 1867. He was 39 years old at the time of this assignment in 1907. He would go on to become a major influence in German aviation, becoming the chief of field air forces in 1915 and chief of staff to the commanding general of the air force in 1916.

[4] Cuneo, op. cit., p. 60.

[5] Ibid., pp. 99-101.

[6] Peter Kilduff, *Germany's First Air Force: 1914-1918* (Motorbooks International, Osceola, WI, 1991), pp. 8-16.

[7] Ibid., p. 9.

[8] John H. Morrow, Jr., *German Air Power in World War I* (University of Nebraska Press, Lincoln, 1982), p. 16.

[9] Werner, op. cit., p. 108. This argument embracing the mystique of the horse as a superior weapon of military transport was to be repeated in many guises and many nations in ensuing years. Twenty-five years later,

on the eve of WWII many general officers of the US army, Poland, Rumania, and possibly the USSR, were convinced that horse-mounted cavalry were more useful than armoured tanks. Thus both the aeroplane and the tank were retarded in their early development because of the romanticism and obsolete thinking of the leaders. George Patton was one of the critics of this outmoded policy. For the most fascinating account of this phenomenon, see Edward L. Katzenbach, Jr., "The Horse Cavalry in the Twentieth Century: A Study in Policy Response", *Public Policy*, 7 (1958), pp. 120-149. Reprinted in *American Defense Policy*, 3rd ed., 1973.

[10] For the best discussion of this topic, see I. B. Holley, Jr., *Ideas and Weapons* (Yale University Press, New Haven, 1953).

[11] Werner, op. cit., p. 108.

[12] Kilduff, *Germany's First Air Force*, op. cit., p. 11.

[13] Morrow, *The Great War in the Air*, op. cit., p. 35. All subsequent references to Morrow are from this volume unless designated otherwise.

[14] Jeff Shaara, *To the Last Man: A Novel of the First World War* (Random House, New York, 2004), Kindle location, 617.

[15] Morrow, op. cit., p. 149.

[16] Kilduff, op. cit., p. 13.

[17] Ibid.

CHAPTER III

[1] *Fieldbook*, pp. 22-23.

[2] Dr. Wiehmann's quote is cited by Professor Hermann Boelcke in his Introduction to *Boelcke's Fieldbook*, p. 23.

[3] Werner, op. cit., p. 15.

[4] *Fieldbook*, p. 23.

[5] Werner, op. cit.

[6] Werner, p. 33. This letter is only available in Werner's biography since it is pre-war.

[7] Ibid., p. 32.

[8] Ibid., p. 42.

[9] Ibid., pp. 54-55.

[10] Aaron Norman, *The Great Air War*, (The Macmillan Company: New York, 1968), p. 48.

[11] Werner, op. cit., p. 68.

[12] Ibid., pp. 69-70.

[13] R.G. Head, "Doctrinal Innovation and the A-7 Aircraft Decisions" in *American Defense Policy*, 3rd and 4th editions (Baltimore, The Johns Hopkins University Press, 1973 and 1977), 3rd edition, pp. 431-445.

[14] Cited by Winter, op. cit., p. 11.

[15] Morrow, op. cit., p. 54.

[16] R.G. Head, Ed., *Contrails 1959-1960: The Air Force Cadet Handbook*, (USAF Academy, Colorado, 1959), p. 195.

CHAPTER IV

[1] Kilduff, *Germany's First Air Force*, p. 10.

[2] *Fieldbook*, p. 33. Note, this is the first letter in the *Fieldbook*.

[3] Werner, op. cit., p. 73. Note: This portion of the letter is *only* found in Werner's biography.

[4] *Fieldbook*, p. 35.

[5] Cuneo op. cit., p. 128.

[6] Manfred von Richthofen, *The Red Fighter Pilot: The Autobiography of the Red Baron*, translated by J. Ellis Barker, (Red and Black Publishers, St Petersburg, 2007), pp. 112-114.

[7] "Oswald Boelcke" (English translation of original Polish) *Armia Niemiecka 1914-1918*. Retrieved: 5 October 2010, and *Fieldbook*, p. 42. The number "50" is documented in secondary sources, but the number is not mentioned by Boelcke in his *Fieldbook*.

[8] Letter, 9 December 1914, *Fieldbook*, p. 46.

[9] Ibid., pp. 46-47.

[10] Morrow, *German Air Power*, p. 26.

[11] Ibid., pp. 27-28.

[12] Ibid., p. 30.

[13] Winter, op. cit., p. 16.

CHAPTER V

[1] *Fieldbook*, letter, 27 January 1915, p. 49.

[2] *Fieldbook*, letter to his parents, 25 October 1914, p. 43.

[3] H.K. Weiss, "Systems Analysis Problems of Limited War," *Annals of Reliability and Maintainability*, 5 (July 1966), as cited in Jack N. Merritt and Pierre M. Sprey, "Negative Marginal Returns in Weapons Acquisition,

American Defense Policy, III, edited by R. G. Head and Ervin J. Rokke (The Johns Hopkins University Press: Baltimore, 1973), pp. 492-493. The graph of this falling attrition curve was influential in selling the concept of the USAF's Red Flag exercise programme to air force leadership and OSD officials in the early 1970s.

[4] Winter, op. cit., caption on photograph 1, opposite p. 32.

[5] This definition is paraphrased from the DOD Dictionary of Military Terms, the official definition being: "Air superiority: That degree of dominance in the air battle by one force that permits the conduct of its operations at a given time and place."

[6] Quote from Basil Collier, Heavenly Adventurer: Sefton Brancker and the Dawn of British Aviation, p. 47; cited in Morrow, op. cit. p. 114.

[7] Quote taken from his interrogation by the British. Morrow, op. cit., p. 171.

[8] Morrow, op. cit., p. 171.

[9] John R, Cuneo, Winged Mars: Volume II, The Air Weapon 1914-1916 (Military Service Publishing Company, Harrisburg, PA, 1947), pp. 159-160.

[10] Morrow, op.cit., p. 91.

[11] See Appendix I.

[12] Morrow, op. cit., p. 104.

[13] Walter J. Boyne, The Influence of Airpower on History (Pen & Sword, Barnsley, South Yorkshire, 2003), p. 14.

[14] Werner, op. cit., p. 106. This list is only found in Werner's biography.

[15] Werner, op. cit., p. 104.

[16] Franz Immelmann, op. cit., p. 28.

[17] Ibid., p.47.

[18] Ibid., p. 79.

[19] Andreas Thies, Boelcke Auction Catalog (Auktionator, Andreas Thies, Nürtingen, April 2001), pp. 210-211.

[20] Franz Immelmann, op. cit., p. 144.

[21] This technical innovation and the rapid evolution of aircraft development and tactics is superbly reproduced by the Public Broadcasting System's video, "First Air War", a NOVA presentation first aired for television on 30 October 2014.

[22] Anthony H. G. Fokker and Bruce Gould, Flying Dutchman: The Life of Anthony Fokker (Henry Holt & Co., New York, 1931), p. 126.

[23] Ibid., p. 127.

[24] Ibid., pp. 134-138.

[25] Aaron Norman and Quentin Reynolds, among them.

[26] John Cuneo, Winged Mars: Vol. II, op. cit., p. 172.

[27] Fokker, op. cit., p. 150.

[28] Boelcke, Fieldbook, pp. 63-64.

CHAPTER VI

[1] Ibid. pp. 64-65.

[2] Werner, op. cit., p. 134.

[3] Norman L. R. Franks, Jasta Boelcke: The History of Jasta 2, 1916–18, (Grub Street: London, 2004), p. 11.

[4] Edward Sims, Fighter Tactics and Strategy: 1914-1970 (Cassell, London, 1972), p. 18.

[5] Boelcke was consistently shy and did not seek publicity. This was not an act, but a true aspect of his personality. Van Wyngarden, op.cit., p. 71.

[6] Wintgens went on to score nineteen victories, with his eighth occurring on 30 June 1916, whereupon he was awarded the Pour le Mérite. This made him the fourth German ace to receive the Blue Max. He was transferred to Jasta 1 in September 1916, where he earned the rest of his victories. He was shot down in flames on 25 September 1916. The lack of confirmation of his first score has caused some lists to contain only eighteen victories. It is not known whether either of his two early July 1916 victories were later confirmed or if he scored another victory later in July. See Franks, Bailey and Guest, Above the Lines: A Complete Record of the Fighter Aces of the German Air Service, Naval Air Service and Flanders Marine Corps, 1914-1918. (Grub Street, London, 1993), pp. 232-233.

[7] Trevor Henshaw, The Sky Their Battlefield, Ed. II (Fetubi Books: High Barnet, Hertfordshire, 2014), p. 17.

[8] Boelcke, Fieldbook, pp. 75-76.

[9] Henshaw, op. cit., p.18.

[10] Gary Sunderland, "Designing Fokker Airplanes," Cross & Cockade, Vol. 30, No. 3 (Autumn 2015), p. 202.

[11] Boelcke, Fieldbook, pp. 78-79.

[12] Greg Van Wyngarden, Jagdstaffel 2 "Boelcke": Von

Richthofen's Mentor. Aviation Elite Units, No. 26. (Osprey Publishing Ltd., Oxford/New York, 2006), pp. 16–17.

[13] Henshaw, op. cit., p. 22.

[14] Hart, op. cit., p. 20.

[15] Boyne, op.cit., p. 78.

[16] H.A. Jones, *Official History of the War: The War in the Air, Being the Story of the part played in the Great War by the Royal Air Force*. (Clarendon Press, Oxford, 1922-1937), Volume II, pp. 156-157. Emphasis added. Cited by Hart, op.cit., p. 21.

[17] Close formation is used for penetrating weather, for routine, peacetime flying, by aerobatic teams, and for flights returning safely from training or combat missions when they are on "initial approach" for a formation pitch out and landing.

[18] Cited in Mackersey, op. cit., p. 30.

[19] Lieutenant M. F. Powell, a quote from Winifred Loraine, *Robert Loraine: Soldier, Actor, Airman*, pp. 217-218; cited by Morrow, op. cit., p. 117.

[20] Shoto Douglas, with Robin Wright, *Combat and Command*, pp. 55-97, cited in Morrow, op. cit., p. 117.

[21] Manfred von Richthofen, *The Red Fighter Pilot: The Autobiography of the Red Baron*, translated by J. Ellis Barker, (Red and Black Publishers, St Petersburg, 2007), p. 64. One of the differences between Boelcke's *Fieldbook* and von Richthofen's autobiography is that Oswald Boelcke actually wrote his own letters to his parents; von Richthofen's memoir was written much later, after the ace was very famous. At least one source wrote that he had a public relations person assigned to him. Her job was to interview von Richthofen and ghostwrite his biography.

[22] Peter Kilduff, *The Red Baron: The Life and Death of an Ace* (David & Charles, Cincinnati, OH, 2008). p. 40.

[23] Ibid., p. 42.

[24] Werner, op. cit., p. 152. This letter is not included in *Fieldbook*.

[25] Bernard Rice, letter, October 23, 1915, as described by his nephew, David Rice, op. cit., p. 189.

[26] Letter to Boeckle's parents. Werner, op. cit., p. 155-157. It is obvious that the letters printed in Boelcke's

Fieldbook were quite heavily edited, as they do not contain the extended descriptions found in Werner.

[27] Kilduff, op. cit., p. 37.

[28] Ibid., p. 154. This award is completely neglected in Boelcke's *Fieldbook*.

[29] Fokker, op. cit., p. 153.

[30] Norman Franks, *Sharks Among Minnows*, op. cit., p. 35.

[31] Ibid., p. 41.

[32] *Fieldbook*, op. cit., pp. 90-91.

[33] Ibid., pp. 41-42.

[34] Cuneo, Vol. II, op. cit., p, 177.

[35] Ibid., pp. 184-185.

[36] Henshaw, op. cit., Tables in Appendix 3, pp. 346-347.

CHAPTER VII

[1] Bernard Rice, letter to his father, 26 January 1916, op.cit., p. 201.

[2] *Anhaltischer Staats-Anzeiger*, Dessau, Thursday, 6 January 1916, p. 1.

[3] Immelmann, *The Eagle of Lille*, op. cit., p. 168.

[4] Kilduff, op. cit., pp. 37-38.

[5] The medal was originally established by Friedrich Wilhelm I, the electoral prince, as the *Ordre de la Generosité* on 12 May 1667. The full title of the organization is: The Order of the Teutonic Knights of St. Mary's Hospital in Jerusalem, and their motto was "Help – Defend – Heal". Friedrich II, who was also known as Friedrich the Great, renamed it the *Orden Pour le Mérite* on 6 June 1740. Friedrich Wilhelm III directed on 18 January 1810, that the Orden would be strictly reserved for war service or bravery against an enemy. In WWI the original requirement for aviators was eight victories, but by late 1916 it was increased to sixteen. Sometime later the requirement became twenty, and finally by 1918 to thirty as the number of high-scoring aces grew. German air service personnel were the smallest group to receive the medal. They were also the most junior as the pilots were young NCOs or lieutenants, and their role was the most glamorous and daring. A total of eighty airmen won the award including: the commander of the air service, his chief of staff, five bomber pilots, nine ob-

servers and sixty-four fighter pilots. The award is the equivalent to the Medal of Honor in the United States and the Victoria Cross in the UK.

[6] *Salt Lake Tribune*, 3 August 1916.

[7] The card is from the collection of Heinz-Michael Raby, and the translation is his.

[8] Werner, op. cit., p. 186.

[9] Ibid., p. 189.

[10] Jon Guttman, *Nieuport 11/16 Bébé vs Fokker Eindecker: Western Front 1916.* (Osprey Publishing Ltd., Oxford, 2014).

[11] Imperial War Museum Documents (IWMDOCS), L. Horridge, manuscript letter, 19 July 1916. Cited in Hart, op. cit., p. 61.

[12] Winter, op. cit., p. 36.

[13] Johan Ryheul, *KEKs and Fokkerstaffels: The Early German Fighter Units in 1915-1916* (Fonthill Media Ltd, London, 2014).

[14] Cuneo, Vol. II, op. cit., p. 209.

[15] Ryheul, op. cit.

[16] Cuneo, Vol. II, op. cit., p. 226.

[17] Ibid., p. 227.

[18] Guttman, op.cit., Location 586.

[19] Cited in Cuneo, Vol. II, op. cit., p. 276.

[20] Ryheul, op. cit., Chapter 17.

[21] Werner, op.cit., p, 180. Again, this letter is totally omitted from Boelcke's *Fieldbook*.

[22] Quote attributed to Oswald Boelcke, but not included with his memorandum on the Fokker E.IV.

[23] Werner, op.cit., pp, 183-185. This report is the sole remaining copy of the several technical documents he submitted to the chief of the German air service.

[24] Fokker, op. cit., pp. 154-155.

[25] Werner, op.cit., p, 186.

[26] Boelcke, op. cit., p. 125.

[27] Christopher Campbell *Aces and Aircraft of World War I* (Book Club Associates: London, 1981), p. 46.

[28] Unidentified editor, "Introduction," to *The Red Fighter Pilot*, by Manfred von Richthofen, p. 10.

[29] Mason, *The Lafayette Escadrille*, op. cit., pp. 67-68.

[30] Boelcke's *Fieldbook*, pp. 134-138.

[31] Ibid., footnote, p. 136.

[32] Letter, June 12, 1915, cited in Werner, op. cit., p. 198.

[33] Boelcke letter of 4 July 1915, reprinted in his *Fieldbook*, pp. 143-146, and cited in Werner, p. 207.

[34] Werner, op. cit., p.145.

[35] Ibid.

[36] *Salt Lake Tribune*, 3 August 1916.

[37] This is a statement from Lincoln's first debate with Stephen Douglas in 1858, cited in "Lincoln," *National Geographic*, April, 2015, pp. 42-43.

CHAPTER VIII

[1] Edward H. Sims, op. cit., p. 3.

[2] As quoted in Franz Immelmann, op. cit., p. 30.

[3] The first seven dicta are taken from Norman Franks' Introduction to Werner's biography; the eighth is a direct quote from Professor Werner's own narrative on page 210.

[4] Sims, op. cit., p. 17.

[5] See the Appendices for other sets of air-to-air tactics. These were due largely to the efforts of two men: Edward (Mick) Mannock for the British, and Albert Duellin for the French.

[6] Robert L. Shaw, *Fighter Combat: Tactics and Maneuvering* (Naval Institute Press: Annapolis), pp. 274-275. This text is extraordinary in its lengthy and extremely detailed descriptions of air combat manoeuvres, such as: one-versus-one, two-versus-one, few-versus-many, and individual tactics like "high yo-yo", "rolling scissors" and "defensive spiral".

[7] Published by Jack Merritt and Pierre Sprey in, "Negative Marginal Returns in Weapons Acquisition," in R.G. Head and Ervin Rokke, *American Defense Policy*, 3rd ed., (The Johns Hopkins University Press: Baltimore, 1973), p. 493, with permission.

[8] Sims, op. cit., p. 16.

[9] Ibid, p. 17.

[10] Werner, op. cit., pp. 247-248.

[11] RAF Museum, R. Rice, manuscript notes, undated. As cited by Peter Hart, *Somme Success*, p. 22. Also see David Rice, op. cit., pp. 169-209.

[12] The full title is Office of the Chief of Naval Operations, "Naval Air Training and Operating Procedures Standardization General Flight and Operating Instructions" (OPNAVINST) 3710.7U, 23 November

2009. Note supplied by Admiral Bud Edney, USN (Ret.), May 2015.

[13] Joint Publication 1-02, *DOD Dictionary of Military and Associated Terms* 08 November 2010, as amended through 15 March 2015.

[14] Letter, 31 July 1916, cited in Werner, op.cit., p. 224, but not printed in Boelcke's *Fieldbook*.

[15] Ibid., p. 228.

CHAPTER IX

[1] Lyn Macdonald, *Somme* (Michael Joseph Ltd., London, 1983) p. 13.

[2] Peter Hart, *The Somme: The Darkest Hour on the Western Front* (Pegasus Books, New York, 2008).

[3] Werner, op. cit., p. 200.

[3] Hart, op.cit., pp. 128-129.

[4] As quoted in Jones, *Official History of the War, Volume II*, op. cit., pp. 271-272.

[5] Werner, op.cit., p. 200.

[6] Werner, op.cit., p. 200.

[7] Morrow, *German Air Power in World War I*, op. cit., p. 152.

[8] Mackersey, op. cit., p. 135.

[9] Ibid., pp. 330-331.

[10] Albert Ball: letter to his family, 16 July 1916, cited by Mackersey, op. cit., p. 122.

[11] Mackersery, op. cit., pp. 122-123.

[12] Whitehouse, op. cit., p. 173.

CHAPTER X

[1] Franks, et.al., *Above the Lines*, op. cit., p. 16.

[2] Franks, *Jasta Boelcke*, op. cit., p. 13.

[3] von Richthofen, op. cit., pp. 95-96.

[4] Franks, *Jasta 2 Boelcke*, op. cit., p. 15.

[5] *Chef des Feldflugwesens, Nr. 14047 Fl. Vom 5.4.1916, Bordbuch fuer dan Flugzeug, Fok. D.III. 352/16, begonnen am: 1 September 1916, beendet am: (blank).* This flight log was provided courtesy of Walter Waiss, colleague of the author's. Waiss is co-author (with Steffen Gastreich) of *Jagdstaffel Boelcke*.

[6] The author's information differs from that of Professor Werner, who wrote that the war diary [not available to the current author] "records nine such flights up to 14 September." p. 236. The Fokker flight logs record sixteen flights including two on 14 September 1916.

[7] Reynolds, op. cit., p. 94.

[8] Barrington J. Gray, "Number One for Jasta 2: An Account of Hptm Oswald Boelcke's Twentieth Victory," *Cross & Cockade*, Vol. 5, No. 3 (1974), pp. 126-129. Werner, op. cit., Appendix, "The Victories of Oswald Boelcke" p. 272. See the expanded list of Boelcke's victories in Appendix B at the end of this volume.

[9] Werner, op. cit., pp. 235-236.

[10] Gray, op. cit., p. 129.

[11] Boelcke, op. cit., pp. 183-185. Also, Werner, op. cit., pp. 233-236.

[12] From a memoir written by one of his pilots and found deposited in his papers. Werner, p. 236.

[13] Werner, op. cit., p. 208.

[14] Ibid., p. 250.

[15] Interview published in the *Salt Lake Tribune*, 3 August 1916.

[16] Alan Bott, *An Airman's Outings*, cited by Norman Franks, *Jasta Boelcke*, pp. 21-22.

[17] Franks, *Jasta Boelcke*, pp. 22-23.

CHAPTER XI

[1] Morrow, op. cit., p. 37.

[2] Morrow, *The Great Air War*, p.162.

[3] Gray, op.cit., p. 207. *Cross & Cockade* also published an excellent article, on the D.I, "Albatros D.I, Flight Technical Report, 1917" by Bill Evans, Vol. 5, No. 4 (1974), pp. 104-116.

[4] R. R. Money, *Flying and Soldiering*, (Ivor Nicholson & Watson Ltd, London, 1936), p. 100, as cited in Hart, op. cit., p. 174.

[5] Hart, Ibid., p. 174.

[6] Data in this section was derived from "Observations On WWI Petrol," The Aerodrome Forum, Author: Kacey and posted by Bletchley, 7 January 2010. His references include: NACA Report #47, "Power Characteristics of Fuels for Aircraft Engines", 1920, no. 4. And an article by Alchim Engels, "Descriptions of WWI German Naphthas and Petrols", Posting on The Aerodrome Forum, 29 July 2002.

[7] Franks, *Jasta Boelcke*, p. 24.

[8] Werner, op.cit., p. 237-238.

[9] Von Richthofen, op. cit., p. 97.

[10] Franks, *Jasta Boelcke*, p. 25.

[11] Boelcke, op. cit., pp. 190-191; Werner, op.cit., p. 240.

[12] Manfred von Richthofen, *The Red Fighter Pilot*, pp. 98-99.

[13] Ibid., p.100.

[14] Mackersey, op. cit., p.132.

[15] Peter Kilduff, *Red Baron: The Life and Death of an Ace*, op. cit., p. 74.

[16] H.A. Jones, *The War in the Air*, Vol. II.

[17] James F. Miller, Albatros D.I-D.II, pp. 49-50.

[18] von Richthofen, op. cit., p. 99.

[19] Trenchard letter to Brancker, 21 September 1916, cited in Mackersey, p.125.

[20] Ibid., p. 127.

[21] McCudden, Flying Fury, op. cit., pp. 124, 128.

[22] Mackersey, op. cit., p.129.

[23] Boelcke, cited in Werner, op. cit., pp. 241-242.

[24] Norman Franks, Hal Giblin, and Nigel McCrery, *Under the Guns of the Red Baron: The Complete Record of von Richthofen's Victories and Victims Fully Illustrated* (Grub Street, London, 1995), pp. 16-17.

[25] Boelcke's letter, 8 October 1916, Boelcke's *Fieldbook*, pp. 191-192. Also, cited in Werner, p. 243.

[26] Ibid., p. 244.

[27] Cited in Henshaw, op. cit., p. 55.

CHAPTER XII

[1] Although there existed some uncertainty about the type of British aircraft, the latest edition of Trevor Henshaw's *The Sky Their Battlefield, Ed. II*, op. cit., p. 56, documents the aircraft as a D.H.2, serial number 2533, flown by Captain H.W.G. Jones of 32 Squadron.

[2] Boelcke, op. cit., p. 196.

[3] Karl Koehler, "Auf dem Wege zur Luftwaffe," *Wehrwissenschaftliche Rundschau*, 16, No. 1 (January 1966), p. 553; cited in Morrow, op.cit., p. 158.

[4] Henshaw, op. cit., pp. 56 and 59.

[5] Letter dated 19 October 1916, Werner, op. cit., pp. 252-253.

[6] Morrow, op.cit., p. 136.

[7] Second Lieutenant Gwilym Lewis, *Wings Over the Somme* (Bridge Books: Wresham:, 1994), pp. 75 and 78, as cited by Hart, op. cit., pp. 211-212.

[8] Franks, *History of Jasta 2*, Appendices C and E.

[9] von Richthofen, op. cit., pp. 99-100.

[10] Van Wyngarden, op.cit., p. 20.

[11] Werner, op. cit., pp. 250-251.

[12] Ibid., p. 245.

[13] Morrow, op. cit., p. 171.

[14] Ibid., pp. 235-236.

[15] Albert Ball, quoted in Chaz Bowyer, *Albert Ball, VC* 2nd ed. (Bridge Books, Wexham, 1994), p. 91; Hart, op. cit., p. 184.

[16] Norman Franks, Appendix in Werner, op. cit., pp. 272-275. This list of victories also appears in Franks' *Jasta Boelcke*, Appendix F, pp. 205-208. The most recent publication of the list is in Steffen Gastreich and Walter Waiss, *Jagdstaffel Boelcke, Band VIII, 1914-1918*, from the Boelcke-Archives. (Helios, Aachen, Germany, 2014). This book provides a marvellous set of photographs from the Boelcke family, Jasta Boelcke and other German fighter squadrons. It also reproduces each page of "The Claim-Books of the Fighter Squadron Boelcke", pp. 33-71, and a translated summary, pp. 83-88. Each of these lists is consistent with Franks' renditions. These victories were also crosschecked with the extensive data in Henshaw, *The Sky Their Battlefield*, op. cit., pp. 56-59.

[17] Henshaw, op. cit., p. 60.

[18] Franks, pp. 16, 33 and 46.

[19] Hart, op. cit., p. 199.

[20] I am indebted to Colonel Gert Overhoff for this observation on the distribution of Boelcke's dicta.

CHAPTER XIII

[1] Quoted in Werner, op. cit., pp. 256-257.

[2] Captain Walter Bloem, "A Talk with Boelcke on the Day of his Death", *The New York Times*, 28 January 1917, Section 3, p. 1. The author cannot verify the authenticity of this article. There were many articles published in newspapers during WWI that had no basis in fact. Norman Franks also reviewed this *New York Times* article and commented that he cannot confirm

it either. He noted the interview may have taken place, but that the facts are not supported by the record. 'The language, even when translated, does not appear too outlandish'. Personal correspondence from Norman Franks to the author, 4 November 2015. We include it here for the possibility that it is correct.

[3] Quote from Böhme's letter of 31 October 1916, Werner, op. cit., p. 258.

[4] Manfred von Richthofen, *The Red Fighter Pilot: The Autobiography of the Red Baron* (Red & Black Publishers, St Petersburg, FL, 2007) p. 101, and *The Red Baron:* Translated by Peter Kilduff, (Bailey Brothers & Swinfen Ltd., Folkestone, 1974), p. 53.

[5] Werner, op. cit., p. 258.

[6] Cited from the newspaper article in the *Dunkirk (NY) Evening Observer*, 4 November 1916, p. 1, which was written in Berlin and cabled by the United Press.

[7] Werner, op. cit., p. 260.

[8] Ibid., pp. 261-262.

[9] Andreas Thies, op. cit., p. 59.

[10] Copy of the proclamation reproduced in Steffan Gastreich and Walter Waiss, *Jagdstaffel Boelcke, Band VIII 1914-1918* (Helios, Aachen, 2014), pp. 306-307.

[11] Van Wyngarden, op. cit., p. 23, and Steffen Gastreich and Walter Waiss, *Jagstaffel Boelcke*, op. cit., p. 225. The wording is taken from Gastreich and Waiss, who derived it from the actual letter.

[12] Jeff Taylor, "A Wreath for Boelcke", *Cross & Cockade*, Vol. 20, No. 4 (1989), p. 217. This demonstration of respect and chivalry was not completely absent from WWII. When Douglas Bader was shot down over German-occupied France in 1941 and made a prisoner, he lost his two artificial legs. Adolf Galland, a prominent German general and fighter ace befriended Bader and arranged for two replacement legs to be parachuted to him via the RAF.

[13] Werner, op. cit., p. 260.

[14] *Anhaltischer Staats-Anzeiger*, 16 November 1916, p. 1, as reprinted in Andreas Thies, op. cit., p. 233.

[15] "German Air Hero Buried Today", *Dunkirk Evening Observer*, 4 November 1916, No. 76, p. 1.

[16] Kilduff, *Red Baron*, op. cit., p. 177.

[17] Andreas Thies, op. cit., p. 82.

CHAPTER XIV

[1] Franks, Giblin and McCrery, *Under the Guns of the Red Baron*, op. cit., pp. 27-39.

[2] Unknown author, "Introduction" to *The Red Fighter Pilot*, op. cit., p. 15.

[3] Kilduff, op. cit., p. 92.

[4] Barington J. Gray and Members of the D.H.2 Research Group, "The Anatomy of an Aeroplane: The de Havilland D.H.2 Pusher Scout: Part 5, In the Field-August, 1916", *Cross & Cockade*, Vol. 22, No. 4 (1991), p. 209.

[5] Ibid.

[6] Werner, op. cit., p. 217.

[7] Christopher Cole, ed., *Royal Flying Corps 1915-1916*. (William Kimber, London, 1969), p.256.

[8] Winter, op. cit., p. 154.

[9] Hart's comment on Boelcke's legacy is from *Somme Success*, op. cit., p. 211.

[10] Cited by Peter Hart in the video, *The Great War in Colour*.

[11] Franks, et. al., *Above the Lines*, op. cit., p. 16.

[12] Cuneo, Vol II, op. cit., p. 229. Cuneo draws this conclusion from the official German monograph on the subject, Reichsarchiv (Germany), *Schlachten des Weltkrieges, Band 20. Somme-Nord. I. Tiel (Berlin)* 1927.

[13] Morrow, op. cit., p. 173.

[14] Ibid., p. 174.

[15] Winter, op. cit., p. 154.

[16] Franks, *Jasta Boelcke*, Appendices C and E.

[17] McCudden, op.cit., pp. 275-276.

[18] Franks, Giblin and McCrery, *Under the Guns of the Red Baron*, op. cit., p. 51.

[19] von Richthofen, *The Red Fighter Pilot*, op. cit., p. 107.

[20] Ibid., p. 108.

[21] Ibid., p. 109.

[22] Quoted by Peter Kilduff, *Red Baron*, op. cit., p. 120.

[23] Franks, Bailey and Guest, *Above the Lines*, op. cit., p. 70.

[24] Morrow, op. cit., p. 234.

[25] Winter, op. cit., p. 156.

[26] Kilduff, op. cit., p. 122.

[27] Norman Franks, Russell Guest and Frank Bailey,

Bloody April…Black September (Grub Street, London, 1995), p. 112.

[28] Ibid., p. 114.

[29] Ibid.

[30] Air Vice-Marshal Arthur Gould Lee, op. cit., p. 3.

[31] Ibid., pp. 217-218.

[32] Ibid., p. 221.

[33] Ibid., p. 225.

[34] Fokker, op. cit., pp. 152-153.

[35] Museum of the US Air Force, fact sheet, "Fokker D. VII", 9 September 2014.

[36] Jack N. Merritt and Pierre M. Sprey, "Negative Marginal Returns in Weapons Acquisition", op. cit., p. 491.

[37] Franks, et. al., *Bloody April…Black September*, op. cit., p. 126.

[38] Ibid., pp. 243-244.

[39] Extracted from Burke Davis' biography, *War Bird*, as quoted by Franks, Ibid., p. 161.

[40] Franks, p. 164. The date is not certain because it was not recorded in official papers, and Bäumer's post-war recollection does not include the date. Franks believes it to be 21 September 1918 when he shot down three RFC bombers.

[41] Russell Guest in Franks, Guest and Bailey, op. cit., p. 164.

[42] Ibid., p. 244.

[43] Franks, *Jasta Boelcke*, op. cit., p, 180.

[44] Ibid., pp. 179-180.

CHAPTER XV

[1] Sims, *Fighter Tactics & Strategy*, op. cit., p. 58.

[2] Mackersey, op. cit., p. 129.

[3] Cited in Joshua Levine, *Fighter Heroes of World War I* (Collins, London, 2008), p. 243.

[4] Frederick Libby, *Horses Don't Fly: The Memoir of the Cowboy who became a World War I Ace* (Arcade Publishing; New York, 2002), p 168.

[5] Karl Bolle, "Jagdstaffel Boelcke", in Lt. General Walter Eberhardt, ed., *Unser Luftstreitkraft: 1914-1918* (Vaterlandish C.M. Weller, Berlin, 1930), p. 136.

[6] Fokker, op. cit., p. 12.

[7] Captain Hans Ritter, *Der Luftkrieg* [The Air War], published in Germany and cited by Professor Werner,

op. cit., p. 246.

[8] Erwin Böhme in Werner, pp. 250.

[9] Cited in Franks, *Jasta Boelcke*, p. 39. The original source for Franks' quote is obviously Werner, pp. 250-251, but a different translation, printed by John Hamilton Ltd, 1933.

[10] A quote from Jentsch's autobiography, *Flieger im Feuer* [Flier on Fire] (Karl Josef Sander Verlag: Magdeburg, 1937), cited by Franks, *Jasta Boelcke*, pp. 151-152.

[11] Gastreich and Waiss, *Jagdstaffel Boelcke*, op. cit., p. 265.

[12] *Fort Wayne (IN) Sentinel*, 27 July 1917.

[13] H.A. Jones, in Raleigh & Jones, *The War in the Air.* 6 vols. (The Clarendon Press, Oxford, 1922-1937), Vol. 2, p. 282.

[14] John Killen, *A History of the Luftwaffe* (Doubleday & Co., Garden City, NY, 1968), pp. 6-7.

[15] Quentin Reynolds, *They Fought for the Sky* (Cassell & Co. Ltd, London, 1958), p. 74.

[16] Daniel Michaels and Sarah Sloat, *The Wall Street Journal*, 13 December 2015, "Snoopy Remembers the Red Baron, but Few Germans Do: Snoopy's famed WWI nemesis isn't on the radar in his home country."

[17] Chapman's "Opponent: Boelcke noted for his Way of Setting Traps for Enemies", *The New York Times*, 30 June 1916.

[18] Franz Immelmann, op. cit., p. 219, and Werner, op. cit., p. 204-208.

[19] Norman Franks attributes this information to the late Ed Ferko. The rumour of Boelcke's involvement was due to a letter Kiffin Rockwell wrote to Chapman's brother, Paul, about Victor being hit across the skull on 17 June in a fight with Boelcke. Personal correspondence with the author, 1 November 2015.

[20] *Dunkirk Evening Observer*, 4 November 1916, No. 76, p. 1.

[21] Milton Bronner, "The War Heroes of Germany", *The Charleston Daily Mail*, Sunday, 25 September 1927, p. 6.

[22] *Charleston* (WV) *Gazette*, 1 September 1935.

[23] Don Cantrell, *Santa Ana (CA) Register*, 6 July 1966.

[24] Cited in Sims, op. cit., p. 5.

[25] Cuneo, Vol. II, op. cit., p. 173.

[26] Ibid., p. 258.

[27] Ibid., p. 259.

[28] "Fourth Class Knowledge," in R.G. Head, Ed., *Contrails 1960-1961: The Air Force Cadet Handbook*, (USAF Academy, Colorado, 1959), p.208.

[29] Whitehouse, op. cit., p. 153.

[30] Ibid., p. 30.

[31] Raleigh & Jones, *The War in the Air*. 6 vols.

[32] I am indebted to Lt Col Ulrich Metternich, GAF, Ret., for this portion of the unit's history. Lt Col Metternich is one of the sponsors of the author in this extended relationship with the 31st Wing.

[33] Interview with Colonel Stefan Kleinheyer, wing commander, 5 August 2015.

[34] R.G. Head, "Wo Finden Wir Oswald Boelcke Heute," *Boelcke Echo*, Issue 3/15, October 2015, pp. 18-20.

CHAPTER XVI

[1] Interview with Colonel Gert Overhoff, 5 August 2015.

[2] *Salt Lake Tribune*, 3 August 1916.

[3] Viktor E. Frankl, *The Will to Meaning: Foundations and Applications of Logotherapy*, (New American Library, New York, 1988).

[4] Winter, op. cit., pp. 174-191.

[5] Air Force Doctrine Document (AFDD) 2-1.1, *Counterair Operations*, 1 October 2008, revised 1 November 2011, p. 2.

[6] Cited in Cuneo, Vol. II, op. cit., pp. 227-228, as referenced in H.A. Jones, *The War in the Air*. Vol. II.

[7] Ibid., p. 266.

[8] Werner, op. cit., p. 128.

[9] AFDD, op. cit., p. 2.

[10] Werner, op. cit., pp. 135-136.

[11] Werner, op. cit., p. 136.

[12] AFDD, op. cit., p. 4.

[13] Franks, op. cit., p. 187.

[14] Werner, op. cit., p. 247.

APPENDICES

[1] There is uncertainty over the 32nd victory as Boelcke described in correspondence on 19 October the aircraft involved as "Vickers single-seaters", the German term used for any pusher biplanes. He also claimed the attack happened in the afternoon. Therefore interpretation of his letter and 100-year-old records have led to two possible vicitims. Trevor Henshaw believes it was 6992 F.E.2B that was shot down whereas Norman Franks believes it was most likely to be A2539 D.H.2. The author acknowledges both arguments but agrees more strongly with Franks that it was the D.H.2.

[2] Miller, *FE 2b/d vs Albatros Scouts*, op. cit., pp.18-19.

[3] Miller, op. cit., pp. 31-32.

[4] The source for the information in this section is Barrett Tillman, "Maxim Machine Gun", in *Flight Journal*, December 2015, pp. 62-63.

[5] Rudolf Hoefling, *Albatros D-II: Germany's Legendary World War I Fighter* (Atglen, PA: Schiffer Publishing, 2002), p. 5.

[6] Ibid.

[7] Fokker, op. cit., p. 149.

[8] *Flight*, 13 January 1916 [Author's note: The date is certainly an error as the D.I was not operational until August 1916]. (*Flight* was a British aero weekly magazine.) Cited in James F. Miller, *Albatros D.I-D.II*, (Oxford: Osprey Publishing, 2012), p. 24.

[9] James F. Miller, *FE-2b/d vs Albatros Scouts: Western Front 1916-17* (Oxford: Osprey Publishing, 2014), pp. 29-39.

[10] Morrow, op. cit., p. 162.

[11] Exact figures are source dependent, but the most reliable seem to be: Miller, *Albatros D.I-D.II*, p. 19; Windsock Datafiles, Albatros D.III, p. 21; Robert C. Mikesh, Albatros D.Va.

List of Terms, Abbreviations and Acronyms

Term	Meaning
Abgeflogen	"Flown out"; worn out from flying, psychologically finished
Abteilung	Section
Ace	A pilot or observer who has shot down at least five aircraft
AEF	American Expeditionary Force
Auftragstaktik	German word for decentralised "mission tactics"
Albatros	The manufacturer of the Albatros aircraft
BAM	Brieftauben Abteilung Metz (Carrier pigeon flying section at Metz; a deception to maintain operational security)
BEF	British Expeditionary Force
Biplane	Airplane with two wings
C-type	German abbreviation for improved reconnaissance biplane
Camel	A famous British aircraft built by the Sopwith company
Chord	The width of a wing from front to back
D-type	German abbreviation for single-seat fighter
DFC	Distinguished Flying Cross
Dr.-type	German abbreviation of Driplane
Eastern Front	The theatre of operations from the Baltic Sea to the Black Sea with Russia and Romania vs Austro-Hungary, Bulgaria, the Ottoman Empire and Germany
Eindecker	German for single-wing airplane
E-type	German abbreviation for Eindecker
Escadrille	French for squadron
Escadrille de chasseur	Hunting/fighter squadron
FFAb	Field Flying Section Artillery (Bavaria)
Feldflieger-abteilungen	Field Flying Sections (FFA)
Feldwebel	Sergeant
Flieger Abteilung	Flying unit/section
Fliegertruppe	Flying troops
Flight	The act of flying; a group of aircraft proceeding together
Fokker	Anthony Fokker; an aircraft made by the Fokker firm
Former	Structural part of the fuselage that determines its shape
GAS/GAF	German air service/German air force; later the Luftwaffe

Geschwader	A German wing organisation with several squadrons
Hauptmann	German rank of captain
Idflieg	War Ministry Inspectorate of Flying Troops
Jagdstaffel/Jasta	Hunting/fighter squadron/Abbreviation of Jagdstaffel
Johannisthal	The main Berlin airfield for non-airliners; location of several aircraft manufacturers
Kasta	Kampstaffel, Reconnaissance/bombing squadron
KEK	Kampfeinsitzer Kommando; single-seat fighter detachment
Kette	German for a Flight, a unit of 5-6 pilots and aircraft; a Staffel could have two Kettes
Kurvenkampf	"Battle of curves"; a turning aerial fight
Leutnant	German rank of second lieutenant
Longeron	Long pieces of wood or metal, attached to formers, to which the fuselage skin is attached
LVG	Luftverkehrsgsellschaft, a two-seat German reconnaissance aircraft
MC	Military Cross (British)
NCO	Non-commissioned officer
Oberleutnant	German rank of first lieutenant
Oberst	German rank of colonel
Oberstleutnant	German rank of lieutenant colonel
Observer	Usually an artillery officer in the back seat who takes notes, draws maps of opposing artillery positions; also a machine gunner
Offz	Warrant officer
OHL	German high command
OzbV	Offizier zur besonderen Verwendung; officer for special duties
POW	Prisoner of War
Pour le Mérite	French, "For the Merit"; the Blue Max
Pusher	An aircraft with an engine and propeller in the rear
RFC/RAF	Royal Flying Corps/Royal Air Force, United Kingdom
Rittmeister	German for cavalry captain; von Richthofen held the rank of Rittmeister
Solo	Flying alone; the first flight alone of a pilot, without an instructor

Sortie	A flight of one aircraft, out and back; one take-off and one landing
SPAD	A French aviation firm, *Societe pour l'Aviation et ses Derives*
Staffel	German for squadron
Taube	"Dove", an early German monoplane
Theatre of War	The area of air, land, and water that is directly involved in the conduct of the war. It may contain more than one theatre of operations
Theatre of Operations	A sub-area within a theatre of war required to conduct or support specific combat operations, geographically separate and usually focused on different enemy forces
Tractor	An aircraft with an engine and propeller in front
Triplane	Airplane with three wings
Uhlan	An elite cavalry unit
VC	Victoria Cross (British)
Vizefeldwebel	Sergeant
Western Front	The theatre of operations from the English Channel to Switzerland with Germany and Austria-Hungary opposed to England and France. Italy was a separate theatre of operations

A NOTE ON SOURCES

The main source for this article is autobiographical – Oswald Boelcke's *Fieldbook*. This small book is a compilation of his letters to his family and a few friends during the war years, from 1 August 1914 through 1916. The original was published in German by his father, Professor Hermann Boelcke, in 1916, only two months after Oswald's death. I donated an original version of that book in German along with an English translation, to the library of the San Diego Air & Space Museum.

In 1932 Professor Johannes Werner published an excellent biography in German, *Boelcke, der Mensch, der Flieger, der Führer des deutschen Jagdfliegerei* (K.F. Koehler Verlag, Leipzig). Werner had been a friend of the Boelcke family and obviously had access to their letters as well as correspondence with numerous surviving members of the German air service. To his (and our) great benefit, Werner puts Boelcke's letters into historical perspective and sketches out the broader aeronautical, strategic and tactical implications of his experience. The only deficiency with Werner's work is that he does not provide references or citations for his many quotes. I have tried to correct that deficiency by citing references and sources. Werner's biography was first translated into English by Claude W. Sykes and published in London by John Hamilton Limited. The English version was reprinted in 1972 by Arno Press, Inc. and by Greenhill Books/Lionel Leventhal Ltd in 1985 and again in 1991. The most current printing is by Casemate Publishers in 2009. Norman Franks wrote an introduction and appendix with a list of Boelcke's victories for the 2009 Casemate and 1991 Greenhill printings. With Casemate's permission I have reprinted Franks' victory list and have added a column showing the aircraft that Boelcke was flying in each encounter.

Norman Franks, *Sharks Among Minnows*, relates the period of the Fokker Eindeckers, July 1915 to August 1916. The best description of Jasta Boelcke's personnel and monthly activities from August 1916 through the end of the war is Norman Franks' *Jasta Boelcke: The History of Jasta 2, 1916-1918*. Greg Van Wyngarden's *Jagdstaffel 2 "Boelcke": Von Richthofen's Mentor*, is also quite good. One of the most comprehensive books on the air war is Trevor Henshaw's *The Sky Their Battlefield, Edition II*, published in 2014. This volume is virtually encyclopedic in its detailed chronological listing of air activities and every British, Dominion and American casualty on every day of WWI.

The best book on the background of the German air service and the first two years of the war is John Cuneo's *Winged Mars, Volumes I and II*. Vol. I covers the history of the service before WWI, and Vol. II, *The Air Weapon: 1914-1916*, follows for these three years. These are perhaps the most detailed historical accounts of the service.

Three additional autobiographies were exceptionally useful: Manfred von Richthofen's, *The Red Fighter Pilot*, Franz Immelmann's biography of his brother, Max, *The Eagle of Lille* and Anthony Fokker's *Flying Dutchman*. Two other volumes on von Richthofen are Peter Kilduff's *Red Baron* and *Under the Guns of the Red Baron*, the definitive study of von Richthofen's eighty victories by Normal Franks, Hal Giblin and Nigel McCrery.

John H. Morrow, Jr.'s two books are the most valuable I have found on the industrial side of WWI aviation. They are *The Great War in the Air: Military Aviation from 1909 to 1921*, and *German Air Power in World War I*.

Many of the photographs and some of the victory data are from Steffen Gastreich and Walter Waiss, *Jagdstaffel Boelcke, Band VIII, 1914-1918*, from the Boelcke-Archives, published by Helios in 2014. Each of these victories was cross-checked against copies of the "Claims Record" printed in this volume.

There are two excellent books on tactics. The first is Edward Sims, *Fighter Tactics and Strategy: 1914-1970*, that provides a detailed narrative of how pilots planned and conducted air combat, including an excellent description of Oswald Boelcke's manoeuvres. Ironically, it does not reprint the actual dicta. The reverse is true of Robert Shaw's unique work, *Fighter Combat: Tactics and Manoeuvring*. Shaw, a US navy fighter pilot, describes in the most exquisite detail complete descriptions of basic fighter manoeuvres and multiple formation tactics (one-on-one, two-on-one, many-versus-many, etc.). This remarkable book uses both engineering formulae and pilot-oriented descriptions of manoeuvres and is probably the most advanced work available to the prospective fighter pilot.

Two other works are also unique in their contributions to this literature. Ian Mackersey's *No Empty Chairs: The Short and Heroic Lives of the Young Aviators Who Fought and Died in the First World War*, is a recent and penetrating portrait of the Royal Flying Corps pilots, policies and peculiarities. The most unexpected book found in this research is Denis Winter's *The First of the Few: Fighter Pilots of the First World War*. This small volume contains the only description I am aware of that focusses on the detailed, distinctive pilot-side of the life, times and habits of RFC pilots, and by extension, all Great War aviators. From recruitment to pilot training to missions in combat squadrons, Winter's research and writing takes the reader into the cockpit of the many aeroplanes they flew in this first great air combat. His descriptions of the physical environment (the cold, hypoxic air at higher altitude, the G-forces, the foul castor oil that spewed from the engine) grab the reader with a vicious intensity. The mental stress was no less debilitating. He describes the psychological effects of flying four to eight sorties a day and seeing pilots disappear from the mess in almost a never-ending stream. They lived with death every day.

These and other works about the men, the aces and the machines are listed in the Bibliography. They are commended to the general reader, the aviation historian and the pilots of the future.

BIBLIOGRAPHY

BOOKS AND ARTICLES

Abbott, Dan-San. "The Camouflage and Markings of the Albatros D.II Aircraft." *WW1 Aero, The Journal of the Early Aeroplane,* #150, November 1995.

"Albatros D.Va: German Fighter of World War I." in *Famous Aircraft of the National Air and Space Museum.* Washington, DC, National Air and Space Museum, n.d.

"The Albatros Fighting Biplane – III". *Automotive Industries.* 6 June 1918, pp. 1095-1097.

Boelcke, Oswald. *Hauptmann Boelckes Feldberichte,* with an introduction by his father Professor Hermann Boelcke, Dessau [in German]. Berlin, Friedrich Andreas Berthes A.-G. Gotha, 1916.

An Aviator's Field Book: Being the Field Reports of Oswald Boelcke, from August 1, 1914, to October 28, 1916, translated from the German by Robert Reynold Hirsch, M.E., with a foreword by Joseph E. Ridder, M.E. National Military Publishing Co., New York, 1917.

Bolle, Karl, Rittmeister a. D., "Jagdstaffel Boelcke," in Walter von Eberhardt, *Unser Luftstreitkrafte: 1914-1918.*

Boyne, Walter J. *The Influence of Airpower on History.* Pen & Sword, Barnsley, South Yorkshire, 2003.

Campbell, Christopher. *Aces and Aircraft of World War I.* Book Club Associates, London, 1981.

Campbell, Joseph. *The Hero with a Thousand Faces,* 2nd ed. Bollingen Series No. 17. Princeton University Press, Princeton, NJ, 1973.

Chef des Flugflugwesens. *Bordbuch für das Flugzeug, Fokker D.III 352/16. Begonnem am: 1 September 1916.* Nr. 14047 Fl. Vom 5.4.1916 (in German).

Cole, Christopher ed., *Royal Flying Corps 1915-1916.* William Kimber, London, 1969.

Connors, John F. *Albatros Fighters in Action.* Squadron/Signal Publications Inc., Carrollton, TX, 1981.

Cronauer, Peter. "Jagdflieger Oswald Boelcke, Erste Schritte zum Ruhn. *Flugzeug Classic,* May 2016, pp.46-49.

Cuneo, John R. *Winged Mars. Volume 1: The German Air Weapon, 1870-1914* The Military Service Publishing Co., Harrisburg, PA, 1942.

Volume 2: The Air Weapon, 1914-1916. The Military Service Publishing Co., Harrisburg, PA, 1947.

Eberhardt, Walter von (Lt. General), ed. *Unser Luftstreitkrafte: 1914-1918.* Vaterlandisch Verlag C. M. Weller, Berlin, 1930.

Flammer, Phillip M. *The Vivid Air: The Lafayette Escadrille.* University of Georgia Press, Athens, 1981.

Fokker, Anthony and Bruce Gould. *Flying Dutchman: The Life of Anthony Fokker.* Henry Holt & Co., New York, 1931.

Franks, Norman L. R. *Jasta Boelcke: The History of Jasta 2, 1916–18.* Grub Street, London, 2004.

Sharks Among Minnows: Germany's First Fighter Pilots and the Fokker Eindecker Period, July 1915 to September 1916. Grub Street, London, 2001.

Franks, Norman, Hal Giblin and Nigel McCrery. *Under the Guns of the Red Baron: The Complete Record of Von Richthofen's Victories and Victims Fully Illustrated.* Grub Street, London, 1995.

Franks, Norman L. R., Frank W. Bailey & Russell Guest. *Above the Lines: A Complete Record of the*

Fighter Aces of the German Air Service, Naval Air Service and Flanders Marine Corps, 1914-1918. Grub Street, London, 1993.

Gastreich, Steffen and Walter Waiss, *Jagdstaffel Boelcke, Band VIII, 1914-1918,* from the Boelcke Archives. Helios, Aachen, Germany, 2014.

Gilbert, Martin. *The Somme: Heroism and Horror in the First World War.* Henry Holt & Co., New York, 2006.

Gray, Barrington J. "Number one for Jasta 2: An Account of Hptm Oswald Boelcke's Twentieth Victory." *Cross & Cockade, The Society of World War I Aero Historians,* Vol. 5, No. 3 (1974), pp. 126-129.

"The Anatomy of an Aeroplane: The DeHavilland D.H.2 Pusher Scout." *Cross & Cockade,* Vol. 22, No. 4 (1991).

Gray, Peter L. and Ian R., Stair. *Albatros Fighters of World War I.* Air History World War I Series, No. 2. Windgran Publications.

The Albatros D.I-D.III. Profile 127. Profile Publications, United Kingdom, n.d.

Greer, Thomas H. *USAF Historical Study 89, The Development of Air Doctrine in the Army Air Arm, 1917–1941.* Office of Air Force History, USAF, Washington, D.C. 1955, reprinted 1985.

Greig, Andrew. *That Summer.* Faber & Faber, London, 2000.

Guttman, Jon. *Nieuport 11/16 Bébé vs Fokker Eindecker: Western Front 1916.* Osprey Publishing Ltd, Oxford, 2014.

Hacker, Major E. W. *Learning from the Past: A Fighter Pilot's Obligation.* Thesis, The Marine Corps Command and Staff College, Quantico, Virginia, 6 April 1954.

Hanlon, Michael E. "From Dicta Boelcke and the SPAD XIII to the Raptor", *Relevance, Quarterly Journal of the Great War Society,* Vol. 19, No. 3, Summer 2010, pp. 27-31.

Hart, Peter. *Somme Success: The Royal Flying Corps and the Battle of the Somme.* Pen & Sword Military, Barnsley, South Yorkshire, 2012.

Bloody April: Slaughter in the Skies over Arras, 1917. Cassell, London, 2005.

The Somme: The Darkest Hour on the Western Front. Pegasus Books, New York, 2008.

Head, R.G. and Ervin Rokke, ed. *American Defense Policy, 3d ed.* The Johns Hopkins University Press, Baltimore, 1973.

Head, R.G. "Albatros D.II" *World War I Aero,* August 2014, No. 220, pp. 76-79.

"Albatros D.II Unveiled at San Diego Air & Space Musuem", *World War I Aero,* February 2015, No. 222, pp.64-68.

Henshaw, Trevor. *The Sky their Battlefield: Air Fighting and Air Casualties of the Great War.* Grub Street, London, 1995.

The Sky their Battlefield II: Expanded and Updated: Air Fighting and Air Casualties of the Great War. Fetubi Books, Hertfordshire, 2014.

Hofling, Rudolf. *Albatros D-II: Germany's Legendary World War I Fighter.* Schiffer Publishing, Ltd., Atglen, PA. n.d.

Holley, I. B., Jr. *Ideas and Weapons.* Yale University Press: New Haven, 1953.

Immelmann, Franz. *Der Adler von Lille.* Leipzig, Austria: K.F. Koehler Verlag, 1934, reprinted as *Immelmann: The Eagle of Lille.* Greenhill Books,

London, and Presidio Press, Novato, CA. 1990.

Imrie, Alex. *German Fighter Units: 1914-May 1917*. Airwar 13. Osprey Publishing Ltd., Oxford, n.d.

Jones, H. A. *The War in the Air*. Vols. The Clarendon Press, Oxford, 1922-1937.

Kilduff, Peter. *Iron Man Rudolf Berthold: Germany's Indomitable Fighter Ace of World War I*. Grub Street, London, 2012.

Red Baron: The Life and Death of an Ace. David & Charles, Cincinnati, OH, 2008.

Germany's First Air Force: 1914-1918. Arms and Armour Press, London, 1991

Billy Bishop, VC. Grub Street, London, 2014.

Kacey. "Observations On WWI Petrol," *The Aerodrome Forum*, posted by Bletchley, 7 January 2010.

Kornerup, A. & J. H. Wanscher. *Methuene Handbook of Colour*. Methuen & Co, Ltd.: London, 1963. First published by Politikens Forlag, Copenhagen, 1961.

Kowalski, Thomas J. *Albatros D.I-D.Va: Legendary Fighter*. Lublin, Poland, Kagero Publishing, n.d.

Lee, Arthur Gould (Air Vice-Marshal). *No Parachute: A Classic Account of War in the Air in World War I*. Grub Street, London, 2013.

Levine, Josua. *Fighter Heroes of World War I*. Collins, London, 2008.

Libby, Frederick. *Horses Don't Fly: The Memoir of the Cowboy who became a World War I Ace*. Arcade Publishing, New York, 2000, 2012.

Longstreet, Stephen. *The Canvas Falcons: The Men and Planes of WWI*. Barnes & Noble, New York, 1970.

Macdonald, Lyn. *Somme*. Michael Joseph Ltd., London, 1983.

Mackersey, Ian. *No Empty Chairs: The Short and Heroic Lives of the Young Aviators Who Fought and Died in the First World War*. Orion Publishing Group, London, 2012.

Mason, Herbert Molloy, Jr. *The Lafayette Escadrille*. Random House, New York, 1964.

McCudden, James T. B. *Flying Fury: Five Years in the Royal Flying Corps*. Doubleday & Company, Garden City, New York, 1968.

Michaels, Daniel and Sarah Sloat, "Snoopy Remembers the Red Baron, but Few Germans Do." *The Wall Street Journal*, 13 December 2015.

Mikesh, Robert C. *Albatros D.Va: German Fighter of World War I*. Smithsonian Institution Press, Washington, D.C., 1980.

Miller, James F. *Albatros D.I-D.II*. Osprey Publishing Ltd., Oxford, 2012.

FE-2b/d vs Albatros Scouts: Western Front 1916-17. Osprey Publishing Ltd., Oxford, 2014.

Morrow, John H., Jr. *The Great War in the Air: Military Aviation from 1909 to 1921*. Smithsonian Institution Press, Washington, D.C., 1993.

German Air Power in World War I. University of Nebraska Press, Lincoln, 1982.

"The War in the Air," in Hew Strachan, ed., *The Oxford Illustrated History of the First World War*. Oxford University Press, Oxford, U.K. 2014, pp. 264-276.

Neumann, George Paul (Major), ed. *The German Air Force in the Great War*. Naval & Military Press, Uckfield, East Sussex, 2004.

Norman, Aaron. *The Great Air War: The Men, The Planes, the Saga of Military Aviation 1914-1918*. The Macmillan Company, New York, 1968.

Osprey Publishing. *D.H.2 vs Albatros D.I/D.II: Western Front 1916*. Osprey Publishing Ltd., Oxford, 2012.

Albatros D.III: Johannisthal, OAW, and Oeffag Variants. Osprey Publishing Ltd., Oxford, 2014.

SPAD VII vs Albatros D.III: 1917-1918. Osprey Publishing Ltd., Oxford, 2011.

Phelan, Joseph A. *Aeroplanes and Flyers of the First World War, Originally titled Heroes & Aeroplanes of the Great War 1914-1918*. Grosset & Dunlap Publishers, New York, 1973.

Pietsch, Thorsten. "Air Ace Oswald Boelcke." Trenches on the Web Bio: Oswald Boelcke. http://www.worldwar1.com/biocgob.htm.

Raby. Heinz-Michael. Letters and Email correspondence. Member of the Boelcke Tradition Association, the organisation that is custodian of the memorabilia in the Boelcke Tradition Room at the Tactical Fighter Wing 31 Boelcke, German air force.

Raleigh, Walter and H.A. Jones. *The War in the Air*. 6 vols. The Clarendon Press, Oxford, 1922-1937.

Reynolds, Quentin. *They Fought for the Sky: The Story of the First War in the Air*. Cassell & Co., London, 1958.

Rie, David. "The Observant Quirk: The Rice Brothers, A Family History of WW1", *Cross & Cockade*, Vol. 20, No. 4 (1989), pp. 169-209.

Richthofen, Manfred von. *The Red Battle Flyer*. R. M. McBride & Co., New York, 1918.

The Red Fighter Pilot: The Autobiography of the Red Baron. Translated by J. Ellis Barker. Red and Black Publishers, St Petersburg, 2007.

The Red Baron. Translated by Peter Kilduff. Bailey Brothers & Swinfen, Folkestone, 1974.

"Dicta-Richthofen: The Last Will & Testament", Translated by Stephen T. Lawson. *Cross & Cockade*, Vol. 23, No. 2 (1992), pp. 65-74.

Rimell, R. I. *Albatros D.II*. Windsock Datafiles. Albatros Productions Ltd., Berkhamsted, UK, 1998.

Ringlstetter, Herbert and Wolfgang Mühlbauer. *Flugzeug Classic, Special 12 Das Magazin für Luftfahrt, Zeitgeschichte und Oldtimer*, 2014.

Ryheul, Johan. *KEKs and Fokkerstaffels: The Early German Fighter Units in 1915-1916*. Fonthill Media Ltd, London, 2014.

Shaara, Jeff. *To the Last Man: A Novel of the First World War*. Random House, New York, 2004.

Shaw, Robert L. *Fighter Combat: Tactics and Manoeuvring*. Naval Institute Press, Annapolis. 1985.

Sims, Edward H. *Fighter Tactics and Strategy: 1914-1970*. Cassell, London. 1972.

Soam, John. "Fighter Pilots Survival Guide," *Air & Space*, Washington, D.C., The Smithsonian Institution. June/July 2014, pp. 28-33.

Sothworth, A. D. Bud. "Albatros D.II and D.IIIa Aircraft." Kookaburra Technical Publications, Dandenong, Victoria, Australia, 1985.

Suderland, Gary. "Designing Fokker Airplanes," *Cross & Cockade*, Vol. 30, No. 3 (Autumn 2015), pp. 196-234.

Taylor, Jeff. "A Wreath for Boelcke," *Cross & Cockade*, Vol. 20, No. 4 (1980), pp. 216-218.

Thies, Andreas. Boelcke: Auction Katalog. A catalogue of the archival items of Oswald Boelcke offered to the public, 16 May 2001.

Tillman, Barrett. "Maxim Machine Gun." *Flight Journal*. December 2015. pp. 62-63.

Traditionsverband Boelcke e. V. *Jagdbombergeschwader 31 "Boelcke": 40 Jahre (1958-1998)*. A History of the Fighter-Bomber Wing 31 "Boelcke": 40 Years (1958-1998). Zentraldruckeerei Koeln: Porz-Wahn, 1999.

Treadwell, Terry C. & Alan C. Wood. *German Knights of the Air: 1914-1918 The Holders of the Orden Pour le Mérite*. Brassey's, London, 1997.

Knights of the Black Cross: German Fighter Pilots of the First World War. Cerberus, Whitechurch, Bristol, 2004.

US Air Force. Office of Air Force History. *The US Air Service in World War I*. Headquarters, USAF: Washington, D.C. The Albert F. Simpson Historical Research Center Maxwell AFB, Alabama. 1978.

Van Wyngarden, Greg. *Jagdstaffel 2 "Boelcke": Von Richthofen's Mentor*. Aviation Elite Units, No. 26. Osprey Publishing Ltd., Oxford, 2007.

Weatherseed, John. "Mercedes Engine History." *The Vintage Aviator*, internet.

Werner, Johannes. *Boelcke der Mensch, der Flieger, der Führer der deutschen Jagdfliegerei*. K.F. Koehler Verlag: Leipzig, 1932; translated and published in English as *Knight of Germany: Oswald Boelcke, German Ace*. John Hamilton Limited: London, 1933. Republished by Casemate: Havertown, PA, 2009, first edition 1985. With an introduction and appendix by Norman Franks, 1991.

Whitehouse, Arch. *Decisive Air Battles of the First World War*. Duell, Sloan and Pierce: New York. 1963.

WindSock Datafiles. *Albatros D.III.*, Herts, 1996.

Winter, Denis. *The First of the Few: Fighter Pilots of the First World War*. University of Georgia Press, Athens, Georgia. 1983.

Wonderich, Marcus, ed. "Oswald Boelcke: Der grosse Lehrmeister," in *Flugzeug Classic Special 12, Militaerflugzeuge des ersten Weltkreigs*. 2014, pp. 96-98.

NEWSPAPERS

A number of newspapers were consulted during the research for this book. Below are some of the newspapers which are referenced within this piece of work.

Charleston Gazette

Dunkirk Evening Observer (NY)

Fort Wayne Sentinel

The New York Times

Salt Lake Tribune

VIDEOS

Wings, 1929

Flight Commander, 1930

Hells Angels, 1930

Dawn Patrol, 1938

The Blue Max, 1966

Fly Boys, 2006

The Red Baron, DVD Video, MMC Art Department, 2010.

The First Air War, a NOVA television video for the Public Broadcasting System, 2014.

INDEX

Squadrons & Wings (by Country)
France

Germany

INDEX